POST-JAZZ POETICS

Post-Jazz Poetics
A Social History

Jennifer D. Ryan

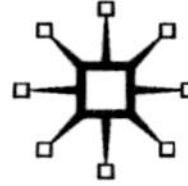

POST-JAZZ POETICS
Copyright © Jennifer D. Ryan, 2010.
All rights reserved.

First published in 2010 by
PALGRAVE MACMILLAN® in the United States – a division of St. Martin's
Press LLC, 175 Fifth Avenue, New York, NY 10010.

Where this book is distributed in the UK, Europe and the rest of the world,
this is by Palgrave Macmillan, a division of Macmillan Publishers Limited,
registered in England, company number 785998, of Houndmills, Basingstoke,
Hampshire RG21 6XS.

Palgrave Macmillan is the global academic imprint of the above companies
and has companies and representatives throughout the world.

Palgrave® and Macmillan® are registered trademarks in the United States,
the United Kingdom, Europe and other countries.

ISBN: 978–0–230–62315–6

Library of Congress Cataloging-in-Publication Data

Ryan, Jennifer D., 1974–
    Post-jazz poetics: a social history / Jennifer D. Ryan.
      p. cm.
    Includes bibliographical references.
    ISBN 978–0–230–62315–6 (alk. paper)
  1. American poetry—African American authors—History and
criticism.   2. American poetry—Women authors—History and criticism.
3. Jazz in literature.   4. Literature and society—United States—
History—20th century.   5. African American women—Intellectual
life—20th century.   6. Feminism and literature—United States—History—
20th century.   7. Poetics—History—20th century.   8. Music and
literature—History—20th century.   9. Williams, Sherley Anne, 1944–
1999—Criticism and interpretation.   10. Sanchez, Sonia, 1934—Criticism and
interpretation.   11. Cortez, Jayne—Criticism and interpretation.   12. Coleman,
Wanda—Criticism and interpretation.   13. Mullen, Harryette Romell—
Criticism and interpretation.   I. Title.

    PS310.J39R93 2010
    811'.5409928708996073—dc22

                                                           2009041140

A catalogue record of the book is available from the British Library.

Design by MPS Limited, A Macmillan Company

First edition: May 2010

10 9 8 7 6 5 4 3 2 1

Printed in the United States of America.

For Grace

CONTENTS

Acknowledgments

This project took nearly eight years to complete, and I am grateful to the many people who offered support, advice, and resources along the way. Adalaide Morris, Doris Witt, Tom Lutz, Corey Creekmur, and John Rapson worked with me on the book's early stages at the University of Iowa. I received countless hours of friendship and help from Robin Barrow, Bidisha Banerjee, Missy Donegan, Sam Metta Bexar, Lori Muntz, Eleanor Nickel, and Amy Spellacy when we all lived in Iowa City. My colleagues and friends at Buffalo State College offered careful readings of the manuscript as it neared completion; thank you especially to Karen Sands-O'Connor, Peter Ramos, and Barish Ali. Thank you also to the poets whose work is featured here; they responded promptly to my inquiries and granted me permission to quote generous excerpts from their poetry. My parents faithfully encouraged me throughout the writing process and during all seasons of life. My brother, my link to all things hip, always checked in to make sure I was taking time for myself. Finally, my husband gave me reasons to keep writing and helped me to treasure the best parts. Tim travels with me in this as in all things.

Permissions

Excerpt from "Solo" from *Festivals and Funerals* copyright © 2009 by Jayne Cortez. Originally published by Phrase Text (1971). Reprinted by permission of the author.

Excerpts from *Jazz Fan Looks Back* by Jayne Cortez. Copyright © 2002 by Jayne Cortez. Reprinted by permission of Hanging Loose Press, Brooklyn, NY.

Photograph of Wanda Coleman by Susan Carpendale copyright © 1988 and 2009 by Wanda Coleman. Reproduced by permission of Wanda Coleman.

Excerpts from *African Sleeping Sickness: Stories & Poems*, Black Sparrow Press, copyright © for Wanda Coleman, 1990; excerpted with permission of the author.

Excerpts from *Bathwater Wine*, Black Sparrow Press, copyright © for Wanda Coleman, 1998; excerpted with permission of the author.

Excerpts from *Imagoes*, Black Sparrow Press, copyright © for Wanda Coleman, 1983; excerpted with permission of the author.

Excerpts from *Mercurochrome*, Black Sparrow Press, copyright © for Wanda Coleman, 2001; excerpted with permission of the author.

Excerpts from *American Sonnets*, copublished by Light and Dust Books and Woodland Pattern Book Center, copyright © 1994 by Wanda Coleman.

Photograph of Harryette Mullen copyright © by Judy Natal. www.judynatal.com. Reproduced by permission of the photographer.

Excerpts from *Blues Baby: Early Poems* by Harryette Mullen. Copyright © 2002 by Harryette Mullen. Reprinted by permission of the author.

Harryette Mullen, excerpts from *Recyclopedia: Trimmings, S*PeRM**K*T, and Muse and Drudge*. Copyright © 1991, 1992, 1995, and 2006 by Harryette Mullen. Reprinted with the permission of Graywolf Press, Saint Paul, Minnesota, www.graywolfpress.org.

Excerpts from *Sleeping with the Dictionary* by Harryette Mullen. Copyright © 2002 by the Regents of the University of California. Published by the University of California Press.

Patricia Smith, excerpts reprinted from *Big Towns, Big Talk* (1992) by permission of Zoland Books, an imprint of Steerforth Press.

Patricia Spears Jones, excerpts from "The Birth of Rhythm and Blues" and "Gossip" from *The Weather That Kills*. Copyright © 1995 by Patricia Spears Jones. Reprinted with the permission of Coffee House Press, www.coffeehousepress.org.

Author photograph copyright © 2009 by Tim Bryant. Reproduced by permission of the photographer.

Introduction: How Do I Make that Sound? A New Feminist Poetics

In his biography of classic blues singer Bessie Smith, Chris Albertson tells the story of a 1928 party hosted by New York journalist Carl Van Vechten and his wife, dancer Fania Marinoff (141–46). Although Smith usually shunned events hosted by white devotees of black life like Van Vechten, she agreed to attend this gathering with niece Ruby Walker and composer Porter Grainger. After Smith sang several numbers, stopping for a drink after each one, Walker and Grainger decided it was time to leave. They liberated Smith from her place at the piano and began steering her toward the door, but Marinoff intervened, spreading her arms and demanding a kiss from Smith. The singer was so irritated by this display of polite white condescension that she shoved her hostess away and swore at her. Marinoff was visibly shocked by the rebuff; however, the trio managed to make their exit without further incident.

A few days later, Smith found the opportunity to entertain a more desirable audience. She and Ruby decided to spend the hours between the matinee and evening performances of their Lafayette Theater show at Percy Brown's, a local speakeasy. On the way back, after having regaled the other patrons with stories of the Van Vechten gathering, Smith was inspired to stage an impromptu musical. She positioned herself on a garbage can in an alley behind the Lafayette. As Ruby danced, enveloped in an oversized fur coat, Smith sang a song from the show's finale, drawing an enormous crowd of clapping, dancing listeners. The performance ended only when Jack Gee, Smith's husband, descended in a rage: Smith had purposely defied his dictum forbidding free public shows.

Bessie Smith's actions in these two instances illustrate her determination to bring her music to an audience already familiar with its themes and history. Many women blues singers conceptualized the blues, even in the face of racial and sexual discrimination, in a manner similar to Smith's: as a forum for public communication, self-definition, and improvisatory performance. Such multifaceted strategies persist across a wide range of black women's artistic practices. In this book, I examine the jazz-influenced poetry of post–Black Arts writers Sherley Anne Williams, Sonia Sanchez, Jayne Cortez, Wanda Coleman, and Harryette Mullen. As conceptually and politically innovative poets, they tie the complexities of African-American feminism to the formal techniques and cultural allusiveness of not only jazz but also late modern experimental poetics. I examine their work's evolution and the implications it holds for the history of black radical poetics by following a genealogical approach. This organizational mode proceeds from what Ann Vickery has termed the "how and why," via social and literary analysis, of each poet and her work (14). Such analysis includes biographical information, the poets' own writings on literature, and theoretical scrutiny of the poetry and its cultural contexts. One essential element of this genealogy emerges from the unique jazz-poetic forms that these poets develop, in which they transform literary conventions through the infusion of social critiques via specific experimental techniques. My discussion also references other poets performing similar compositional experiments in order to illustrate the convergence of critique and form during particular historical moments. By aligning my literary analysis with contemporary developments in jazz and feminism, I locate each poet's work in a related but unique moment in the history of American avant-garde art.

The five poets featured in this study invoke Bessie Smith's signature flaunting of social conventions in their jazz-influenced pieces. Sherley Anne Williams, for example, redefines blues culture as a source for modern feminism by representing Smith's voice and body through demonstrations of agency rather than spectacular objectification. Sonia Sanchez, on the other hand, revises Black Power conceptions of African-American culture by creating recognizably feminist perspectives framed in the new jazz elegy and blues haiku forms. Jayne Cortez, another participant in Black Arts activities, highlights connections between musical performance and political critique through surrealist images of the abused environment. As a self-identified South Los Angeles poet, Wanda Coleman legitimizes the harsh details of a geography marked by unacknowledged deprivations, interrogating the ways in which the controlled publication and dissemination of texts collude in supporting persistent social problems. Finally, Harryette Mullen challenges the linguistic boundaries of poetic tradition through her work's references to Language poetics, women's participation in blues and jazz culture, and prose-poetic catalogues.

In spite of their revolutionary status within the history of Western poetry, these poets acknowledge and build upon the work of their artistic precedents. Their lineage includes Lucy Terry, who authored what critics believe to be the first poem published by an African American, "Bars Fight," in 1746, and Phillis Wheatley, who lived her entire life as a slave and published the first book of poetry by an African American, *Poems on Various Subjects*, in 1771. The history of twentieth-century African-American women's poetry extends these moments of innovation through such periods of intense creative activity as the Harlem Renaissance, when writers like Helene Johnson, Georgia Douglas Johnson, Gwendolyn Bennett, and Angelina Weld Grimké investigated racial politics through the lens of women's experiences. Their focus on socially charged topics like black women's physical beauty and sexual oppression gave rise to a new political poetry, one with its own set of compositional rules. This poetics was predicated on the rejection of structural conventions like meter, rhyme, and form at a time when many male Harlem Renaissance writers were producing sonnets and odes faithful to the European literary tradition. Important stylistic innovations thus resulted from rhetorical defiance.

These writers' preoccupation with giving creative voice to the peculiar social position in which black women found themselves in early twentieth-century America informed radical midcentury artistic movements as well. The Black Arts Movement, an effort in the second half of the 1960s and the early 1970s to organize African-American writers and artists around black nationalist politics, counted poets Sonia Sanchez, Nikki Giovanni, Carolyn Rodgers, and June Jordan among its most active participants. By developing a poetics based in political themes, confrontational rhetoric, and stylistic devices meant to imitate spoken-word performance, these women writers challenged the popular notion that Black Arts and Black Power, the concurrent political movement, were primarily led by men. Today, African-American women poets recognize their precedents' achievements while seeking out new methods by which to explore and add to black literary and social traditions.

HISTORY AND THE CULTURAL ROOTS OF INNOVATION

Although black women's poetry responds to many different cultural, literary, and historical factors, references to two major cultural events recur throughout the body of twentieth-century work: slavery and the evolution of jazz. Attempts to reconcile two such different thematic influences—an exploitative socioeconomic institution and a culturally specific art form—struggle with the basic contradictions that exist between their origins and their complex historical effects. This struggle in itself helps to produce jazz poetry's unique structural and ideological elements. The added inflection of women's particular political concerns gives the poetry a unique position within dynamic African-American literary traditions.

Slavery and abolition provide vital source material for an overwhelming number of black writers; jazz poets acknowledge both literary forerunners and the social impetus behind the work in their references to this history. Indeed, evidence of the institution's influence over later social conditions has shaped the history of African-American literature as a whole. In Harriet Jacobs's *Incidents in the Life of a Slave Girl* (1861), the narrator points out the particularly devastating effects that slavery wreaks on women and children: "[W]omen are considered of no value, unless they continually increase their owner's stock. They are put on a par with animals" (380). The ideological lessons imparted by such narratives appear in many later fictional accounts as well. Sherley Anne Williams's *Dessa Rose* (1986) considers the fate awaiting a young, pregnant slave woman imprisoned for fleeing her owner and finding refuge on a plantation owned by a white woman who is having an affair with one of her male slaves. Toni Morrison's *Beloved* (1987), perhaps the literature's most famous example, grows out of the real-life story of runaway slave Margaret Garner, who attempted to kill her own children rather than see them taken back into slavery. Such histories testify to the inescapable burden that slavery has placed upon both survivors and descendants. For women, that burden has been further complicated by the enforced absence of emotional, sexual, and biological self-determination.

Slavery's centuries of abuse and repression provided the social inspiration for jazz. As an art form, jazz derives from several different musical traditions, including African tribal rhythms, traditional Christian spirituals and hymns, gospel, and early forms of blues music. As a cultural practice, jazz has enabled communication, often subversive in nature, that challenges prevailing social norms. Jazz's origins can be traced back to the methods of communication that slaves used while working on plantations and in private homes. Their field hollers and ring shouts helped to preserve African heritage, convey plans for escape, and resist the social customs imposed on them by white slaveholders. Blues music, jazz's closest artistic relative, evolved from the call-and-response strategies of early African-American gospel music and the themes of loss and hope common to slavery-era songs. Blues performance then enabled economic freedom, social mobility, and expressive potential for some early-twentieth-century black women. Their lyrics explored social inequality, domestic abuse, sexual autonomy, and other controversial topics in the only public arena available to a severely marginalized group.

However, in spite of jazz's ongoing popularity in stages ranging from swing to fusion, its practitioners have repeatedly experienced racist social conditions and often found their talent exploited as well as rewarded by white audiences. These circumstances are compounded for black women in jazz, who have contended with patriarchal attitudes, sexual stereotyping, and economic disparities as well as racial discrimination. Linda Dahl points out, for instance, that many jazz artists considered their groups' black women singers the visually appealing "fronts" to a band rather than serious musicians (122). Beate Gersch argues that gender roles have helped to shape the direction and nature of developments in the history of jazz since "[j]azz performances . . . have been one of the few areas in American culture in which the black man has been able to exercise power and display his masculinity without threatening the assumed superiority of the white male" (46). While gender roles and racialized relationships have changed significantly since the early twentieth century and continue to shift in unpredictable ways, such mindsets persist in some quarters. Such attitudes also pervaded the Harlem Renaissance and the Black Arts Movement, which attempted to redress racial injustice without considering the complex intersections of gender and sexuality. Many African-American women pursuing careers in jazz and literature have therefore endured a vexed relationship to political discourse and artistic craft. Their commitments to social justice and creative freedom, as well as the outsider status resulting from other groups' exclusionary attitudes, have motivated them to oppose historically established inequalities.

Black feminist critics understand this opposition as a necessary step toward defining an independent consciousness. Many writers agree, in fact, that their work depends upon a conceptualization of the multiple factors that impact black women's experiences. Deborah K. King labels such an interactive rather than additive notion of oppression "multiple jeopardy" (297), suggesting that "black women must develop a political ideology capable of interpreting and resisting that multiple jeopardy" instead of a conservative view of their experience (310). According to King, this resistance includes "the visibility of black women," their right to self-determination, challenges to mainstream social structures, and an acknowledgment that theory cannot fully account for the complexities of experience (312). Most black feminist critics recognize a need to theorize inclusively while accepting the specificities of personal experience. Patricia Hill Collins understands African-American feminist experience as dialectical in nature, engaged in fighting "the suppression of Black women's ideas" with "intellectual activism in the face of that suppression" (5–6). Rose M. Brewer points out that black feminism's attention to the concept of multiple jeopardy and the particular perspective of its theorists distinguish it from other feminist traditions, rendering new conceptual frameworks necessary (236). This attention to intersecting social factors and specificity of theoretical perspective defines black feminist thought, the principal political stance that motivates African-American women's jazz poetics. At the same time, however, these writers acknowledge the "*intersectionality* of social movements," the fact that "privilege and oppression, and movements to defend and combat these relations, are not in fact singular" (Ferree 10). Their work seeks to address the broader spectrum of women's experiences with both creativity and deprivation.

Black women writers redefine traditional forms of creativity in order to underline the urgency of their challenges to mainstream ideologies. Their work often references domestic problems and intracultural disputes as well as issues of social policy. Darlene Clark Hine and Kathleen Thompson detail, for instance, women's struggles with black men who vent frustration through sexual harassment and abuse (301). These women increasingly voice an awareness that the threat of rape and other forms of violence could come from black men's hands as well as white men's (Hine and Thompson 302). Divisions have also existed since the 1970s among black women, self-proclaimed feminists included, over sexual discrimination, racial conflicts, economic disadvantages, and the difficulties of defining worthy social roles. Michele Wallace's condemnation of relationships between black men and white women in *Black Macho and the Myth of the Superwoman* (1978), for example, drew criticism from several quarters. Her argument that gender equality needs to be addressed before black women can address racial politics set her apart from many contemporaries. This situation articulated the tensions that often have accompanied black women's efforts to characterize their subject-positions.

Paula Giddings, writing a few years after Wallace, stakes out a contrasting position in her history of African-American women in the United States, *When and Where I Enter: The Impact of Black Women on Race and Sex in America* (1984). Her title comes from "The Status of Women in America," an 1892 essay by scholar-activist Anna Julia Cooper: "Only the black woman can say, 'when and where I enter, in the quiet, undisputed dignity of my womanhood, without violence and without suing or special patronage, then and there the whole . . . race enters with me'" (qtd. in Giddings 13). This quotation illuminates Giddings's argument about the dual importance of sex and race in the history of African-American women's experiences as well as her belief that "racism is still the salient issue" (350). Her chapter on black America's ultimate failure to support the presidential campaign of black Congresswoman Shirley Chisholm also examines the particular kinds of sexism that black women face.

The contrasts in argument and rhetoric between Wallace and Giddings illustrate the potential for combustion that exists among different feminisms. While many black feminist writers acknowledge the need for progressive political stances when theorizing the intersections of gender, race, sexuality, class, and other identity factors, their conceptions of such paradigms take a potentially infinite number of forms. The jazz poets in this study create innovative, socially driven art that contributes to black feminism's dynamic perspectives on American society and culture.

THEORIZING JAZZ POETICS

Jazz poetry, as a theoretical term, accounts for the complexities and contradictions of both artistic innovation and social inequities. Unlike most other schools or movements in experimental poetics, it addresses specific cultural moments, seeking to transform the structures and connotations of language in order to reimagine the contexts of jazz performance and composition. Jazz poetry's links to both textual practice and musical performance blur conventional divisions between artistic categories. Music and text share compositional elements; a text's musical influences enable it to resonate within a wider range of cultural and literary traditions. As a subgenre of experimental poetics, jazz poetry incorporates compositional elements such as jazz-based metaphors, thematic tributes to legendary jazz performers or performances, textual imitations of the sound of jazz, textual imitations of the techniques used to compose or perform it, and references to social issues with which jazz has historically been associated.

Poets represent jazz as a performance strategy through nonreferential uses of language like sound poetry or via a combination of formal techniques such as scat syllables, anagrammatic rearrangements of words, unusual visual spacing, and the traditional AAB blues-lyrics song form, in which the speaker states a problem in the first line, repeats it, and then offers a solution or resolution in the third line. These compositional strategies, often inspired by specific performers or famous moments in the music's history, suggest that poets use jazz to address explicit cultural agendas. The poetry also evokes Carolyn Forché's concept of "the social," a key dimension of political poetry that she defines as the "space between the state and the supposedly safe havens of the personal" (31), through calls for social change, tributes to African-American cultural history, and recognition of others' artistic innovation. In their attention to the multiple jeopardy of black women's subject-positions, African-American women jazz poets situate their work in the context of other political interventions. Their exclusion from both the male performance spaces of jazz and many largely white, mainstream feminist movements motivates their definition of a specifically black feminist jazz poetics.

As this formulation suggests, the poetry's political impulse emerges from the intersections of racial identity, feminism, and experimental art. This union of social, political, and artistic concerns defines the history of black women's musical creativity as unique among traditions of public expression. Linda Dahl argues that African-American women began working in minstrelsy, vaudeville, and musical comedies soon after the Civil War in order to take advantage of a rare form of social mobility (10). Angela Davis agrees with Dahl, pointing out the opportunities to travel that early blues singers like Ma Rainey and Bessie Smith enjoyed. She identifies a newly "emancipatory quality about their music" that could be attributed to their physical freedom (Davis 72). In spite of poets' attention to these accomplishments, however, previous histories and analyses of jazz poetry have failed to take into account the innovations of women writers, just as the history of experimental poetics traditionally has neglected black work.

The history of written jazz poetry dates back to 1912, when Vachel Lindsay published "The Congo," a controversial portrait of so-called primitive elements that some contemporaries would come to associate with the Harlem Renaissance.[1] Since that time, the term "jazz poetry" itself has occupied a marginal yet tenacious position in American literary studies; critics have disagreed over accepted definitions of its formal elements and its position in the history of poetry. Sascha Feinstein, author of *A Bibliographic Guide to Jazz Poetry*, an annotated guide to nearly every jazz poem published in a magazine, journal, or book through 1997, lists a Carl Sandburg poem published in the 1916 collection *Chicago Poems* as the earliest jazz-influenced piece (77), though jazz poetry's frequent republication and anthologization make this fact difficult to confirm. Feinstein suggests that the earliest published example by an African-American man was Raymond Garfield Dandridge's 1920 poem "De Drum Majah" (*Bibliographic Guide* 23), though he labels Langston Hughes "the Father of Jazz Poetry" because of his work in *The Weary Blues* (1926) and because he became "one of the first writers to experiment with poetry read to jazz" (*Bibliographic Guide* 44).[2] While many otherwise well-known poets dabbled in jazz themes and forms in the early twentieth century— including Hart Crane, in "For the Marriage of Faustus and Helen" (1926), and E. E. Cummings, in several poems from *&[Ampersand]* (1925)— Feinstein's bibliography accords precedence to those authors who wrote a significant number of jazz poems, who demonstrate a practical knowledge of the music in their work, who elegize lesser-known musicians, and, of course, who write what he considers well-crafted poetry.

This last criterion in particular demonstrates the subjectivity that has shaped writers' approaches to the history and definition of jazz poetry. Sascha Feinstein wrote the only book-length study of jazz poetry as an autonomous genre, *Jazz Poetry: From the 1920s to the Present* (1997), which renders his theory all the more relevant. He characterizes jazz poetry as "any poem that's been informed by jazz music" (2). Acknowledging the challenges of attempting to capture the sounds of performed jazz in concrete poetic imagery, he admits that so many types of jazz poems have been written that they defy clear categorization. Feinstein organized his book in a call-and-response fashion, alternating chapters on black work with those on white critique or reappropriation. This approach allows him to examine the discrepancies and moments of overlap between these groups (10).[3] Although the rash of musicians' drug-related deaths during the bebop era sparked an increase in jazz-based elegies, Feinstein concludes that later jazz poetry has taken a "rather quiet and strongly narrative" turn that reflects an absence of revolutionary energy (164). Some of the poets Feinstein discusses exhibit this tendency; however, he omits mention of most women jazz poets, whose work, even in more recent decades, incorporates radical themes and compositional strategies.

Stephen Henderson's 1973 anthology of African-American poetry, *Understanding the New Black Poetry: Black Speech and Black Music as Poetic References,* may be the most significant critical precedent to Feinstein's work. Henderson's introduction provides a thorough analysis of black experimental poetry that critics still cite today; the collection includes poetry by Margaret Walker, Gwendolyn Brooks, Margaret Danner, Sarah Webster Fabio, Mari Evans, Sonia Sanchez, Nikki Giovanni, Audre Lorde, Betty Gates, and several other black women poets. He argues that black literary accomplishment exists in both oral and written traditions ("Introduction" 3); like many black feminist theorists, he claims that "the ethnic roots of Black poetry . . . are ultimately understood only by Black people themselves" (7–8). Henderson also understands women's work as a key element of African-American poetic traditions, even if he does not define the specific thematic and structural elements that they have pioneered.

Although Henderson does not label the poems in his anthology "jazz poetry" per se, the volume's emphasis upon the theme of "black music" and its inclusion of several jazz-based poems used as illustrations suggest that he defines a poetics grounded in blues and jazz elements. His definition of black experimental work derives from three basic elements: theme, structure, and saturation.[4] The poetry that he sees as truly "black," for example, often focuses on one of several broad themes: liberation, the developing "historical consciousness of the people," literacy, folk life, and realistic depictions of contemporary society (13–14). African-American speech and music, including oral performance traditions, inform such poems' structures ("Introduction" 31).

In addition to the recurring themes that he identifies, Henderson analyzes the base elements of common structural techniques in some detail, including "virtuoso naming and enumerating," "jazzy rhythmic effects," "virtuoso free-rhyming," "hyperbolic imagery," "metaphysical imagery," "understatement," "compressed and cryptic imagery," and "worrying the line" (33–41).[5] Black poetry also makes use of mascon words, which Henderson defines as "words and constructions [that] seem to carry an inordinate charge of emotional and psychological weight" and "have levels of meaning that seem to go back to our earliest grappling with the English language in a strange and hostile land." The word "mascon" derives from a NASA term for concentrated lunar matter that exerts a greater gravitational pull; Henderson identifies mascon words and phrases as those possessing *"a massive concentration of Black experiential energy,"* for instance, "roll" (44–45; original italics). Mascon words contribute to a work's "saturation," the degree to which it contains identifiably black characteristics and ideas. The reader must possess an insider's knowledge of that blackness and be able to perceive "the *depth* and *quality* of experience which a given work may evoke" (Henderson 64; original italics).

Some more recent critics have explored the social and historical contexts of jazz writing in order to quantify more precisely the impact that jazz has had on black experimental texts. Aldon Nielsen stresses the political inclinations and artistic innovations of both jazz poets and musicians in *Black Chant: Languages of African-American Postmodernism* (1997). Here he draws readers' attention to the work of lesser-known African-American writers, calling for a revision of the twentieth-century American literary canon through a recognition of "the suppressed Africanity of international modernism" (7).[6] In his collection of essays entitled *Discrepant Engagement: Dissonance, Cross-Culturality, and Experimental Writing* (1993), Nathaniel Mackey glosses the title phrase as the "rickety, imperfect fit between word and world," analogous to the noise made by the block upon which a weaving loom sits. This description of the sounds that creation makes derives from the weaving metaphor central to the mythology of the African Dogon tribe (19). Mackey adopts it as a means of explaining both the historically situated nature of black experimental poetry and the influence of jazz in African-American writing and criticism.[7] He understands jazz as a major factor in several poetic situations that arise out of the need to scrutinize social inequalities from new perspectives: plays between content and form manifested in a sense of "insubordination" and marginality, recognizable markers of black experience, voices of the "orphan" or socially excluded, and the "fissures and fractures" of ideas that interact dissonantly (1–21). Like Nielsen's "black chant" and Baraka's "changing same," Mackey's terminology suggests that a working definition of jazz poetry must include a political consciousness, formal characteristics, and substantial thematic references to jazz as a specifically African-American cultural product.[8]

As another concept that contributes to an inclusive definition of jazz poetry, the blues highlights the central importance of the genre's social history and interdisciplinary nature. Jazz poets have consistently incorporated blues themes and forms, in spite of the fact that some early-twentieth-century black writers like Frances Harper and Charles Chesnutt used their fiction as a forum in which to denounce blues-influenced poetry (Herron 18). Blues music originates in African-American cultural traditions and retains historical links to jazz; most popular in its "classic" and "country" forms in the early twentieth century (Gioia 12–20), it preceded most major jazz styles and has formed an important musical corollary to jazz's ongoing development. It has also exercised significant thematic and formal influences over various stages in the history of jazz poetry. In *Blues, Ideology, and Afro-American Literature: A Vernacular Theory* (1984), Houston Baker terms blues' history of cross-influences over black music and literature the "blues matrix." He argues that the blues underlies most black writing, claiming that it can help to reveal such writing's vernacular dimensions and complexities to perceptive readers.

Sherley Anne Williams also wrote some important criticism on the interventions that the blues makes in American literature. Guided by Stephen Henderson's work, she outlines in "The Blues Roots of Contemporary Afro-American Poetry" (1979) nine major ways in which blues culture has inspired the themes of black poetry. Williams's ideas proceed from the premise that "in some contemporary Afro-American poetry, the devices and structures of the classic blues form are transformed, thus allowing the poetry to function in much the same way as blues forms once functioned within the black communities across the country" ("Blues Roots" 73). The blues themes and devices she defines include "the communal nature of the relationship between blues singer and blues audience"; an interest in acting rather than reflecting on problems (74); "the use of verbal and musical irony"; a focus on concrete experiences (75); "worrying the line" through the use of repetitions "with a difference"; depictions of "particularized, individual experience rooted in a common reality" (77); assertions of self-identity (80); literal rather than symbolic meaning except in reference to sex and physicality (81); and Henderson's own "mascon" images (82). Williams's categories, although wide-ranging, do not include form. Karen Jackson Ford notes that most theorists of blues poetics make a similar omission ("Writing Paper Blues" 90) but claims that "blues poems also have their own ground—the page—and their own terms—literary terms—that are necessary to the understanding and appreciation of *blues on the page*" (93; original italics). Some critics like Paul Oliver oppose Ford's notion that blues poetic forms possess subversive elements by claiming that the form cannot be separated from the music (8–9); however, the fact that blues music has facilitated increased economic mobility for some African Americans and enabled the communication of socially subversive ideas suggests that it possesses a significant political potential.[9]

Most histories that analyze jazz- and blues-influenced literature mention women poets only as side notes, though Feinstein lists Mina Loy's 1921 poem "Mexican Desert" and her 1923 piece "Crab-Angel" as well as Amy Lowell's 1927 "Jazz Dance" as the earliest jazz poems published by women (*Bibliographic Guide* 59). The earliest jazz poem by an African-American woman seems to have been Helene Johnson's "Poem," about a young black banjo player, first published in James Weldon Johnson's 1922 *Book of American Negro Poetry* (Feinstein, *Bibliographic Guide* 48) and reprinted in Maureen Honey's anthology, *Shadowed Dreams: Women's Poetry of the Harlem Renaissance* (1989). African-American women's jazz poetry receives little attention in either work, however. This study sets out to correct that omission by filling in the gap between the material experiences of black women writers and their standard critical representations. The themes and structural features specific to feminist jazz poetry indicate that black women jazz poets refuse marginalization by participating in contemporary political arguments. Jazz-inspired compositional techniques and themes enable these poets to articulate the social issues unique to black women by using experimental literary techniques and invoking a historically African-American cultural product. Such issues include nationally defined economic disparities, domestic abuse, body image, consumerism, women-centered histories, environmental conservation, and the problematic negotiation of black women's bodies through the often hostile geographies of modern society.

WRITING POST-JAZZ

Post-Jazz Poetics is the first book-length examination of women jazz poets that links an avowedly feminist politics to jazz-inspired compositional strategies. Many gaps in the literature on experimental poetics and African-American writing provide evidence of the need for this research, including the fact that in the three most substantial anthologies of jazz poetry published today,[10] the work of women poets makes up less than one quarter of the content. As discussed above, the culture of jazz music historically has underrated the work of its female practitioners as well. The concept of "post-jazz" defines a poetics in which writers seek to extend the formal and contextual traditions established by their literary precedents while acknowledging the importance of that history. To write "post-jazz" poetry does not require that poets discard the music's influences as no longer relevant; rather, this work has already absorbed and incorporated jazz elements, reworking them into a vocabulary familiar to readers who may (in addition, perhaps, to knowledge of the music) already know poetry by Amiri Baraka, Gwendolyn Brooks, Michael Harper, Hayden Carruth, and many others. African-American women's jazz poetry takes this musical language as a given, not merely celebrating performance and performer, but using the new vocabulary that music enables as a vehicle for focused feminist analyses. The poetry's politics also exists in the kinds of sound it makes: the rhythms and wordplay integral to jazz traditions illuminate the logic of black women's transformative roles in American society.

African-American women's contributions to the history of American culture have been underrepresented not only by the artistic and critical traditions within jazz (and jazz poetics) but also by social and literary-critical feminist movements. The dominant trends of US social history underscore black women's often unsatisfactory relationships to both political and artistic movements. Marginalized within the public forums of feminism and jazz, they have also dealt with the fallout of governmental decisions that overlook the nuances of race, class, gender, and sexual preference. Hine and Thompson explain how, even though laws such as Title VII of the 1964 Civil Rights Act made significant provisions for gender equality in the public and private spheres, black women have continued to face obstacles to their rights as citizens in the workplace and at home and as cultural representatives. In spite of their central roles in the United States' still-unfolding history of civil struggle, these women remain enmeshed in the contradictory social effects of post–Civil Rights attitudes. This book attempts to rectify such marginalizations by drawing critical attention to the particular innovations and social meaning that their words convey.

Post-Jazz Poetics contributes a new perspective to revisionist histories of African-American women by positioning a previously overlooked mode of literary analysis within the relevant social history. The connections that I identify between jazz-based formal innovations and political statement define feminist jazz poetry as an important subgenre of contemporary experimental poetics. Black women jazz poets write in a "third language" spurred by the exclusion of African-American women from white feminist practices and the predominately male culture of jazz performance. Each writer's work engages in a dialectic exchange with contemporary jazz and feminist movements in order to identify an alternate space for the creative acts of black women. Beate Gersch suggests that readers did not begin to recognize and seek out black women's jazz-influenced work until "the emergence of black feminism and a gradual inclusion of women's voices in literature canons and literary criticism" (50). Their absorption and transformation of the textual innovations that jazz enables, alongside a consistently radical political consciousness, expand the poetry's aesthetic possibilities beyond the definitions imagined by earlier contributors to the history of jazz poetics.

I examine, therefore, both the poetry's experimental linguistic elements and the new poetic genres that have evolved through transformations of poetic conventions and new approaches to traditional forms like the elegy and the sonnet. Many critics and poets, including Aldon Nielsen, Nathaniel Mackey, and Harryette Mullen herself, emphasize the need to theorize the forms, structures, and visual elements of African-American poetry alongside the work's aural and rhetorical impact. As Meta Du Ewa Jones has pointed out, "scholarship on orality in African-American litera-ture is too often bonded to the notion of the 'vernacular' as the authen-ticating stamp upon the critical packaging of Black poetry" (70). At the same time, because many black writers have composed pieces originally intended for verbal delivery, scholars have neglected "the achievements of their compositional effects on a *textual* level" (Jones 77); instead, "the musically influenced *sounds* within African-American poetry must be consistently linked to their *signs*—their visual dimensions" (Jones 87; original italics). Investigating the interactions between this poetry's vari-ously oral and textual elements yields essential insights into its long-term social and literary influences.

The chapters of my study follow an organization inspired by the chron-ological history of developments in blues and jazz music; my argument presumes that both social message and formal structure define the impor-tance of this poetry's innovations. I begin with the work of Sherley Anne Williams, whose poetry examines the blues-based feminism embodied by Bessie Smith as both a professional singer and a black woman living in early twentieth-century America. In Chapter 1, "Finding Her Voice: The Body Politics of Sherley Anne Williams's Blues," I argue that Williams uses regionalist themes and blues references to highlight the restrictions historically placed upon black female bodies and to advocate a politics of community. Angela Davis has noted the revolutionary possibilities that blues singers represented; their music offered "a cultural site where masses of black women could associate themselves aesthetically with travel as a mode of freedom" (67). Williams depicts Bessie Smith as a representative blueswoman in many of her jazz poems in order to suggest that Smith's body, a mobile site of both white and black fascination, symbolized agency for black women, as did her public attitudes and daring lyrics. Her body's movement through a variety of geographies often considered off-limits to African Americans during the Jim Crow era both mirrors and challenges the regionalist sensibilities of much blues music. My readings of her poetry allow me to conclude that Williams uses blues references in her poetry as a means of validating black women's physical presences in the face of artistic and social marginalization.

In Chapter 2, "Nationhood Re-formed: Revolutionary Style and Practice in Sonia Sanchez's Jazz Poetics," I read Sanchez's jazz poems in the context of her shifting political and artistic affiliations. During her participation in the Black Arts Movement and in Black Power organizations like the Nation of Islam, Sanchez explored the performance techniques of bebop as a vehicle for both formal poetic innovation and political statement. After she repudiated the ideologies of Black Power, Sanchez sought out the blues as historical source material and formal model for her work. These creative decisions resulted in the consolidation of two important jazz-poetic forms: the jazz elegy and the blues haiku. Jahan Ramazani's and Melissa Zeiger's theories of the elegy inform my readings of Sanchez's elegies as key contributions to the emerging jazz elegy tradition, which reimagined poetic conventions in order to address contemporary issues. Drawing on Frenzella Elaine De Lancey's theorization of Sanchez's new haiku form as well as more traditional theories of the haiku, I demonstrate how Sanchez reconceptualizes the haiku as a specifically feminist poetic form through invocations of blues history. Her feminism derives from a fundamental belief in the social relevance of experimental poetry, further reinforced by her work as a teacher and an advocate for hip-hop musicians.

In Chapter 3, "Talk to Me: Ecofeminist Disruptions in the Jazz Poetry of Jayne Cortez," I begin my analysis of Cortez's jazz poetry from her early relationship with jazz saxophonist Ornette Coleman. Her exposure to Coleman's free jazz sessions helped give direction to her work's jazz references and provided the early impetus for her own live performances. I also align Cortez's frequent use of repeated-line blues forms with the call-and-response method common to gospel music in order to argue that her poetry is formally rooted in the performance traditions of blues and jazz. Her jazz poetry's often disturbing images of violated bodies and the natural world, as well as the political rhetoric that draws on jazz-based slang as a marker of authenticity, recall the concerns of ecofeminist writers like Greta Gaard and the compositional strategies of surrealist writers such as Aimé Césaire. These images and rhetoric also resonate with blues lyrics, which commonly incorporate surrealist imagery and irony to heighten their rhetorical effect. Cortez's interest in the material consequences of environmental violations enables her to reframe surrealist discourse as feminist and to understand ecofeminist struggle as both environmental and racial.

In Chapter 4, "Shape Shifting: The Urban Geographies of Wanda Coleman's Jazz Poetry," I focus on the work of Wanda Coleman, a talented and prolific Los Angeles writer who has received less critical attention than she deserves. Here I link her revisions of traditional poetic forms like the sonnet to a range of jazz influences and to the peculiar geographies of neglected American social strata. Her poetry proposes urban landscapes as a literary alternative to the visions of New England and New York offered by other regionalist writers. Coleman depicts the socially marginal spaces of America's working-class urban neighborhoods, particularly those of southern Los Angeles, highlighting their lopsided relationship to the institutions that regulate the nature of American citizenship. Her *American Sonnets* series, which she wrote as part of three different books of poetry, both defies the conventions of the traditional sonnet form and employs jazz-influenced compositional strategies in order to advocate new modes of creation.

In Chapter 5, "Jazz's Word for It: Harryette Mullen and the Politics of Intellectualism," I investigate the jazz references of Mullen's poetry as evidence of the fragmented compositional techniques and global scope of postmodernist jazz styles. The idea of a "third language" originates in Mullen's own scholarship; in her work, this term signifies her incorporation of highly academicized formal techniques such as those of the Language group alongside a range of African-American textual and oral traditions. This approach enables her to define a new brand of intellectualism in which innovative poetic language helps to promote political change. Like Williams, Sanchez, Cortez, and Coleman, Mullen uses blues elements as a means of shaping feminist statements: here, as a vehicle for a revisionist history of black women's achievements. Her work's transformations of traditional poetic forms and even individual words themselves create a textual approximation of improvisatory jazz performance that challenges the accepted discourses of art and society.

In the book's conclusion, "'Too Many Books For Our Eyes': Future Politics, Future Poetries," I contend that these writers' attention to social and aesthetic contexts signifies a new strand in the history of radical black poetics. Their work consistently manifests an awareness of the many factors that can complicate literary reception, yet they champion art as an important barometer of social change; the poetry's social messages render it immediately responsive to shifts in popular rights and attitudes. As Gregory V. Thomas suggests, for instance, "the similarities in the process through which . . . jazz and Afro-American literature achieved institutional and canonical status can reveal much about cultural change and cultural politics" (303). These poets' commitment to creating a place for black women's voices within the already marginalized discourses of jazz and feminism calls for more critical attention to black women writers and proposes a new set of political and aesthetic concerns. All five of these writers contest poetic conventions even as they demonstrate their familiarity with literary tradition. Their jazz-based revisions of forms and styles suggest that they are rewriting the literary and social practices from which their voices have been excluded, even as the complex range of feminisms in which they participate supports the notion of a transnational feminist politics.

This jazz poetry reflects many of the important social and literary changes of the past several decades. As influential public and professional presences, these poets create work that protests social oppression as well as ideological and artistic marginality. They reappropriate musical references and techniques from the traditionally male-centered arena of jazz and define political positions that serve as correctives to the exclusionary ideologies of mainstream white feminism. These contributions to black feminist thought are written in a third language that dates back to Bessie Smith's public defiance of convention. Indeed, the "post-jazz" vocabulary of Williams, Sanchez, Cortez, Coleman, and Mullen makes possible a new poetics and a new politics: a poetics born out of the contradictory history produced by jazz and the cultural remnants of slavery, and a politics that seeks to promote real social transformation by changing the very words we want to use.

CHAPTER 1

FINDING HER VOICE: THE BODY POLITICS OF SHERLEY ANNE WILLIAMS'S BLUES

IN *BLUES LEGACIES AND BLACK FEMINISM*, her 1998 study of the careers of classic-blues singers Gertrude "Ma" Rainey, Bessie Smith, and Billie Holiday, Angela Y. Davis quotes a 1925 *Vanity Fair* article by Carl Van Vechten that encapsulates the essentialist attitude held by some white patrons of Harlem Renaissance artists. His admiration of Smith's exoticized physique dominates his description of her onstage presence:

> [A] great brown woman emerged. She was at this time . . . very large, and she wore a crimson satin robe, sweeping up from her trim ankles and embroidered in multicolored sequins in designs. Her face was beautiful with the rich ripe beauty of southern darkness, a deep bronze brown, matching the bronze of her bare arms. Walking slowly to the footlights . . . she began her strange rhythmic rites in a voice full of shouting and moaning and praying and suffering, a wild, rough, Ethiopian voice, harsh and volcanic, but seductive and sensuous, too, released between rouged lips and the whitest of teeth, the singer swaying lightly to the beat, as is the Negro custom. (147)

Van Vechten's words, while intended to pay tribute to Smith's musical talent, succeed instead in emphasizing the ideological distance between performer and audience, between a professional black female singer and an upper-class white male critic. I begin my study with this example not to draw my readers' attention to a series of Manichean oppositions but to suggest that black women's creative work grows out of realities much more complex and dynamic than Van Vechten's perceptions indicate.

Bessie Smith repeatedly overstepped the bounds of social expectations, as the introduction's opening anecdote demonstrates, in order to pursue her right to the expressive and personal freedom that sensibilities like Van Vechten's forestalled.

As an African-American performer who relied only upon her own skills for professional survival in the early-twentieth-century entertainment world, Bessie Smith could not afford to subscribe to reductive stereotypes of black femininity that recalled either the plantation South or white fantasies of jungle-inspired blackness. Her valorization of her body's physical presence—and, through it, her beliefs about one's right to self-determination—stemmed instead from a conception of female empowerment that presaged not only the Civil Rights and Black Power movements but also later black feminist theory's investment in the intersecting categories of gender, race, and class. Davis notes, for instance, that Smith spent a great deal of money on jeweled performance outfits meant to dazzle her audience, as did the other blues performers of her day (137). Her onstage visibility allowed her to pose her physical bulk as a threat to would-be abusers of black women in order to call attention to "domestic violence in the collective context of blues performance," proving to her audience that it was "a problem worthy of public discourse" (Davis 28). Smith asserted her physical presence against social violence off-stage as well, even single-handedly threatening a group of Ku Klux Klansmen who had pulled down her performance tent in the middle of a song (Albertson 132–33).[1] Far from allowing her body to remain a passive object of contemplation for observers like Van Vechten, Smith transformed her striking physical presence to arguably feminist ends, promoting personal liberation and social expression.

Sherley Anne Williams explores the feminist potential that Bessie Smith represents in her jazz-poetic portraits of the singer, drawing an analogy between blues performance and political statement. Roughly one-third of the poems from her two books of poetry, *The Peacock Poems* (1975) and *Some One Sweet Angel Chile* (1982), use jazz references and themes. Several of these poems are written in the traditional AAB blues-lyrics song form or employ improvisational techniques such as repetitions with a difference and nonreferential sound syllables. The poetry exemplifies Williams's own notion of a blues aesthetic: political statements that spring from the attitudes and music of early female blues singers like Smith. These poems' imbrication in both social and geographical discourses signals Williams's pointed assessment of the connections between regulating public movement and restricting private bodies. She valorizes the visually marked and marginalized—female, black, economically disadvantaged—as a means of social protest. These elements enable

Williams to advance a social critique that links Smith's musical creativity with her physical experiences of oppression.

Williams's jazz poems take four major forms: imitations or revisions of blues lyrics, first-hand reminiscences about performances or performers, apostrophes to performers by speakers living at a later time, and retellings of history that are framed in the musicians' own voices. Although several different blues and jazz contexts are evoked in the poems, the 19 portraits of Bessie Smith that form the central section of *Some One Sweet Chile*, subtitled "Regular Reefer," dominate Williams's work. Williams extracts some of her poetic material directly from Chris Albertson's biography *Bessie* (1972), which features first-hand interviews with several of Smith's family members. Williams also chooses to portray blues performance almost exclusively through the lens of female experience, a rare choice within an African-American literary tradition that, as late as the 1970s, defined musical influences primarily in terms of spirituals and jazz. Although women blues singers like Smith made significant social gains for black women in the 1920s, they are largely absent from Harlem Renaissance women writers' fiction, as Cheryl Wall points out (70). When blues references appear in a major work, "[b]lues women were even less likely than their male counterparts to have their music acknowledged as art" (Wall 64). Some Black Arts leaders, such as Maulana (Ron) Karenga, also denigrated the blues as a stagnant art form. Williams, however, chooses to validate Smith's life and art as evidence of early black feminist work.

Bessie Smith's tumultuous but groundbreaking career; her insistently nonconformist public presence; the implications her actions held for social perceptions of race, gender, class, and sexual preference; and her continued popularity with contemporary blues and jazz fans make her a rich choice for the subject of these poems. In an interview with Deborah McDowell, Williams explains her own preference for blues and jazz as a cultural model in terms of the music's ongoing appeal: "Although blues singers, jazz singers traditionally start out very young, they always grow up; their audience aged with them and at the same time older people were listening to them, too" (201). Changing blues and jazz styles also reflect the impact of social conditions on artists' politics.

Williams's poetic representations of Smith articulate the tensions between popular representations of black women's bodies and the popular appeal of their voices in performance arenas. Her foregrounding of Smith's body calls attention to the challenges Smith faced both in performance and in real life. Williams took on similar challenges when dealing with the restrictions that society places on black women. She notes that while choosing books to read even early in life, she "was led, almost inevitably . . . to the autobiographies of women entertainers" because they had overcome obstacles and "turned their difference into something that was respected in the world beyond their homes" ("Meditations" 196). Williams also found that the young women who formed her home community had no literary counterparts (197). As a poetic subject, Bessie Smith enabled Williams to address both public perceptions of and private communities among black women. She focuses on Smith's skin color and body size, drawing her readers' attention not to the popular commercial appeal of Smith's lyrics and flamboyant performance style but to the self-presentation that helped her to succeed professionally in spite of an often hostile society. The poems illustrate Smith's agency through the excessive qualities of her performances, such as her public alcohol use and overtly sexual behavior. Williams explores the historical context and geographical locales of Smith's life, as well as the subversive potential of the blues Smith sang, in order to highlight her conscious defiance of the social roles often prescribed for women.

Hazel Carby observes that "as early as 1905 the major discursive elements were already in place that would define black female urban behavior throughout the teens and twenties as pathological" ("Policing" 740). Blues singers like Smith harbored a potential threat to social standards of behavior in their ability to move unchecked among performance arenas and to spend money as they chose. Defining their lifestyle choices as "pathological" enabled society to maintain some rhetorical control over their bodies in public forums like magazine articles even as their talents were exploited. Williams's poetry underscores the physical aspects of Bessie Smith's identity in order to erase this harmful stereotype—the mute but dangerously sexual black female body—from the public discourse of Smith's time. The geographical themes and the politics of women's bodies featured in Williams's work demonstrate that Bessie Smith and other classic blues singers created a blues legacy that is both political and aesthetic.

Many critics have discussed the links that eighteenth- and nineteenth-century cultural commentators drew between African heritage and deviant sexual behavior in women. E. Frances White suggests that Darwin-era beliefs in the inherently biological basis of race and gender link them in the popular imagination (83). Sander Gilman argues that, in fact, "[t]he perception of the prostitute in the late nineteenth century . . . merged with the perception of the black" (248), while Myriam J. A. Chancy asserts that the increasing "sexualization of Black women meant that they were held accountable for both their perceived wantonness and the perceived sexual aggressiveness of Black men" (102). These examples indicate that the burden of African-American bodily representation has, quite literally, rested on black women.

Colonialist treatments of black women's bodies and physical geographies reinforce the historically perpetuated linkage between black women and social deviance. Radhika Mohanram conceptualizes the "black body" as an entity "perceived as being out of place, either from its natural environment or its national boundaries" (xii), because geography itself "is saturated with relations of domination which are relevant to the construction of identity." Women play the central role in this equation, according to Mohanram, since their bodies represent a site at which "place, race, and gender" interact (xv). Jane Kuenz describes black women's bodies as both the site of spectacular fascination and "the terrain on which is mapped the encroachment and colonization of African-American experiences . . . by a seemingly hegemonic white culture" (421). Alison Easton agrees, theorizing that "body and history are bound together . . . [and] one cannot write one without the other" (57).

Bessie Smith's unregulated body and attitudes attracted unwelcome social attention, yet she refused either to conform to expected modes of behavior or to avoid the public eye. Her body's history thus exceeds the limits imposed by contemporary notions of propriety. Williams's poetic reimaginings of Smith are deliberately positioned in opposition to such colonialist views, achieving what Kuenz lauds in Toni Morrison's novels, a revision of "the specific stories, histories, and bodies of African-Americans . . . which, if written, will make disinterestedness and its unproductive or damaging results impossible" (430). Williams's work offers a productive means of understanding black women's relationships to their bodies as active rather than passive.

Mainstream social discourses traditionally interpret black women's bodies as powerless. In order to recoup the ground lost through this long-standing stereotype, feminists need to read their physical manifestations as elements of women's dynamic subjectivities. Jane Desmond suggests that critics can "continue to analyze 'difference' while avoiding its implicit reification . . . [by] concentrat[ing] on the discursive construction and activation of various categories of difference, on their interaction, and on the ways these concepts and categories are buttressed and naturalized through their anchorage on the body" (121). Patricia Hill Collins advocates an "Afrocentric perspective" on beauty (89), for example, as an alternative to familiar stereotypes of black women, while Dorothy Roberts argues that "a vision of liberty that respects the reproductive integrity of Black women is a critical step toward a just society for everyone" (312). In my analyses of Williams's Bessie Smith poems, I read both the geographical positioning and the physical characteristics of Smith's body as markers of her independence. Her participation in early-century blues culture afforded her the personal and expressive freedom necessary to provide a new feminist model of the politics of the body for African-American women.[2]

"RETURNING TO THE BLUES": WILLIAMS'S BLUES POETICS

Sherley Anne Williams was born in Bakersfield, California, on August 25, 1944, and spent her childhood in Fresno. She lived under relatively impoverished conditions, often picking cotton to help support the family; both of her parents died before she finished high school (Anderson 491). This circumstance forced the remaining family members to accept welfare assistance (M. Henderson 764). Many of Williams's Bessie Smith poems portray the experiences Smith had before achieving commercial popularity. This choice of subject may have been prompted by Williams's own early familiarity with the particular difficulties of being a working-class African-American woman. She had discussed her desire to give a voice to this group from the beginning of her career (Anderson 491). As one of four sisters, one of whom returned home to care for Williams after her marriage broke up (Howard 344), Williams spent much of her early life observing the hardships that accompany the lives of working-class black women. These experiences suggest that she interpreted Bessie Smith as both a symbol of the unique characteristics of black women's social experiences and a participant in the feminist dimension of the blues.

In the course of her creative and scholarly work, Williams developed a threefold conception of a blues aesthetic. According to her theorization, blues qualities exist in the social relevance of blues singers' personal experiences; in the blues performances that gave singers an opportunity to articulate feminist beliefs; and in specifically black accounts of history and language. In her interview with Claudia Tate, Williams describes blues culture in its broadest terms as "a body of continuous expression that encompasses popular Afro-American music." The essence of blues culture consists in its delineation of "some kind of philosophy, a way of looking at the world" that provides both "a basis of historical continuity for black people" and "a ritualized way of talking about ourselves and passing it on" (Tate, "Sherley Anne Williams" 208). In this definition, blues music and the bodies of its performers carry similar significances: the people who share their experiences and the "ritualized" expression of those experiences shape the blues as much as do its compositional elements. Blues performers treat their music as a physically performative medium, in which the facial movements necessary to produce its particular vocal techniques echo the music's rhetorical expressions of bodily longing. Rather than understanding the blues as an ideological "catch-all" for racial experience inaccessible to those who live outside black culture, Williams here refers to the formal techniques and themes shared by artists who create blues-influenced pieces.

Williams also notes that the blues allows artists to frame debates about the intersections between social issues and romantic relationships: "You can, of course, write blues about other kinds of subjects, but generally the blues has dealt with intimate situations" (Tate, "Sherley Anne Williams" 209). She illustrates the intermingling of public and private spheres in the blues by describing her own introduction to the music in the 1960s, when she "began to delve into the blues as an act of quiet rebellion against the cultural nationalist who proclaimed the blues counterrevolutionary because they were 'morose' songs that reminded people of 'slavery times'" ("Returning" 819). Here Williams points to the historical tension in the Black Arts community between favoring jazz as an "intellectual" black music and maintaining fidelity to blues as jazz's source. Cultural critics like Maulana Karenga, leader of Black Power organization US, established a tradition in which jazz is linked to revolution and social change, while the blues, rooted in the hardships of the Reconstruction and Jim Crow eras, evokes protest and despair.[3] Considering the thematic importance of blues influences in her own work, Williams offers the idea that "the blues is about dialogue; its story is one of frustrated union" in which the conversation takes place "between equals" ("Returning" 821). Blues situations occur in specific historical moments, and the music's female subjects stand on equal footing with men and with lovers of both sexes.

Williams highlights the intermingling of private and public lives as well as the typically feminist rhetoric of blues lyrics in her Bessie Smith poems. She demonstrates the lyric potential of blues' spoken word and sung components through revisions or imitations of preexisting lyrics, while drawing on the lyrics written by women blues singers themselves as sources. As regards the formal components that her poetry and their music share, she posits that "in the same way that modern poetry rejected the formulaic use of rhyme and meter, blues prosody rejected the mnemonic call and response pattern . . . of the classic form, replacing it with suggestion and implication" (822). Although the AAB-patterned stanzas Williams and other blues poets often employ may imply call-and-response, the recurring lyric voice of her poetic narratives blurs the line between individual and communal experience, enabling one woman's voice to express the desires of many.

Williams's blues poems mimic the general form and themes of Bessie Smith's lyrics while also making use of nonstandard punctuation, irregular spacing, dialect inflections, and references to details of Smith's personal life. These additional elements remind the reader of the oral nature of the poems' source while invoking the lyrics' historical context, their function as a means of social protest, and their subjects' relevance to the harsh realities of many African-American women's everyday lives. A poem that occurs about midway through *Some One Sweet Angel Chile*, entitled "the hard time Blues," presents the image of a husband's love as a tangible, consumable product that sustains his lover even as he violates his marriage vows. The physical act of cooking and its edible products stand in for intimacy in order to draw an unmistakable parallel between bodily love and the body's very survival. Williams begins her re-creation of Smith's song with an italicized line, *"It wa'n't all moanin and cut'in the fool,"* which suggests that the speaker anticipates criticism of her domestic and professional lives. These words seem intended to address popular conceptions of blues performance and the lifestyle associated with it, offering, instead of the wild times of drinking and dancing associated with the so-called Jazz Age, the "hard time blues." The lifestyle of black female entertainers commonly included hard work, disappointment, and abuse, rather than the self-indulgence that some popular accounts of Bessie Smith's life imply. The line's isolation in white space on the page, its italicization, and its lack of end punctuation multiply emphasize this statement, suggesting that performers could find no alternative to these conditions.

Beginning with the poem's first full stanza, Williams draws on the traditional AAB blues-lyrics structure. Here the speaker berates herself with the thought that all her work "for sparkle and shine" (line 2) has been rewarded only with a two-timing husband. Even as she describes the material wealth gained by musical performance, she realizes that these superficial gains have been essentially meaningless: her attention to appearances caused her to overlook what was really going on at home. The stanza finishes with reference to the low quality of both husband and mistress, the monetary nature of the narrator's assessment persisting in her use of the descriptors "two bit" and "ain worth a dime" (line 4). Williams's use of the lyric voice emphasizes the speaker's position as breadwinner, the person in charge of her household's finances. This clear marker of autonomy refuses popular perceptions of African-American women's social status in the early twentieth century.

In the next stanza, the lyric's tone shifts significantly. The narrator illuminates the true nature of the husband's transgressions with his mistress for the first time, as the reader-listener discovers that "[h]e baked her biscuts [*sic*], baked em soft and brown" (line 5) while his wife was out earning their living. This line, which summons up images of warmth, sustenance, and intimacy, recalls the references to "bake my jelly roll" that recur in many blues pieces. Both examples refer to sexual relations, but within the enclosed space of the home. The adjectives "soft and brown" refer not only to the edible products of a comfortable domestic life but also to the sensual pleasures of lovemaking that fill the space the speaker left free while she "was out singing in the town" (line 7). The speaker's repetition of this intimate scene a second time with a difference—"Baked her biscuts [*sic*], baked em in my bed" (line 6)—reflects her outrage at this betrayal, while the line more explicitly links the two domestic activities of cooking and sex. At this point, the speaker flouts the social conduct expected of contemporary women, as she publicly describes the nature of the physical relationships taking place in her home. The sensory adjectives she employs to evoke images of baking bread and what her audience would ordinarily expect to remain a private scene in bed resonate with the revelatory power of narrative. Her skin color also reminds her audience that she interrogates not just female relationships to sex but black female ones. The speaker's identity as a black woman infuses that subject-position with agency and belies nineteenth-century preconceptions about "wanton" female behavior.

The italicized performance direction included to the left of the poem's next line, "I could not co-operate with this 'Love' plan" (line 8), instructs the performer to speak the line. While this direction comes from the original Bessie Smith tune, it also triggers the idea that the poem—at first glance a printed artifact inert on the page—demands performance to generate meaning. Williams's source for the poem, Bessie Smith's real-life blues performances, reasserts itself through the interruption of this spoken line, which appears isolated from the three three-line stanzas that make up the rest of the poem. The final stanza acknowledges this interruption in its first line, which, unlike the first lines of the previous two stanzas, is enjambed and contains a period that also interrupts the narrative flow: "Well. The rising sun / ain't gon set in the East no mo" (lines 9–10). The opening interjection arrests movement for a moment as the speaker pauses; the action continues only when she passes judgment on her truant husband. "The rising sun" appears on one line to emphasize the illusory optimism of the image as well as the unstoppable trajectory of its referent; however, the next line immediately undercuts this image, suggesting that the movement of the center of the universe—the place her husband formerly occupied—will be altered by her injuries. The speaker then follows the performance direction on the left-hand side to repeat the line, with another alteration, as she draws attention to her declaration with "I say" (lines 11–12). This line, remarkable for the openly erotic connotations of "rising sun" and "setting in the East," is also the only line taken without alteration from Bessie Smith's original lyrics to "Hard Time Blues" (Davis 286).

The piece's final line, a spoken yet exclamatory decision to leave the husband, seems to diminish the lyrical nature of the preceding lines, but in fact embodies the tension between independence and a need for personal affirmation through love that characterizes so many blues lyrics. This final line assigns the full weight of blame to the husband by switching from third- to second-person address of the guilty party. The ending exclamation mark renders the fact that he has "let yo good woman go" (line 14) less an occasion for tears than anger in the eyes of the speaker. The poem ends on a note of strength that asserts the crime without hesitation and leaves no room for reparation, suggesting in the end that a violation of the private activity of sustenance—because that activity stands in as a metaphor for sexual activity—cannot be forgiven. The ambiguity of speaker inherent to blues performance also ensures that Smith's own history of extramarital affairs will not undermine the message of this musical-poetic discourse.

"[T]he hard time Blues" depicts several of the major topics of Williams's blues-influenced work: food and sexuality, financial and bodily independence, and historicized perspectives on women blues musicians' lives. The specific textual strategies that Williams employs to communicate these themes—stage directions, spacing, punctuation, biographical references—act in the service of her blues aesthetic, which seeks to convey the particular worth of black creativity as well as its historical evolution. Williams sums up this aesthetic in "Blues is Something to Think About," the second poem by this title in *The Peacock Poems* (a fact that in itself suggests a kind of conscious self-revision). Describing the blues as "a traditional situation / with a new response" (lines 2–3), Williams suggests that the black language inherent to the blues changes unpredictably as it incorporates revisionist perspectives on history.

"THIS COULD BE THAT ROAD": REGION AND THE BODY

The nomadic dimension of Sherley Anne Williams's experiences, another possible motivation for her choice of Bessie Smith as poetic subject, developed during the course of her graduate education and professional career. After receiving her bachelor's degree from California State University, Fresno, in 1966 ("In Memoriam" 64), she studied first with poet and critic Robert Hayden at Fisk University and then with Sterling Brown at Howard University.[4] She received a master's degree in American literature from Brown University in 1972 (M. Henderson 764). During her graduate education, she taught in the African-American studies program at Brown and at Federal City College in Washington, D. C. (Anderson 491; Howard 344). Her geographic mobility during this period highlights the diversity of her literary mentors and suggests that her scholarly interests in history, literature, and cultural theory originated in part in a sense of physical transience or displacement. Like Smith, she sought professional advancement through changes in physical situation.

In Williams's work, a strong sense of geographical locatedness is linked to the persistent discrepancy between the position that black women occupy in society and the recognition that they deserve. In her 1983 interview with Claudia Tate, just after the publication of *Some One Sweet Angel Chile*, she describes the professionally fraught position of African-American women writers, who have often had to struggle for intellectual recognition among their black male peers. The strength Williams believes that she and her contemporaries possess exists in their "same sense of commitment, that rock-hard will," which allows them to focus on "understanding the self, the family, and the community" in lieu of trying to address broader, less concrete issues. Their writing offers more political immediacy as a result, Williams claims, since it poses questions such as "what are we going to do about the here and now, me and you?" (Tate, "Sherley Anne Williams" 206). One answer to this question lies in Williams's project of portraying the lives of "lower-income black women" as a means of exploring the knowledge they can offer the socially aware reading public (Tate, "Sherley Anne Williams" 207). This textual link to her childhood indicates that personal experience has helped to determine her work's themes.[5]

Like Bessie Smith, Williams lived a mobile existence as a publicly recognized black female professional. Although she did not begin writing for a public audience until after college, she published her first piece in an East Coast journal: a short story, "Tell Martha Not to Moan," printed in *Massachusetts Review* in 1967 (Anderson 491).[6] This story narrates the relationship between Martha and her lover, Time, who educate one another about the things their lives lack: racial pride on Martha's part and a sense of manly responsibility on Time's. Although Martha finds herself alone and pregnant at the end of the story, her new sense of identity as both an African American and a woman, living in a small town rather than in New York as Time has elected to do, illustrates the joint valorization of physical traits and geographical locale that would characterize Williams's later work.

Williams's poetry, in spite of its social relevance, does not appear at first glance to engage seriously with either the 1980s political conservatism contemporary to her writing or the consequent poverty and unemployment suffered by American minority groups in particular. However, her commentary on African-American female authorship is aligned with the broader efforts of women of color to define the issues ignored by the primarily white, middle-class second-wave feminist movement.[7] Her attention to community, a theme common to much black feminist theory, suggests that her writing shares a goal with the national movement: rewriting the domestic space as a source of feminist agency. At the same time, she complicates the feminist movement's original goals by calling attention to the experiences of working-class black women. Williams's use of domestic themes as a vehicle for political messages can also be understood as a means of fostering what Francesca Sawaya has called "a black political community that could counter the 'force of prejudice'" (72). Sawaya interprets the presence of regionalist themes in the work of some African-American women writers as attempts both to "counter the racist regionalism of white Southern writers and to authorize their own political voices" through the cultivation of specifically black fictional communities (74). While Williams's poetic invocations of region do not reference identifiably Southern communities, her emphasis on the connections between themes of travel and African-American history positions her work in the context of blues culture, itself defined by activist messages.

Williams's regional themes often derive from poetic scenarios based in the home and the performance arena, drawing connections between community-building and political awareness among black women.[8] Geographical mobility and expressive license afforded classic-blues singers like Bessie Smith a unique forum for socially relevant communication. Smith's travels between the American South and North and her function as a symbol of social mobility for black women operate as central tropes in Williams's poetry. Angela Davis and Hazel Carby have both noted the revolutionary possibilities historically embodied by blues singers, whose music "permitted the women's blues community—performers and audiences alike—to engage aesthetically with ideas and experiences that were not accessible to them in real life" (Davis 66) and created "a web of connections among working-class migrants" (Carby, "Policing" 754). Through their subject matter and rhetorical approach, women blues singers anticipated many of the goals of later black feminist movements: social and political freedom, self-determination, communal solidarity, and fair labor practices. Williams depicts the contexts of Smith's career as a blues performer in terms of both Smith's achievement of these goals and the places where such social interactions occurred.

Bessie Smith has also come to be associated with a specific geographical location through the widely publicized and spectacularly violent nature of her early death, an incident upon which Williams's narrator reflects in the last of her Bessie Smith poems. Smith was injured in a bizarre automobile accident on September 26, 1937, when manager and lover Richard Morgan ran her car into a National Biscuit Company truck stopped on the side of a dark highway outside Clarksdale, Mississippi. The accident sparked accounts written by Morgan himself, the attending doctor, Smith's adopted son Jack Jr., and jazz enthusiast John Hammond, although no one has been able to determine whether racism was a factor in the untreated blood loss that caused her death about eight hours later (Albertson 218–26).[9] Smith's failure to achieve a major comeback, which had seemed to be in the works at the time of her death, coupled with this suspicion of racism, assured her a legendary status that was augmented by the appearance of several works on her life in the coming years.[10] The key attraction of this story for the general public remains the picture of a mute and violated black female body whose geographical mobility resonates in some contexts with tragedy rather than freedom.

Williams references key elements of Bessie Smith's biography like her death in order to establish an important link between the politics of the body and the politics of the region in her work. Smith's body, an emblematic black woman's body, functions in the poetry as a conflicted site of public expression, self-definition, and violation. As her ability to travel freely indicated her status as an icon of feminist self-sufficiency, so Smith's sudden extinction within the familiar geography of her travels symbolizes the continued social barriers to black women's professional achievement. The many popular representations of Smith's body in both performance and death align it with Diane Roberts's theory of the relationship between race and region: socially symbolic black bodies like Smith's can become entangled in a "war over the body" in which "[t]he body is defined and circumscribed according to gender, race, and class" (2). Roberts points out that such struggles over physical and geographical representation are historically informed, involving traditional stereotypes as much as recent events (22). For Williams, Smith embodies not only the social freedom owed to African-American women but also the ways in which women have been physically censured. Retelling the events of Smith's life allows her to create a specifically "black political community," as her work, like that of other regionalist African-American women writers, "authorizes [her] voice through and against the canons that sought to define [her]" (Sawaya 85). In Williams's poems, Smith's body and voice reenter the performance space while refusing to legitimate the spectacle of her death.

The final poem of the Bessie Smith group in *Some One Sweet Angel Chile*, "down torrey pines road," highlights the connections Williams draws between regional location and bodily experience. In this narrative, which sketches a car ride down a road running north and south through La Jolla, California, the speaker draws a parallel between her own journey in the present and the journey Smith took to her death. The speaker reflects that "this could be that road / in Mississippi" (lines 1–2) in spite of the chronological and geographical differences between herself and Smith. The effect of the moonlight is the same, the way it "washes / out all colors" (lines 5–6) as well as the trees and shadows and curves in the road that must also have been among the last sights Smith saw before her fatal accident. The fact that the potential for physical harm exists in both places suggests that the two women's situations might also be linked by shared experiences of racial discrimination. If Smith's ability to travel distinguished her from other contemporary black women, and her life was abruptly cut short in the course of that travel, then, too, the speaker's mobility might be curtailed by outside threats waiting down the road. Although mainstream society no longer condones the segregation embodied by "the Jim / Crow ward in the hospital / that used to be there" (lines 16–18), a sense of menace persists. The speaker faces that menace as she imagines Smith might have, "dar[ing] each curve to / surprise me" (lines 19–20) in the same manner with which daily obstacles must be dealt; in this case, the "rear-end of some truck" meeting her "before I can stop" (lines 22–23) suggests an immediate bodily threat.

This sense of peril diminishes in the poem's final stanza, when the speaker signals a biker passing her on the road, feeling anxious that his lack of visibility at night might endanger him as it did Smith. Unlike the subject of her memory, this narrator successfully reaches "the traffic light at the / summit" (lines 28–29) and reaffirms her own life by reminding herself that "this is not / the road to Clarksdale" (lines 29–30). Her life need not take the same path as Smith's, and yet, as she goes, she repeats "over and over / what my name is not" (lines 31–32): reiterating Smith's presence as a mantra to forestall the accident she herself might have had and to pay tribute to Smith's enduring symbolic weight in the lives of black women. Williams's decision to interpolate a response to the events of Smith's life through the voice of a sympathetic modern narrator signifies a conscious resistance to the narratives that exploit the violent nature of Smith's death. The invocation of Torrey Pines Road, one of the largest thoroughfares in La Jolla, also situates the potential violation of the narrator's body within a specific geography, just as Smith's body will forever be associated with "the road to Clarksdale." La Jolla lies south of Bakersfield, Williams's birthplace; the two cities are visually linked on political maps by Torrey Pines, which extends through the countryside between them. Smith's journey south toward Clarksdale and the hoped-for resurgence of her career linked past and future lives; the narrator's journey south between Bakersfield and La Jolla embodies the feminist progress toward self-determination that Williams envisions for black women.

Some of Sherley Anne Williams's contemporaries also draw connections in their poetry between regionalist themes and blues' and jazz's social resonance. Their understandings of the music's geographical significance often translate into metaphorical representations of African-American history rather than reimaginings of the politics of black women's bodies. However, the preponderance of regionalist motifs in women's jazz poetry suggests that these poets share an understanding of both politics and black creativity as physically located. This sense of physical situation further complicates long-standing theorizations of African-American jazz poetics. For example, Amina Baraka's explorations of jazz and place appear in a volume she coauthored with husband Amiri Baraka, *The Music: Reflections on Jazz and Blues* (1987). In the poem "Birth Right," she advocates seeking out the expression of oppressive circumstances in jazz in order to help alter the course of history. The speaker, a mother, hopes her children "carry the blues in their throat" (line 2): "perhaps," she speculates in the poem's final line, "that's how they will survive racism" (15). Blues manifests through the body, so it must serve as a tool of historical protection more than mere entertainment.

Ntozake Shange offers a jazz-inflected vision of the role that geography has played in African-American history in the third section of *A Daughter's Geography* (1983). "From Okra to Greens / A Different Kinda Love Story" consists of 12 poems arranged in a loose allegorical narrative that describes the romance of "Okra" and "Greens," two characters whose food names, each associated with the cultural traditions of a specific region, point to their contrasting backgrounds.[11] The seventh of the poems in this section, "Okra to Greens: A Historical Perspective of Sound/Downtown," depicts time passing by referencing the legendary performances of such musicians as Pharaoh Sanders, Lee Morgan, Albert Ayler, and Sun Ra. The poem's narrator, Okra, longs to relive these magical moments yet realizes that she is "not 19 years old/in tie-dyed jeans" (line 16), as she was when she first heard the performances; rather, "it's ten years later/& the changes are transcribed" (line 21). The fact that her access to these performances is now limited to recordings illustrates Okra's weariness with her up-and-down relationship with Greens. Her readiness to redefine the insubstantial relationship between them and settle down also connotes a broader desire to reconcile the various regions and ethnic groups of the United States. The geographical associations of jazz musicians' mobile existences and the travel themes common to the blues trigger the poem's conclusion.

In her last book of poetry, *This Is My Century: New and Collected Poems* (1989), Margaret Walker describes the geographical locations and broad compass of African-American history using a jazz-inflected vocabulary. Unlike Williams's work, her poetry clearly draws on European poetic forms, grammar, and diction and makes little use of dialect or Stephen

Henderson's mascon words. Jazz and blues references enable her to create a revisionist version of American history: she lists examples of black accomplishments in a poetic catalogue in order to contrast the artistic innovations of black and white society. In Section IX of "This Is My Century: Black Synthesis of Time," the speaker links the history of black music to the literal movement of the black diaspora. The opening statement that "I heard the drums of Africa / and I made the music of Spain" (lines 5–6) culminates in a celebratory catalogue of jazz history: "All the Calypso brothers / have danced music in my head / and all my beautiful jazzy greats / like old Satchmo, / the Duke, the Count, the Duchess, the King / the Queen, Prince, and Princesses / they were the sons and daughters of royalty / in my dynasty" (lines 9–16). Here the climax of the poem positions the titles assumed by such jazz musicians as Louis Armstrong, Duke Ellington, Count Basie, and King Oliver in relation to their participation in ethnic, geographical, and artistic lineages. Walker's concluding lines—"I am a black mother / running from slavery" (lines 19–20)—root this lineage in not only the physical experiences of oppression that shape black heritage but also African-American women's role in overcoming such obstacles. For poets like Baraka, Shange, Walker, and Williams, jazz represents the fame and occasional rewards of black accomplishment, but the historical strength of black women enables its artistry.

CONSTRUCTIONS OF BESSIE SMITH: WRITING A NEW BLACK FEMINISM

Sherley Anne Williams not only worked to develop a critical link between geographical themes and blues lifestyles in her creative work but also refined her notion of what a feminist blues aesthetic might entail through her professional activities. Teaching played a prominent role in her career, allowing her to draw productive connections between her personal past and her writing. After finishing her graduate work, she accepted a position in the Literature Department at the University of California, San Diego, which she retained until her death in 1999. Here she earned tenure in 1975 and was chair of her department from 1977 until 1980. Williams also served as a Senior Fulbright Lecturer at the University of Ghana and was a visiting professor at the University of Southern California, Cornell University, Stanford University, and Virginia's Sweet Briar College.[12] These experiences demonstrate Williams's professional commitment and diversity of scholarly interests. Throughout her career, feminist conceptualizations of social relationships recurred as a bridge between often disparate projects.

Williams's only book-length work of criticism, *Give Birth to Brightness* (1972), examines what she characterizes as a "neo-black" theme: portrayals of the heroic "streetman" whose life manifests a "distinctive fusion of rebellion and group consciousness" (214). Although she focuses on the work of male writers such as Jean Toomer, Langston Hughes, Ralph Ellison, Sterling Brown, Richard Wright, Amiri Baraka, James Baldwin, and Ernest Gaines, her argument illustrates a humanist social vision in which the rights of black men and black women receive equal attention.[13] Her celebration of black male accomplishment stands in contrast to the writings of some black feminists of the period—most notably Michelle Wallace, who attributes what she calls "a growing distrust, even hatred, between black men and black women" to racism and "an almost deliberate ignorance on the part of blacks about the sexual politics of their experience in this country" (13).[14] Williams's views in this book reflect the black cultural nationalism of the Black Arts Movement and demonstrate that her specifically feminist politics emerged later in the course of her career.[15]

For Williams, recuperative work on women's literature demanded an ethic similar to that she assigned to African-American literary theory. In "Some Implications of Feminist Theory" and "Some Implications of Womanist Theory," she concludes after looking at writings by Deborah McDowell and Barbara Smith that feminist critics should consider men's writings as well as women's in order to "confront black male writers with what they have said about themselves" and to perform "a thoroughgoing examination of male images in the works of black male writers" ("Feminist Theory" 44). The second of the two articles follows the first almost word for word; one key difference between the two lies in her substitution of Alice Walker's term "womanist" in place of "feminist." Williams defines womanist thought as a theory "'committed to the survival and wholeness of entire people,' female *and* male, as well as to a valorization of women's works in all their varieties and multitudes" ("Womanist Theory" 517). Framed in this way, her notion of critical inquiry implies that feminism is a humanist philosophy relevant to any analytical context. "Womanism" in fact seems to anticipate third-wave feminist thought. Her poetry, on the other hand, manifests an identifiably black feminist sensibility.

Two poems from *The Peacock Poems* can serve as an illustration of Williams's early feminist politics. Both poems are entitled "Any Woman's Blues," the title of a popular Bessie Smith tune; the thematic differences between the first and the second poem describe a progression from oppressive conditions to independence for the speaker. The first "Any Woman's Blues" in fact comprises three shorter poems: "Blues is Something to Think About" (subtitled "the last verse of *One-Sided Bed*

Blues," a longer poem published in *Some One Sweet Angel Chile*); "The Valley"; and an untitled, italicized prose reminiscence about an earlier period in the speaker's life. "Blues is Something to Think About" takes the AAB blues-lyrics form in order to articulate the melancholy experience of being "alone so mucha the time" (line 2). The speaker seeks relief since the absence of her "man is messin with [her] mind" (line 6). This piece's juxtaposition with the next two poems, both of which are prose descriptions of California's San Joaquin Valley, creates a stark contrast between the failure of her relationship and its geographical situation. Williams refuses the link often drawn in blues lyrics between transient lifestyles and personal loss in order to suggest that self-actualization does not depend upon outside circumstances.

Williams faithfully records details of the San Joaquin Valley's climate and industry in "The Valley," drawing the conclusion that "[t]he Valley is not the most fertile farming area in the world. It is the richest" (*Peacock Poems* 12). The italicized paragraphs on the next page intersperse the speaker's experience of driving between Los Angeles and Ashley, California, to see an obstetrician with a description of the Valley that acknowledges the simultaneously beautiful and utilitarian nature of its landscape. Like her body, the Valley manifests both fruitfulness and manmade scars; a semantic slippage between "fertile" farmland and "rich" oil wells positions the speaker in the interstices of gratitude and regret, looking back at what she has lost but also ahead to what approaches in her future. This persistent sense of movement and changing perspective implies that the speaker has left a damaging relationship behind her yet is haunted by the memory of what she has given up. In the end, she decides to make the best choice possible to maintain her own richness.

In the second "Any Woman's Blues," subtitled *"every woman is a victim of the feel blues, too,"* four verses in AAB form narrate the speaker's resolution both to create a new life and to encourage the same independence in other women. She has relinquished the melancholy tone of the pining lover; instead, she acknowledges that she should "need mo'n jest some man to set me right" (line 6). She advises others to recognize the opportunities that change brings, reframing the rejection depicted in the first version of the song as an opportunity to move on to new experiences. Although she sings the blues, this speaker asserts that she hasn't given up: "Naw. My song ain't through" (line 24). The thematic progression from the first "Any Woman's Blues" to the second suggests that Williams's emerging feminist thought privileged independence and self-validation. Her later Bessie Smith poems would reinforce this notion of feminist expression through their explorations of Smith's physical and creative freedom.

Bessie Smith's function as a representative image of black women in Williams's poetry illustrates Leslie Dunn and Nancy Jones's notion of an "embodied voice": a performative voice attached to a visually "different" body that opposes hegemonic patriarchal structures. Peter Antelyes, one contributor to Dunn and Jones's collection, *Embodied Voices: Representing Female Vocality in Western Culture* (1994), posits that Bessie Smith's "performances were built around her ability to ground her voice in her body" (216), which rendered her voice an instrument of physical and artistic desire for her audiences. Antelyes concludes that Smith's simultaneous public representation of body size, gender, and race constituted a theatrical "paradox of embodiment and indeterminacy" that both fascinated audiences and uneasily transgressed social boundaries (217). Smith's open acknowledgment of her alcohol use and bisexuality, coupled with her obvious pride in the physical attributes of gender and race, presented just such a paradox to many contemporary viewers who may have wished to enjoy her music divorced from her physical presence.

Chris Albertson's biography allots a substantial amount of space to various accounts of Smith's physical presence and reputation. Her manner of dress, sexual exploits, weight and stature, and obvious pleasure in eating and drinking form the center of several prominent anecdotes, like the one that opens the introduction to this book, that are used to explain Smith's public effect. Ruby Walker, the niece of Smith's second husband Jack Gee and her longtime tour companion, notes, for example, that her aunt's wealth changed only those personal habits directly related to public appearance: "'[A]t home,'" she explains, "'she was still the same old Bessie, slopping around in her slippers, her hair flying all over the place, and cooking up a lot of greasy food'" (Albertson 60).[16] Williams represents blues culture as a source for emerging black feminism in the 1970s and 1980s by allowing Smith's voice and body to permeate her poetic narratives through demonstrations of agency rather than spectacular objectification.

The poem "fifteen," for instance, the third of the Bessie Smith group in *Some One Sweet Angel Chile*, explores bodily markers of difference and ends with the conclusion that one's physical experience helps to determine one's destiny. Here Williams re-creates the first encounter between Bessie Smith and Ma Rainey, her predecessor and mentor in blues performance. Interpreting the lines on Rainey's face allows the poetic Smith to anticipate the marks her own future will leave on her; significantly, the first communication between these two blues legends is silent, as they look into one another's faces. As narrator, Smith notes that Rainey's "big / boned face" (lines 3–4) bears lines representing the defining circumstances of her life: race, sexuality, and maternity. This last aspect has written itself most visibly on her face, in "the brackets / round

her mouth [that] stood fo / the chi'ren she teared / from out her womb"
(lines 10–13), suggesting that her life's hardships shape each word she
sings and speaks.

When Rainey finally talks to Smith, her words are not set off from the
poem's text by quotation marks; instead, they blend into the surrounding
lines through enjambment and dialect inflections. As Rainey asks her
young colleague to sing something, she tests Smith's ability not by listen-
ing to her words, but by "looking in / my mouth" (lines 19–20), as if
for physical confirmation of her musical gift. Smith herself understands
this strategy, replying in kind with the private observation, in the poem's
concluding lines, that Rainey's very scrutiny helps to complete the song,
since "no matter what words / come to my mind the / song'd be her'n jes
as / well as it be mine" (lines 21–24).

Because physical traits are deliberately read here as signs of talent,
Williams's re-creations of Rainey and Smith oppose one facet of bell
hooks's argument in her 1992 essay, "Selling Hot Pussy: Representations of
Black Female Sexuality in the Cultural Marketplace." Hooks raises legiti-
mate concerns about the historical exploitation of black women's bodies
in order to claim that the "representation of black female bodies in
contemporary popular culture rarely subverts or critiques images of
black female sexuality which . . . still shape perceptions today" (114).
Many theorists of black popular culture share this supposition with good
reason. Williams, on the other hand, revises her audience's perceptions
of Rainey's and Smith's physical characteristics by framing their physi-
cal imperfections, associated in the poem with both sexual choice and
social experience, as signs of agency rather than passivity. Additionally,
in spite of hooks's claim that "many black women singers . . . have culti-
vated an image which suggests that they are sexually available and licen-
tious" (117), the excessive sexuality with which both Rainey and Smith
are sometimes associated is transformed here into a private source for
creativity, cultivated in an inner space ("She was looking in / my mouth")
and inaccessible to public gazes. Hooks's conclusion at the end of her
article that excessive sexuality can be more productively interpreted as "a
powerful declaration of black female sexual subjectivity" (128) resonates
with the argument of Williams's poem, in which bodily characteristics
facilitate private communication.

One of Amina Baraka's jazz poems also considers how the politics of
women's public performances contributes to feminist sensibilities. Like
the poems by Baraka, Shange, and Walker discussed in the previous sec-
tion, this piece uses jazz to position its subject's life within a chronology
of black history. Though the poem's politics relates to the broader
context of African-American culture rather than to the specific sites of

black women's bodies, it further demonstrates how women jazz poets draw connections between performance and black feminist statement. Baraka's "For the Lady in Color," an elegy for Billie Holiday included in *The Music: Reflections on Jazz and Blues*, envisions Holiday's ability to overcome the social stigmas of gender and skin tone as the heat concentrated in the center of a candle flame. The poem's speaker tempers the admission that she is mesmerized by the power of Holiday's musical gift with the assertion that the pure joy of creation alone did not drive her music; rather, the hardships that every African American faces inspired her to sing. In spite of her elegiac tone, the narrator refuses to romanticize either the singer's life or the world that loved her music. By the end of the poem, the speaker's revelation that "the darker you are / the harder you fall" (lines 46–47) transforms her blues from an elegy into a manifesto. She restates the piece's opening thesis with a subtle but essential addition, noting that the power of Holiday's music continues to enthrall her, not because of its intrinsic aesthetic qualities but because it motivates listeners to act against social inequalities. Her elegy thus refigures the music as a vehicle for political expression. Rather than merely admiring Holiday's artistic talent, the poem's speaker compares performance to protest in order to argue that Holiday's onstage appearances were political acts.

Williams's Bessie Smith poems, like Baraka's tribute to Billie Holiday, portray Smith's public acts as feminist. In addition to highlighting her body size and skin color, the poems point to Smith's openly sexual persona as an important component of her physical agency. Sexual freedom accompanied the social and economic independence that Smith gained through her career. The anecdotes most commonly told about her life center on her more intimate exploits, while she favored writing explicit lyrics to attract listeners.[17] Hazel Carby argues in "It Jus Be's Dat Way Sometime: The Sexual Politics of Women's Blues" that blues singers offered "an alternative form of representation, an oral and musical women's culture that explicitly addresses the contradictions of feminism, sexuality, and power." Their music functioned as an important social "discourse that articulates a cultural and political struggle over sexual relations" (231). The expressive openness with which singers like Smith treated issues of sexuality not only attracted audiences but also represented one of their music's strongest ideological appeals. Indeed, blues singers served important social functions for their audiences, who looked to them for entertainment and validation of private beliefs and desires. Tony Bolden suggests that "[p]art of the resistive challenge in the blues idiom involves its rejection of traditional Christian views toward the body" in favor of "physical pleasure" (*Afro-Blue* 49). Smith embodied both resistance and enjoyment for her listeners.

In Williams's Bessie Smith poems, sexuality and public success together signify feminist empowerment. "The Empress Brand Trim," for example, features a brief history of Smith's rise to fame alongside several well-known anecdotes about Smith's impulsive public—and private—actions. Here Williams achieves a unique tribute to Smith by combining historical details from her life with fictionalized representations of the singer herself and her real-life niece. Beginning with her first impressions of Smith after she married uncle Jack Gee, the poem's narrator, named Ruby Walker after Smith's niece, unfolds a series of images that reveal the sources of Smith's physical attraction for audiences and lovers alike. Ruby does not stint in relating Smith's transgressions, admitting that not only was she regularly attracted to "womens and / mens" (lines 34–35), but she pursued women "on the Q.T." (line 36) so that Jack would not find out about these more scandalous affairs.

According to the poem's narrator, Smith held the power in her relationship with Jack, since there "wasn't nothing / he could do about / the mens" (lines 38–40), but the steps she took toward self-sufficiency also implied gains for black women in a broader sense. As Ruby, the narrator notes that her "whole / life changed" (lines 13–14) after watching Smith rehearse in her home and realizing that physical size and skin tone did not dictate her aunt's success. Ruby compares her own beauty and talent at the time to Smith's less socially acceptable appearance, commenting with admiration on the fact that "She carried herself / like she didn't know she / was ugly, almost / like she didn't know she / was black" (lines 21–25). Here the breaks in the enjambed lines both draw attention to Smith's physical characteristics and divorce the sum total of her persona, represented by the pronoun "she," from its superficial visual traits. "Was ugly" and "was black" also suggest that the narrator had come to believe, after witnessing Smith's actions, that the singer's once negative qualities had become assets. This shift indicates that her audience endorsed Smith's disregard for social conventions. The narrator also references two famous stories about Smith's public behavior in the poem: that she disguised herself from overly zealous fans in Chicago by wearing sunglasses, and that she once single-handedly dispersed a group of Ku Klux Klansmen who were planning to pull down the circus tent under which she was performing in Concord, North Carolina. Albertson notes that after the intruders were gone, she dismissed this incident with "'I ain't never *heard* of such shit,'" just as the narrator Ruby quotes her in the poem (133; lines 32–33; original italics).

The last stanza of this poem also highlights Smith's proactive stance toward her sexuality, when the narrator gives an example of her physical attractions for many men. Although Ruby describes Smith as "bigger and darker" than her niece (line 16), she admits that Smith would choose to flirt with the "finest brown" (line 42) man she could find by brazenly commanding him to "pay homage to the / Pussy Blues made" (lines 45–46). Smith herself fosters a link between her musical talent and her sexuality in the poem, lending credence to Williams's supposition that women's bodies can serve as a central source of feminist agency. In the poem and in real life, Smith drew attention to the contrast between her body and that of her conquest by presenting her obviously darker skin and heavy woman's body as signs of power. The narrator ends the poem with a simple acknowledgment of Smith's success in both her musical and her personal life: "And they always did" (line 47)—listen and gravitate toward her. Her body, both in performance and in leisure, enabled her to promote notions of feminist independence and self-reliance.

In some poems, Williams complicates this theory of feminist performance by invoking the complex social and racial climate in which Smith lived. The first poem of the Bessie Smith group, "Regular Reefer," for example, introduces Smith's body as a legitimate ground for self-validation but also raises questions about the means by which she chose to nourish it. Her consumption of drugs and alcohol, both of which were legally prohibited during the peak of her career, signifies her rebellion against social restrictions and underlines her ability to constitute her own body. The poem's placement as the introduction to this section suggests that Williams intends to create an accurate portrait of Smith rather than an unreservedly positive one. The poem's title, printed entirely in capital letters, appears at the right margin on the bottom of page 36 of *Some One Sweet Angel Chile*, while the poem's text appears on the facing page, 37. This disjunction between title and text suggests the disjunction between public and private perceptions of Smith, a complex subject-position that arguably characterized many black women's experiences during the early twentieth century. The repeated negative of the poem's first line, first lowercased and then capitalized, reiterates this complexity.

The denial advanced by the first seven lines of the poem—"no No. / Bessie / didn't / smoke / pot Not / Bessie / nothing like that"—does not lead to a fulfillment of the reader's expectations about legality, propriety, or any number of other possible reasons why Ruby Walker, also this piece's stated narrator, might be denying Smith's drug use. Instead, lines 8 and 9 rephrase the original, unspoken accusation, claiming that Smith just used "REGULAR REEFER." This seeming tautology, rather than merely restating the terms of the accusation, questions the nature of the terminology in order to offer a more precise version of history. Substituting "REEFER" for "pot" enables the narrator to substitute the slang vocabulary more appropriate to Smith's time period, the 1910s through the 1930s, for later, incorrect representations of her life. The wide, fragmentary spacing of the lines gives the poem a spiral-like appearance, suggesting that "reefer" smoke drifts lazily through the air—or that the speaker might be blowing smoke back into the accuser's face:

> no No.
>
> Bessie
>
>   didn't
>
> smoke
>
>   pot Not
>
>   Bessie
>
> nothing like that—
>
>   just
>
> REGULAR REEFER.
>
>   —ruby walker—

Smith's consumption of an obviously illegal substance takes center stage in this first piece in order to demonstrate how her experiences have been marked on her body. The poem communicates both sympathy and defiance to other women faced with the same problem of defending their subjectivity. Williams's attribution to "ruby walker" at the end of the poem clarifies its narrator and adds a note of historical authenticity. Chris Albertson, who relied heavily on interviews and contemporary periodicals for the background information to his biography of Smith, points out in his introduction that both Ruby Walker and Maud Smith, widow of Smith's brother Clarence, provided invaluable insight but had never before been approached for interviews (11). Williams's use of this text as source material for both "Regular Reefer" and "The Empress Brand Trim" indicates that she recognized its potential for highlighting the feminist dimensions of Smith's cultural legacy through the words of her sisters in the music business. In fact, Williams takes the complete text of "Regular Reefer" from a comment Ruby Walker made to Albertson on the nature of drug use in 1930s Harlem: "Smoking 'reefers' was so common in Harlem during the thirties that many older blacks find it hard to believe that today's highly controversial 'pot' refers to the same thing. 'No, no,' says Ruby, 'Bessie didn't smoke pot, not Bessie, nothing like that—just regular reefers'" (Albertson 189).

This use of a "found" text illustrates Williams's belief in the centrality of narrative to poetic composition, as she discusses in her interview with

Deborah McDowell: "I always think in terms of story: even in the poems, I'm talking about narrative. Even though there may not be an actual character appearing there, there is always a sense of voice" (196).[18] Williams's depictions of the feminist acts Bessie Smith performed are grounded in the politics of her black female body. Her feminist acts constitute both physical and creative expression, exploiting her freedom to transcend boundaries between social classes, races, genders, and public versus private spheres. By highlighting the many barriers that Bessie Smith sought to surpass, Williams's blues poems anticipate the multiple jeopardy theorizations of later African-American feminist theory.

CONCLUSION: STANDING OUT, SPEAKING OUT

The major subjects of Sherley Anne Williams's jazz and blues poetry articulate the historical oppression of black women's bodies and the paradox inherent to their positions as objects of both surveillance and dismissal. In her work, Bessie Smith's professional experiences of expressive freedom and creativity define a historically situated blues aesthetic, while Smith's ability to move at will through the potentially threatening performance environment of the American 1920s and 1930s ties social debates about African Americans' physical movement to public attempts to regulate the appearances of black women's bodies. The centrality of South-North migration patterns in the Bessie Smith poems raises important questions about the social and symbolic freedoms allowed black women, who traditionally have had to negotiate the perils of both public geographies and social discourses. These topics suggest that Williams's work is founded in a specific notion of black feminism: autonomy constituted through free physical movement and bodies validated for their physical difference.

Williams suggests that feminist strategies of communication and community can offer a resolution to the issues inherent to women's participation in artistic and social arenas. In her analysis of the growing popularity of rap music, "Two Words on Music: Black Community," for example, she argues that "spontaneity, improvisation, and participatory re-creation . . . have traditionally defined black expressive culture" (164). Such qualities exist in rap, but not in the disco music to which rap responds (Williams, "Black Community" 165), which follows a pattern of white codification and black creative response similar to the swing-bebop conflict of the 1930s and 1940s. Williams suggests that African-American rappers have communally resisted disco's rhythmic uniformity in order to define a new and uniquely black musical creation, just as women blues singers' compositions represented a communal yet innovative expressive space. Blues culture privileges geographic and social mobility; its most popular performers are those who draw their audience's attention to the paradox of America's limited freedoms. Blues performance also compelled white audiences in the early part of the century to confront and accept the perceived double threat of black female bodies in public spaces. Such bodies called attention to what audiences might have seen as excesses—abundant flesh, sexual appetite, the consumption of drugs and alcohol, material wealth, and even protests against social and economic injustice—but their appetite for blues music had to outweigh their discomfort with such excessive displays.

The valorization of the body that Williams identifies as feminist produces complex results in the performance space itself. Here, for performers like Bessie Smith, the white audience's gaze can have a reverse panoptic effect whereby a room full of faces serves to fix the lone performer into place on the isolated circle of the stage. The stage, a privileged space in which singers enjoy fame and garner wealth, may at first seem to operate entirely in opposition to other enclosed spaces that "permit an internal, articulated, and detailed control . . .[and] render visible those who are inside it" (Foucault 172). However, in performance, different forms of control can combine to ensure that even during the apparent anonymity of "the spectacle of public events," "the uninterrupted play of calculated gazes" circumscribes women blues singers' movement (Foucault 177). Even if women like Smith purposely refuse to conform to the status quo, their symbolic weight as property of the patriarchal system and subjects of the domestic sphere can at times diminish their autonomy. In a performance scenario that ostensibly rewards vocal expression, the ring of gazes prohibits uncontrolled movements, and the promise of future performances as well as financial solvency depends upon performers' continued adherence to certain social norms. The relationship between black performer and audience is twice as uneven as that between white performers and their audiences, since a racial barrier compounds the financial dependency upon a paying crowd. For Bessie Smith, this public forum was still a historically exceptional one, accessible only to a few in the early postbellum period. Her success in the public realm of performance rendered her the ideal subject for Sherley Anne Williams's poetic critique of such social inequalities.

Sherley Anne Williams died July 6, 1999. In her last critical publication, "Telling the Teller: Memoir and Story" (1996), she emphasizes the need to look beyond history and autobiography to fiction, which she characterizes as a story about "the making of someone," describing a "process" and "always present" (183). Her blues poems acknowledge history and biography but use them to imagine the effects of social inequalities on living, material bodies moving through the real spaces of American society. James Cone has described the blues as *"existential;* that is, they assume that reality [is] inherent in historical existence and not in abstract essence" (112; original italics). The politics of Williams's Bessie Smith poems issues from a feminist conceptualization of blues performance as real social practice and historical event. Like the other practitioners of a post-jazz poetics discussed in this study, she integrates the music contemporary to her poetry's subjects and uses its language to explore the possibilities and the limits of emerging feminist thought, in this case the revisions to second-wave feminism advanced by women of color. A similar process informs the development of Sonia Sanchez's jazz-poetic forms, as she delves into the expressive potential of the Black Arts-era jazz elegy before turning to the feminist sensibility of her signature blues haiku. Sanchez's active participation in contemporary social movements helped her to define, in the end, a more politically immediate feminism than Williams's.

LETTERS

NATIONHOOD RE-FORMED: REVOLUTIONARY STYLE AND PRACTICE IN SONIA SANCHEZ'S JAZZ POETICS

IN SEVERAL INTERVIEWS, Sonia Sanchez illustrates the difficulty of pursuing creative work by recounting an incident that took place when she was 12 years old. She had chosen to compose a rhymed poem about George Washington's famed crossing of the Delaware River to satisfy a writing assignment commemorating the Presidents' Day holiday. Sanchez's sister found the poem and read it aloud to the family while Sanchez was busy washing dishes; their appreciative laughter humiliated the young author. After that day, Sanchez concealed her interest in writing, even getting out of bed in the middle of the night so she could work on pieces she had hidden under the bathtub (Cornwell 10; Melhem, "Will and Spirit" 74; Reich 85). Though it highlights her characteristic shyness in public, this incident belies the success Sanchez found in her later career as poet, teacher, and activist. Many of the pieces from her first published book of poetry, *Home Coming* (1969), urge her audience to find self-confidence in personal worth, as she does. "[P]oem," for example, begins, "i am black / beautiful" (lines 3–4). Sanchez's early reluctance to share her work even within the relative safety of her home also suggests, however, that she was already attuned to the signifying power of the writing process.

As Sanchez made the transition from schoolgirl amateur to activist presence during the Black Arts period of the 1960s and 1970s, her understanding of textual signification merged with her developing interest in improvisatory performance. In a 1999 interview with David Reich, she describes her first public poetry reading at a Harlem bar, in company with Amiri Baraka, Askia Touré, and others:

> Someone—I don't know who—pulled the plug on the jukebox, and that got everybody's attention. We said, "We want to read some poems," and before the people in the bar could moan because the music's gone, we started to go "pshom t-t-t-t," staccato-style, "d-d-d-d"—you know, like machine guns. And of course we used a couple curse words because we knew that would gather them. People stopped when they heard the curse words. After we got them, we didn't use any more curse words, but they were listening now. (Reich 81–82)

The performers' use of onomatopoeic syllables and obscenities, both intended as provocative verbal acts, points to the activist impulse behind Black Arts performance and composition practices. Sanchez describes the encounter using period-specific discursive markers. "Pulling the plug" on an ordinary evening's entertainment, announcing the intention to replace canned music with live reading, and improvising vocal sounds inspired by the violent noises of guns and curses introduced the new role that poetry would play in the coming years of social conflict. These performance techniques intruded upon listeners' consciousnesses and drew an unmistakable parallel for them between art and politics.

Sanchez's experiences at home with her family and with the other Black Arts poets—among whom she was often the only woman, with the exceptions of Nikki Giovanni, June Jordan, Carolyn Rodgers, and sometimes Gwendolyn Brooks—suggest that she could not separate the mode of her poems' performance and delivery from their content. Her poetry's themes and rhetoric consistently reflect the ideological shifts she underwent over the course of her career. Compositional strategies such as linguistic abbreviations, erratic capitalization, and nonstandard spacing appear not only in Sanchez's 1970s work, for example, but also in the poetry of Black Arts writers like Amiri Baraka (LeRoi Jones), Rodgers, Giovanni, and Haki R. Madhubuti (Don L. Lee). In the introduction to *Home Coming,* Madhubuti argues that "[t]he black artist is dangerous. Blk/art moves to control the negro's reality; moves to negate the influences of the alien forces. Sonia's word usage is positive" (7). Here Madhubuti suggests that Sanchez's innovative use of language, an integral component of Black Arts writing, helps to define a specifically black language opposing white social and literary traditions.

The vocal improvisations of the Harlem bar performance also indicate that the improvisatory ethic of jazz performance informs

Sanchez's typographic and linguistic experimentation. Post-swing, audience perceptions of the connection between jazz and social statement strengthened considerably; musicians cultivated the esoteric solos of bebop and the fragmented, atonal harmonies of free jazz in order to articulate contemporary struggles for civil rights (Kofsky 242). As a jazz poet, Sanchez explores jazz musicians' major accomplishments and creates textual approximations of jazz performance techniques. She and her Black Arts contemporaries built their work's themes upon the continuing evolution of bebop and free jazz styles. Evolving from a "musical revolution made . . . by sidemen, not stars" to a fragmented marker of the social and artistic uncertainty inherent to modernity (Gioia 204, 275), jazz provided a means by which at least one of America's politically invisible populations found a voice. The artistic innovation that the poetry and the music shared was further inflected by the tenets of Black Power, particularly black cultural nationalism.

Sanchez lived and worked within both the Black Arts Movement and the Nation of Islam; much of the poetry she composed during the 1960s and 1970s advocates black nationalist ideologies. Most black writers interpreted the social unrest generated by what Manning Marable calls the failure of the second Reconstruction and the ongoing force of the Civil Rights Movement as a demand for a unified political message. At the same time, Elisabeth A. Frost argues that the experimental work of some American women poets "can be read as seeking a feminist practice that, often inevitably, involves considerable ambivalence toward existing avant-garde agendas" (*Feminist Avant-Garde* xviii). For Sanchez in particular, avant-gardism emerged in the 1960s out of an effort to reconcile the "competing identities" of racial loyalty, formal innovation influenced by black music and vernacular speech, and black feminist thought (Frost, *Feminist Avant-Garde* 66). Her complex social agenda translated into a sometimes conflicted experimental poetics.

Sanchez's work under the auspices of the Black Arts Movement and the years she spent with the Nation of Islam resulted in two poetic forms that are central to her oeuvre: the jazz elegy and the blues haiku. During the early years of Black Power, broken social contracts from the Civil Rights period often sparked confrontations between black activists and representatives of white authority, like the police. The deaths of many African-American leaders, including Martin Luther King Jr. and Malcolm X, generated both outrage and anguish in the black community. Additionally, the sometimes privileged lifestyles that bebop musicians experienced on the social fringe triggered a rash of drug-related deaths. Artists like Sanchez reacted to the deaths of their social leaders and comrades through an outpouring of work produced in an elegiac mode. The traditional elegy derives from a complex series of tropological conventions such as pastoral settings and rhetorical gestures toward consolation. Black poets developed an entirely new set of elegiac conventions in order to pay tribute to cultural martyrs like Malcolm X and John Coltrane. The unitary ideologies espoused by Black Power—what Stokely Carmichael and Charles V. Hamilton label "a call for black people in this country to unite, to recognize their heritage, to build a sense of community . . . to reject the racist institutions and values of this society" (44)—contributed to the political impetus that motivated Sanchez and her contemporaries to exploit the connotative possibilities of the mid-twentieth-century jazz elegy.

In spite of her prominence in the movement and her many collaborations with other writers, however, Sanchez decried women's often powerless positions in the hierarchy of some Black Arts organizations. Her poetry's politics shifted after the mid-1970s, as she began to oppose the misogynistic elements of black nationalist ideology. She created a new poetic form, the blues haiku, in part as a vehicle for political statement alternative to the narrow ideological focus of other Black Arts practitioners. Once a faithful adherent of the Nation of Islam, Sanchez became an artistic provocateur who defined her own critiques of American racial politics.

Although her development of the blues haiku did not occur as a direct result of her disaffiliation with the Nation of Islam, Sanchez turned blues themes to new ends in her poetry after the mid-1970s. After that point, jazz and blues carry a social signification within the work that extends beyond the immediate political connotations of bebop and postmodern styles. Maulana Karenga, leader of the Black Power organization US, wrote in 1968 that "the blues are invalid; for they teach resignation, in a word acceptance of reality" (38). Sanchez rejected this belief, popular among many Black Arts writers. Instead, her work's blues themes underline arguments in favor of feminist and racial equality in an approach similar to Sherley Anne Williams's; her blues haiku's political connotations undermine Karenga's dismissal of the music. William W. Cook suggests, in fact, that Sanchez might have begun writing haiku and tanka "because they are like blues lyrics in their compression and obliqueness" (698). Her expansion of the blues' connotative range produces associative links between blues' traditional subjects and contemporary social injustice.

Sanchez's evolving poetics mirrors the fundamental shift in her role as an African-American female artist that she experienced from the 1980s on. During the late 1960s and early 1970s, the period of her adherence to Black Power, her work contains many statements that uncritically reflect popular ideology. As she gains increasing critical respect as a Black Arts practitioner in the later 1970s, her work diverges, formally and thematically, from that of her contemporaries. Finally rejecting the elitist ethic perpetrated by the male leaders of Black Power, Sanchez creates a feminism grounded in the traditional blues lyrics subjects of love, loss, and self-sufficiency. She also builds her work upon the activist impulse that makes her a well-known advocate for students and a younger generation of black artists.

BLACK POWER'S JAZZ ELEGY: THE ROOTS OF A FEMINIST POLITICS

Sanchez's work focuses on the imbalances in power that characterize American society at every stage in her career. Kathleen Crown notes that, during her Black Power years, "Sanchez's nationalist agenda is set in tension with her feminist consciousness of women's secondary place within the movement as unseen and unheard supporters of men" ("Collector" 34). This tension, manifested in a persistent ambivalence toward the emotional support and ideological leadership of men, would continue to inform Sanchez's creative work as well as her political activism until her formal break with Black Power organizations in 1975. Initially, however, her poetry's politics took its cue from the black nationalist agenda that blossomed in the 1960s as a result of Harlem Renaissance and Civil Rights efforts. In an interview with Herbert Leibowitz, she commented on the 1960s link between form and content in black poetry: "For many of us our change in style was synonymous with a change in content. This forged a new and exciting creation, movement" (367). Sanchez helped to create the jazz elegy[1] as part of her work within this movement. Her childhood experiences cultivated a love of and commitment to jazz that would remain a key element of her poetry even through a series of significant ideological shifts.

Sanchez was born Wilsonia Benita Driver in Birmingham, Alabama, on September 9, 1934, to Lena Jones and Wilson L. Driver, a jazz drummer. Her mother died when she was one year old, and her grandmother, who raised her after that, died when she was nine. Sanchez lived with her father and sister Patricia from then on (Melhem, "Will and Spirit" 73; Salaam, "Love and Liberation" 60). Although Sanchez has often commented on the shyness and stuttering that caused her to avoid others' company during her childhood (Leibowitz 358; Kelly 680; Tate, "Sonia Sanchez" 139; Reich 82), she maintained a fierce loyalty to her family, particularly its female members. She often refers to her mother's presence and her grandmother's participation in her childhood. Joanne Gabbin also tells the story of a trip Sanchez made to the South after college to find traces of her mother's history. Lena Jones Driver turned out to have been "the daughter of a black plantation worker and her white boss by the name of Jones" ("Southern Imagination" 191). Sanchez experienced firsthand the conflicting relationships that distinguish African-American social history and chose to make this story part of her own foundation. She also made the decision to reshape her name, cutting "Wilsonia" down to "Sonia" and assuming the surname of her first husband as her professional name.

Sanchez's father provided her with an education in jazz and blues performance that prepared the ground for her later jazz pieces. He played drums with the first jazz band established in Birmingham, 'Fess Whatley & the Jazz Demons, and counted some later well-known jazz players among his students, including Papa Jo Jones of the Count Basie Orchestra (Spady, "Centrality" 55). He also took Sanchez and her sister to meet musicians like Billie Holiday, Art Tatum, and Sid Catlett at New York City club performances (Melhem, "Will and Spirit" 86). Sanchez understands her father's pedagogical role as one of the most significant elements of these experiences; as she puts it, "we were expected to excel" (Spady, "Centrality" 59). The experiences of listening to these legendary performers and watching her father cultivate his children's exposure to specific elements of black culture provided her with the intellectual confidence necessary to succeed as a poet, activist, and teacher. Sanchez once questioned her new pastor at a New York Lutheran church about the ideas she had gained from a reading of Thomas Paine's *The Age of Reason*. When he dismissed them as blasphemy, she promptly left the church (Spady, "Consummate Teacher" 19; "Centrality" 62). Her need for intellectual challenge exceeded her ability to trust blindly in others' conceptions of faith. This tendency would later motivate both her explorations of the jazz elegy's connotative potential and her rejection of Black Power ideologies.

Sanchez possessed a strong sense of her work's political potential from the start of her career. Although she describes her early poems as "introspective, poetry that probably denied or ignored that I was black," her social consciousness developed quickly.[2] She coupled her experiences as a black woman with those of such openly antiestablishment poets as Pablo Neruda, finally concluding that "the personal was the political" (Leibowitz 364).[3] After she took a writing course at New York University with poet Louise Bogan, Sanchez began to link politics and creativity much more explicitly. She organized a writers' group outside the class and through this activity met Amiri Baraka and Larry Neal, with whom she began to stage readings at local clubs and bars (as in the second anecdote that opens this chapter). Her first publications appeared in the *Liberator,* the *Journal of Black Poetry, Negro Digest,* and *Black Dialogue* (Salaam, "Sonia Sanchez" 297). During this period she also joined the New York chapter of the Congress on Racial Equality (CORE) and the Reform Democrats Club (Gabbin, "Southern Imagination" 193; "Sonia Sanchez" 537). This dedication to political involvement shaped her work's tone and themes.

In spite of her activist work, Sanchez has shielded her private life from view during much of her career, perhaps because she was investigated by federal agents in the mid-1960s after suspicions arose that she was teaching "subversive" materials (Reich 80; Tate, "Sonia Sanchez" 136). The breakup of her marriage to Albert Sanchez, father of her daughter Anita, took place during this period. With her second husband, poet-activist Etheridge Knight, whom she married in 1968 and divorced in 1970, she had twin sons, Morani Neusi and Mungu Neusi, with whom she has often been photographed (Melhem, "The Will and the Spirit" 138). She has been married at least once more: the dedication to *Love Poems* reads "To my husband John." The fact that most commentators know little about these relationships suggests that Sanchez's commitment to political outspokenness was limited only by her desire to protect her family from public scrutiny.

Sanchez's personal turn to Black Power ideologies came, as it did for so many African Americans, as a result of the need to take positive action against social inequalities. The communal aspect of Black Power attracted many activists. Floyd Barbour's anthology of cultural criticism on the period, *The Black Seventies* (1970), employs several rhetorical and structural devices typical of the manner in which Black Power activists sought to cultivate nationwide solidarity. In his foreword, Barbour notes that the anthology's three sections—Outward, Inward, and Forward—represent the intertwined social and philosophical arenas in which struggles for black identity are waged (ix). The body of the anthology also begins with a "Black Declaration of Independence" and ends with a letter from H. Rap Brown, Black Power activist and chairman of the Student Nonviolent Coordinating Committee (SNCC), who was instrumental in establishing the Black Panther Party (Barbour 1, 311–13).

These rhetorical gestures are intended to link Black Power's theorists to citizens engaged in ongoing struggles in their everyday lives. One of the anthology's contributors, James Boggs, warns his readers against a "false consciousness" that spawns only talk instead of action (40), arguing that the movement primarily seeks to decrease the United States' reliance upon capitalist structures by increasing general political consciousness (43). Sanchez's books from the height of Black Power, the mid-1960s through the 1970s, include *Home Coming, We a BaddDDD People* (1970), *Love Poems* (1973), and *A Blues Book for Blue Black Magical Women* (1974). Her condemnations of the United States' capitalist democracy strongly resemble Boggs's. "[R]ight on: wite america" asserts, for example, that mainstream America places a high value on conservatism, while "a/ coltrane/poem," whose social critique I discuss in more detail below, condemns capitalist excesses.

One of the drawbacks of a large-scale program like Black Power, however, existed in its promotion of a fairly uniform ideology, one that did not take into account the complex concerns that individuals face, particularly women. Its initial focus on civil rights expanded into general anti-integrationist and pan-African sentiments fueled by the writings of Martinique social critic Frantz Fanon (Marable 107). Malcolm X, one of the movement's most visible leaders, urged his followers to seek "racial pride, strength, and self-definition" by rejecting Martin Luther King Jr.'s philosophy of nonviolence and identifying their status as a colonized people, an approach that emulated Fanon's ideas in *The Wretched of the Earth* (Van Deburg 2–5). Sanchez espouses the views of Malcolm X, Fanon, and the movement's other leaders in several of the poems from her earlier collections. Although some of these pieces foreshadow the feminist agenda of her later work, such calls for women's self-empowerment sometimes yield to racial concerns. She often couches her arguments for racial equality or autonomy in rhetoric specifically attributable to Black Power organizations, as in the dedication to *A Blues Book for Blue Black Magical Women*, which pays tribute to the Nation of Islam.

While Sanchez was participating in Black Power activities, she developed a jazz elegy that reflects the simultaneously grieving and angry tone of elegies written by contemporaries like Michael Harper. This form also illustrates the formal properties like phonetic spellings, slash marks, and repetitions that she shared with other Black Arts writers. Sascha Feinstein notes that poets wrote more jazz poetry in the 1970s than in any previous period, due in large part to the fact that so many jazz musicians had died in the 1960s as a result of drug use or illness. He characterizes these poems, written in an elegiac mode, as belonging to one of two major types: "grave expressions of sorrow that look at tragedy simply as tragedy" or poems that urge readers to "learn from and not perpetuate the reprehensible treatment of great jazz artists" (*Jazz Poetry* 146). Many jazz elegies also acknowledge the tragic deaths of Civil Rights leaders and other public figures. Sanchez's elegies engage with this pattern in jazz-influenced literature.

Sanchez's jazz elegies also provide political commentary through references to nonmusical historical events. Carole Stone has hypothesized that the simultaneously personal and social language of political protest authorizes the voices of women poets, who have been marginalized within the traditionally male world of elegiac conventions (84–86). Women elegists historically tend to focus on the personal consequences of loss rather than the space of absence within a broader social landscape. Their work can thus offer examples that support context-specific political arguments. Recent literary history reflects this trend in the development of the elegy as a form, since twentieth-century political conflicts have prompted radical changes both in readers' perception of literature's social efficacy and, more particularly, in the poetic strategies that can effectively express grief. Sandra Gilbert calls the post–World War I elegy an antipastoral form based in "*unbelief* in traditional strategies of consolation" and "*disbelief* in the reality of the individual death itself" (182; original italics). The events that Sanchez and her contemporaries witnessed during the Civil Rights and Black Power eras certainly produced both unbelief and disbelief. Jazz musicians' often wrenching deaths positioned them as symbols of social dissension.

Jahan Ramazani and Melissa Zeiger have theorized additional stages in the evolution of twentieth-century elegies. Ramazani cites modern elegists' tendency to deny self-consolation and give into anger at the loss (4–5), while Zeiger notes the permeation of the elegiac mode into genres other than poetry (1). These observations suggest that late-twentieth-century elegies depict anger at death rather than acceptance, highlighting the public act of protest instead of the private work of mourning. In Sanchez's elegies, angry responses to a loved one's death fuel the broader protests against social inequality that Carole Stone describes. Her work's prose and musical elements also indicate that the boundaries of her poetic elegy are malleable.[4]

Sanchez's other variants on elegy conventions include a uniformly lowercase alphabet, erratic spacing, and abbreviated words.[5] These traits help Sanchez to approximate jazz improvisation techniques on paper; such formal innovations escape the limits of traditional poetic forms, surprising rather than satisfying expectations in a manner similar to jazz performance. Poems' repeated lines and unevenly spaced appearance on the page also help to simulate jazz's syncopated rhythms and thematic variations. The elegiac properties of such traits exist in the textual resemblance to aural improvisation: a poem's unconventional visual characteristics pay tribute to a particular musician's talents in improvisatory performance and composition. By pioneering performance techniques that reshaped their music, experimental jazz and blues musicians like John Coltrane, Miles Davis, and Billie Holiday also expressed a desire to focus on specifically black cultural elements. Joanne Gabbin understands

Sanchez's similar tendency to reject mainstream language use in favor of linguistic experimentation as literary "aberrations" that "reflect her view of American society, which perceives blacks as aberrations" ("Southern Imagination" 181). Allusions to a musician's death also provide the jazz elegist with a means by which these "cultural notions of representation, identity, gender, sexuality, and the body [are] tested and rethought" (Zeiger 167). Sanchez developed her own jazz elegy through both formal and thematic explorations of cultural identity.

One of Sanchez's earliest elegies, "liberation poem," represents a recognizably feminist perspective on Black Power conceptions of African-American culture.[6] The poem at first seems to advocate Maulana Karenga's notion that the blues connotes only "resignation."[7] Beginning with the assertion that "blues ain't culture" (line 1), the speaker defines this foundational black music instead as the essence of conflict and deprivation. The blues articulates hardship, providing merely an easy descriptor for hard times. Since both John Coltrane and Billie Holiday helped to perpetuate the "myth" of blues' value in black culture through their music, the poem expresses mourning at their reception within an unjust society. All of the trains have been "derailed" (line 23), a reference to Coltrane's 1957 album *Blue Train,* while the speaker refuses to answer the question implicit in "Am I Blue," the title of one of Holiday's signature tunes.

In spite of this critique of her music, the poem serves as an elegy for Holiday, who died in 1959 after suffering the ill effects of drug use and kidney failure (Gioia 181–82). Dropping her censure of the singer's blues even as she acknowledges Holiday's revered position in cultural history, the speaker addresses Holiday with tenderness, providing an answer to the question posed in her tune through a stand against social oppression. This rejection of conventional blues attitudes does not employ the music's traditional AAB lyric form, posing instead a direct challenge to black America, yet its tribute to Holiday implies that the blues undergirds even this revolutionary act. Sanchez's rhetoric recalls the forceful public statements of black nationalist organizations like the Black Panther Party; her piece's feminist politics stems from its transformation of lyrics sung by a black female jazz artist into what may very well be a war slogan. The speaker's final assertion that she is "ready" remains open to the reader-listener's interpretation.[8] If she will not succumb to the "resignation" that some observers attribute to the blues, she must be ready for aggressive action.

Writing on a piece from *Home Coming,* the elegy "Malcolm," Houston Baker observes that "[e]legiac conventions linking elegist and subject are preserved, and the conjunction between a sympathetic nature and mortal 'man' is summoned in the traditional manner." As Ellen Zetzel Lambert suggests, the elegist reframes the mourner's pain and suffering as reflective questions about the nature of the loved one's death. However, the speaker's rhetorical self-presentation undercuts these apparent links to the pastoral in Sanchez's work through "a defiant tone that resists simple mourning" (Baker, "Our Lady" 182). In "liberation poem," Sanchez refigures the blues as a source of provocative rhetoric, in spite of her lingering ambivalence toward feminist statement.

A similarly conflicted approach to feminism characterizes some of Sanchez's other poems from her Black Power years, including the Billie Holiday elegy "for our lady," also published in *We a BaddDDD People*. This example lacks the overtly militant rhetoric of "liberation poem," centering instead on the intimacies of personal relationships in a lyrical mode that anticipates her later love poems. Here the poem's underlying assumption that a woman's success depends upon a man's support undercuts the speaker's assertion that Holiday's artistic potential remained unrealized.

Sanchez portrays Holiday's words in "for our lady" as an implicitly political force with the power to effect change on both sides of the color line, but this power functions only conditionally. She might have wielded it in a socially productive manner, the poem suggests, "if someone / had loved u" (lines 2–3). Elisabeth Frost argues that these lines articulate Sanchez's move toward "revolutionizing conceptions of gender within the black community" (*Feminist Avant-Garde* 88). Although the poem concludes with a characteristic openness to possibility, its repetition of the idea that Holiday's savior would have been male contradicts black feminist notions of female experience and community. On the other hand, the piece's title recalls reverential epithets used by adherents to a Marian cult, implying that Holiday's social power transcended the transient earthly connections of physical romance. In the end, the poem's gender politics eludes simple definitions.

Sanchez herself admits that Black Power ideologies produced complex racial and gender politics. Her affiliation with the Nation of Islam suggests that spirituality ranked high in her priorities, while the organization's strict governance of women's lives conflicted with her nascent ideas of feminist responsibility. She joined the Nation in 1972 because she was a single mother of three children and felt that "[t]he Nation was one of the places to receive a good education at the time; it was a place to go for some kind of protection" (Kelly 683). Her publicity photographs from this period depict her as a conscientious mother and obedient devotee of Black Islamic principles. In the photographs included on the back covers of both *A Blues Book for Blue Black Magical Women* and *Ima*

Talken Bout the Nation of Islam, a one-poem broadsheet published by Truth Del. Corporation in 1971, Sanchez is shown standing with her arms around her twin sons. She wears a scarf over her hair and a modest, loose-fitting dress that recalls the traditional Muslim style of feminine dress known as *hijab.* Sanchez dedicated *Blues Book* to her father and to Elijah Muhammad.

Sanchez's personal beliefs remained in conflict with some elements of Nation ideology throughout her three-year tenure there, a philosophical schism reflected in many poems from that period. Although she "thought it was important for [her children] to be around people who had a sense of nationhood, a sense of righteousness and morality," she opposed many members' belief that women should be "in the background" of the movement. As she puts it, "My contribution to the Nation has been that I refused to let them tell me where my place was" (Tate, "Sonia Sanchez" 139). She also taught her fellow female adherents about the benefits of birth control (Reich 80); Nation members eventually accused her of being "a *revolutionary* Pan-Africanist and socialist" who did not follow the precepts of militant black nationalism (Kelly 683; original italics). Like Elaine Brown, who gained a position of leadership in the Black Panther Party while asserting that she and her sisters in the struggle "had no intention . . . of allowing Panther men to assign [them] an inferior role in [their] revolution" (192), Sanchez espoused the basic tenets of Black Power while dismissing elements of the philosophy that could place black women in a position inferior to black men.[9] Analyzing the themes of Sanchez's poetry from this period, Elisabeth Frost argues that "she challenged sexist avant-garde rhetoric in order to consider seriously questions about gender" and to undermine Black Power's "deployment of a fixed notion of the black woman" (*Feminist Avant-Garde* 68). This evidence of rebellion against Black Power beliefs indicates that Sanchez's politics came to resemble the beliefs of contemporary black feminists like Michele Wallace and Angela Davis.

Personal relationships further complicated Sanchez's evolving feminism. Her relatively brief marriage to Etheridge Knight, which ended before her affiliation with the Nation of Islam, left her with three children to raise alone and psychic scars from battles with Knight's severe drug addiction (Melhem, "The Will and the Spirit" 138). Two of her poems from *Love Poems* illustrate an uneasy mixture of feminist self-assertion, couched in blues-influenced rhetoric, and expressions of traditional Islamic spirituality. "Old Words," a poem divided into three sections with a brief introductory stanza, offers a reading of Billie Holiday's social significance that seems to revise Sanchez's earlier presentation of blues attitudes. The second half of the poem's first section commands the absent Holiday to "sing away that ill wind / blowing you no good." and to contribute her "fruit" to the wider world (lines 30–31). The poem validates two of Holiday's most famous tunes—"Ill Wind" and "Strange Fruit"—in order to defy personal misfortune. The speaker claims a solidarity with Holiday; her music signals both feminist community and individual accomplishment. Sanchez reconciles these apparently antithetical forces by invoking the traditionally communal environment of blues performance and the personal autonomy its lyrics promote.

The rhetorical gestures of "Poem No. 14," which appears several pages later in *Love Poems*, undermines the straightforward celebration of Billie Holiday's music that Sanchez creates in "Old Words." Here the speaker describes herself in simple but strong terms as "i. woman. / of this western tribe" (lines 4–5), but the poem centers on her decision to worship Allah through his incarnation in a human being. Although her supposition that nothing can be more important than paying tribute to Allah echoes many traditional examples of religious discourse, her deity's embodiment in the figure of a male spiritual leader stands in troubling contrast to other poems' assertions of feminist self-sufficiency. Haki Madhubuti reminds us that "the unofficial position of the Nation of Islam was to read little other than the recommended text" and that there are relatively few references to Sanchez's newfound spirituality in this book ("Sonia Sanchez" 429). The presence of both self-abasement and self-assertion in these pieces indicates that Sanchez spent the mid-1970s working to reconcile the sometime contradictory agendas of feminism, nationalism, and religion.

Sanchez's best-known jazz elegy also negotiates the contradictions that exist among political affiliations while anticipating the lyrical qualities of her later feminist pieces. "a/coltrane/poem," from *We a BaddDDD People*, highlights Sanchez's characteristic formal experimentation. Tone, theme, varying capitalizations, and textual imitations of saxophone playing demarcate three distinct sections that join a celebration of Coltrane's musical accomplishments with a condemnation of discriminatory practices in the United States. This piece speaks to a key moment in the history of Black Arts and later black poetics. Sascha Feinstein observes that because so many poets, like Sanchez, wrote tributes to Coltrane, the "John Coltrane poem" has become the most popular type of jazz elegy (*Jazz Poetry* 118).[10] Kimberly Benston, who labeled Coltrane "the signal mythic figure presiding over the contemporary thrust of African-American poetics" (184), suggests that jazz elegists are motivated by "a larger awareness of death and the consequent struggle for spiritual and communal recognition" (120). Coltrane assumes a central place in the pantheon of jazz subjects because he allowed fans to see an "incessant upheaval of self-transformation" at work in both his personal life and his music (Benston 127, 137). Indeed, he achieved such a broad and immediate social appeal that fellow artists wrote an unprecedented number of songs in his honor; for both fans and musicians, he came to represent a unique combination of "artistic innovation with therapeutic, redemptive spirituality" (Early 373). Similarly, poets writing Coltrane poems build upon Coltrane's "tireless . . . experimentalism" by interrogating the intersections between his work and the challenges that human existence poses (Benston 144, 148). Because he represents not just a pinnacle in the history of jazz innovation but also a spiritual renegotiation of the space between social protest and artistic transcendence, Coltrane's very death manifests as a moment of "cultural redefinition" in which the bereaved give up mourning in favor of defiance (Benston 146). His weight as a cultural icon helped to produce the particular traits that now define the jazz elegy.

Sanchez's Coltrane poem employs several traits peculiar to the new tradition of jazz elegies: it expresses anger at an untimely death rather than mourning quietly, it re-creates the music that Coltrane played, it provides the poet's personal feelings about the loss, and it draws attention to the social inequalities that may have contributed to the death. Perhaps most significantly, Sanchez, like many other jazz elegists, sets her poem in an urban environment that remains indifferent to Coltrane's absence. Nature no longer engages in the act of mourning; both the elegist and her subject instead find themselves alone.[11] Sanchez observes that she sees Coltrane's music as a vehicle for spiritual relief: like a prayer, "his music kept a lot of people alive at a time they wanted to be kept alive" (Finch 36). The first section of "a/coltrane/poem" combines a tribute to one of Coltrane's famous albums with a meditation on the musician's death. The speaker asks, "are u sleepen / brotha john" (lines 11–12), undermining the piece's celebratory opening, which references Coltrane's well-known revision of the *Sound of Music* tune "My Favorite Things." This juxtaposition of a revised tune with the English lyrics to traditional French song "Frère Jacques" uneasily positions Coltrane in opposition to the Western folk-music canon. Coltrane's nickname, "brotha john," reminds audiences that he subverted white Western cultural heritage by mining more conventional songs for jazz riffs. Sanchez's elegy for Coltrane further defies traditional form by serving as a farewell to accepted musical function as well: "Frère Jacques" now serves as a call to action rather than as a nursery rhyme. The poem's speaker introduces this second elegiac possibility with a statement that contrasts visual presentation with an aggressively critical tone meant to startle the reader-listener. The anger in these words belies the rhetorical tranquility that lowercase type and the preceding song lyrics suggest.

Textual imitations of Coltrane's performance style and references to another of his more popular albums, *A Love Supreme,* introduce the next section, a 50-line indictment of social inequalities in the United States. Here two pages' worth of screaming capital letters arrest the reader's attention, targeting the purveyors of white capitalism. The poem presents violence as the only solution to these master builders' exploitation. Even sympathetic whites do not escape these accusations, as Coltrane's seemingly superhuman musical ability, invoked as a series of screeches, motivates the speaker to demand that someone pursue immediate justice. This section ends with a long cry, uninterrupted by syllable breaks or punctuation, that underscores both the worst result of oppression, death, and the urgency of the poem's message. Sanchez builds a textual scream whose continuous string of capital letters exceeds conventional boundaries of diction and decorum.

In spite of the unrelenting anger expressed in the second section, the poem takes on a lyrical tone in the third and final section, reframing Coltrane's performance techniques as gestures toward reconciliation and forgiveness. The repeated words and letters that stand in for Coltrane's rapid melodic improvisations advance a last call to the poem's audience, to achieve solidarity and work toward a more positive future. Parenthetical directions in the left margin guide the reader-performer to sing the section, while the nonsense syllables of "da" and "dum" also encourage the performer to eschew the condemnatory sax lines of the previous section in favor of humming Coltrane's now gentle tune. This vocalization recalls the scat syllables of jazz-singing as the speaker ends with a final, nearly mythic invocation of her poem's subject.[12]

Although Coltrane himself resisted the idea that any specific political intent motivated his musical composition, he conceded in an interview with jazz critic Frank Kofsky that "in any situation that we find in our lives, when there's something we think could be better, we must make an effort to try and make it better. So it's the same socially, musically, politically, and in any department of our lives" (435). More to the point, he noted that "jazz . . . is an expression of music; and this music is an expression of higher ideals, to me. So therefore, brotherhood is there; and I believe with brotherhood, there would be no poverty. And also, with brotherhood, there would be no war" (Kofsky 436).[13] Gerald Early suggests that, in spite of these rather broadly idealistic sentiments, Coltrane's remarks illustrate "the ever-growing tendency in jazz to become more nihilistic and more self-consciously technical in its attempt to serve the psychological needs of its marginalized, intellectual audience as well as to become more anti-intellectual as it aspired for transcendence" (379). In "a/coltrane/poem," Sanchez interprets the cultural impact of his music as a sign of African-American empowerment and solidarity. The poem's forceful rhetoric advocates Black Power principles, for which Coltrane's music and life become a powerful vehicle. The unique formal properties of her jazz elegies—scat syllables and repetitions that represent instrumental music, linguistic abbreviations and expansions, performance directions, and so on—distinguish her work while preparing the ground for future innovations.

Sanchez's jazz elegies rely upon both formal innovations and contemporary black nationalist ideology, yet her work betrays an inconsistent perspective on feminism through the late 1970s. She continued to argue for women's equality in public arenas like the Nation of Islam. In her poetry, however, speakers reference the blues in order to reject the negative connotations of the past, ask for male protection, and recognize women's particular cultural accomplishments. Perhaps this erratic representation of blues-inflected feminism may be attributed to what Jahan Ramazani has called blues' "rhetoric of dialectical redemption," in which the overwhelming negativity of the blues' traditional subjects weakens the potential self- or communal affirmation that performance offers (141). Sanchez found one way of subverting this dialectic in her invention of a new jazz-influenced poetic form, the blues haiku.

BLACK ARTS, BLUES FEMINISM, AND THE NEW HAIKU

Sonia Sanchez's break with the Nation of Islam in 1975 symbolized a formal disaffiliation with the basic ideologies of Black Power. Her ongoing work within the Black Arts Movement nevertheless strengthened her position as a member of the avant-garde in poetics and social activism. Eugene Perkins describes Black Arts as a movement that sought to connect African Americans across the nation, uniting diverse interests in the name of "revolutionary" art (86, 88). Black poets led the drive to produce such art, demonstrating Black Arts' "integrity and functionality" through "*real* poems . . . *real* in the sense that one can *almost feel, hear, smell, and see* that which the poem is attempting to illustrate" (Perkins 89; original italics). Julian Mayfield calls this invocation of the real a sign of "racial memory . . . the unshakable knowledge of who we are, where we have been, and . . . where we are going" (27). These definitions draw an important connection between activist themes and concrete imagery, suggesting that poetic content determined rhetorical presentation. Sanchez composed many Black Arts poems using blues lyrics and images, particularly those drawn from the work of women blues singers, to shape political messages. This poetic framework indicates her new understanding of the blues aesthetic as an appropriate and desirable vehicle for feminist statement.

The Black Arts Movement's concrete products included both jazz-influenced art and the poetry broadside, an innovative publishing forum in which Sanchez participated.[14] James D. Sullivan suggests that the typographical innovations of 1960s broadsides subvert the "mainstream graphic vocabulary" in which conventional presses have tended to publish even formally innovative poetry (35). The audiences for whom broadsides were intended also undermined the predominance of mainstream presses by buying and supporting independent publications. This act enabled them both to participate in "a material political practice" and to demonstrate their "solidarity with a specific cause" (Sullivan 45–46). Independent publishers like Dudley Randall argued on behalf of the efficacy of African-American art as an instrument of social change through these pieces (Sullivan 51).[15] Jazz, a theme in many such socially motivated publications, offered the figure of the jazz musician as "the leader of rebellion against postwar conformity and the spiritual agent of the politically powerless" (Thomas, "'Communicating'" 291). For Sanchez, the socially "real" elements of Black Arts existed in a combination of typographical subversion and politically driven content, both of which she cultivated through her work's jazz- and blues-influenced poetic devices.

Sanchez's politics and poetry both took a decidedly feminist turn as her position solidified as one of the Black Arts Movement's most prominent representatives, male or female. She became, in spite of the movement's predominately male leadership, a symbol of black women's political power in the midst of social and creative turmoil. Many of the Black Arts Movement's chroniclers cite Amiri Baraka as its leader and position Haki Madhubuti in the forefront of public developments. Most critics date its beginning from 1965, since Malcolm X's assassination on February 21, 1965, prompted Baraka's decision to leave Greenwich Village and to sever his affiliations with the Beat poets and the New York School, in order to found the Black Arts Repertory Theater School in Harlem (W. Cook 684–85; Salaam, "Historical Overviews"). William Cook has even labeled Baraka's *Black Magic,* published in 1969, the first "official" Black Arts text (687), although Sanchez also published her first book in 1969. She notes that Baraka was the first person to call her a poet; one night at the Five Spot in New York, he called out, "'Hey Sanchez, someone said you're a poet . . . would you send me some of your work?'" (Finch 42). Critical evaluations of Black Arts have only recently begun to reflect accurately the perceptions and relationships at work within this group. In his discussion of the movement, Cook cites just Sanchez and Nikki Giovanni

(Gwendolyn Brooks is seen as a major influence) as central women poets. Cherise A. Pollard notes, however, that many black women poets and artists of the 1960s and 1970s "worked both within and against the men's assumptions about the relationships between race and gender and art and politics" by engaging with subjects like "race riots, poverty, and institutionalized racism, as well as traditional issues such as rearing children and romantic relationships" (173, 179). Sanchez's work adds more complex dimensions to both critical and popular accounts of Black Arts.

While on the one hand the dearth of criticism on women's Black Arts work reflects the widespread omission of black women's poetry from anthologies and critical analyses of poetic movements, on the other it points to the social pressure that Sanchez faced. Her poetry's themes and evolving formal traits reveal not only artistic isolation but also racial and gender discrimination. In 1971, Sebastian Clarke noted that she was "very much concerned with the (white) woman liberation movement and its subversive relationship to Black women" (97). This attitude suggests that Sanchez sought to define a specifically black feminism, one Joyce A. Joyce later described as "the role Black women must play in society," which "begins with the relationship of the mother to the child . . . [and] the need for Black women to love themselves and to love and respect their Black men" (82). This formulation of Sanchez's politics underscores the themes of love, community, and racial heritage that inform her feminist poetics.

Sanchez secured her position as one of the Black Arts Movement's creative leaders by developing the blues haiku, a new poetic form whose subtle blues allusions frame perspectives on revisionist history and feminist politics. Indeed, as William Cook suggests in a discussion of her work more generally, here she "returns blues, repudiated by Karenga, Baraka, and others, to the center of poetic discourse" (698). Varying examples of her haiku form appear in several books: *Love Poems, I've Been a Woman* (1978), *Homegirls and Handgrenades* (1984), *Under a Soprano Sky* (1987), *Wounded in the House of a Friend* (1995), and *Like the Singing Coming off the Drums* (1998). Theorists of the traditional haiku define the form in terms of a single "high moment" (Yasuda 179) in which the poet "virtually becomes the object [of the poem] and realizes the eternal, universal truth contained in being" (Giroux 45–46). Many writers agree that the haiku's three lines of 5, 7, and 5 syllables in length should break into two unequal halves following a pause at the end of one of the first two lines (Akmakjian 12). Although this pause gestures toward a moment of epiphany, haiku convention also dictates spontaneity and an emphasis on the mundane and impersonal (Akmakjian 14). Haiku most often portray an interaction with nature, but that subject does not preclude the appearance of "[l]oneliness, death, and sickness" (Giroux 113). This indirect link with elegiac subjects suggests an ontological parallel between the jazz elegy and the blues haiku: both draw inspiration from the fundamental inequalities of U.S. social conditions.

The attributes of Sanchez's blues-derived haiku bear a strong resemblance to the original function of haiku—once introductory verses to longer linked poems known as renku—as a form of greeting or "interaction between the author and some other" (Higginson 68, 72–73). This element highlights a parallel between haiku function and the call-and-response strategies of blues and gospel performances. William J. Higginson argues that late-twentieth-century writers of haiku interpret its traditional subjects loosely; the "season" words through which haiku express an affiliation with nature can evoke "an idea, a notion, [or] a thought based on many specific experiences, collected by a group" (102). The social agendas of Sanchez's blues haiku grow out of a similar sense of collective female experience and protest. In "Refusing to Be Boxed In: Sonia Sanchez's Transformation of the Haiku Form," Frenzella Elaine De Lancey characterizes Sanchez's approach to haiku-writing as "revolutionary," describing her recurrent themes as evidence of a politics that combines an Afrocentric worldview with feminist values (30). She discards some of the more rigid elements of the traditional haiku, often drawing her subjects from introspective musings rather than observations of "external nature" ("Refusing" 25). Her reenvisioning of the form achieves a kind of "'linguistic manumission'" (35), a freedom from the constraints of conventional typography, that echoes her earlier rebellions against mainstream publishing. Sanchez herself states that her haiku are meant to connect human beings with ideas that exceed the scope of everyday existence; this process occurs within nature but also exploits the more "surreal" possibilities of image and idea that the haiku's "flash of insight" enables (Finch 43).

Sanchez exploits the expressive possibilities of syntactical markers in order to expand the haiku's powers of signification. Joan Giroux notes, in fact, that English works well as a medium for haiku composition: it encourages the use of "ordinary words" as a means of communicating concrete imagery (120), incorporates the usage of assonance and alliteration common to some English poetic forms (129), and gains valuable meaning from the rhetorical associations of the semicolon, colon, and dash (133). Sanchez also uses the form to respond to specific periods in her life, since it enables her to "compress a lot of emotion" and to "reflect on it, smile, and gain some insight" (Salaam, "Sonia Sanchez" 303). In her interview with Danielle Alyce Rome, Sanchez asserts that "a poet is indeed a creator of social values" that can be explored in more than one genre (229); her decision to bring contemporary feminist insights to bear on the ancient haiku form demonstrates this process.

Sanchez's earliest blues haiku offer a perspective on female self-sufficiency that links personal fulfillment to sexual satisfaction. *Wounded in the House of a Friend* includes two haiku whose speaker examines the usual blues subject of unrequited love, chastising her listener for her naiveté:

> all this talk bout love
> girl, where you been all your life?
> ain't no man can love. (82)
>
> ain't no curves in his
> talk girl can't trust a man with
> no curves on his tongue. (93)

The speaker in both instances is confident yet cynical, her attitude toward the unnamed "girl" almost dismissive. The poem's tone and focus on male betrayal recall female gossip, yet its blues ambience suggests that women possess the power to change situations like this one. Sanchez creates a narrative situation that also invokes the history of feminist blues statements, embodied in the professional autonomy enjoyed by blues singers like Ma Rainey and Bessie Smith. The second haiku underlines this blues reference through the repetition with a difference seen in the phrases "no curves in his / talk" and "no curves on his tongue." Although this kind of reiteration occurs in the AAB form of traditional blues lyrics, it also emphasizes the multiple connotations of "curves." "Curves in his talk" clearly points to the verbal flattery that might be expected of a lover, while "curves on his tongue" suggests an attention to physical lovemaking. The speaker cautions her listener because she perceives that neither aspect exists in the relationship.

In later books, such as *Like the Singing Coming Off the Drums*, Sanchez's blues haiku portray the complexities of romantic love. The gradual disillusionment of the poems' speaker over the course of several disappointing and even dangerous experiences suggests that Sanchez now follows a more rigorous feminist politics. Elisabeth Frost argues that in poems like these she "explores an idea neglected in Black Arts theory: Intimate relationships reflect and can change political realities" (*Feminist Avant-Garde* 92). This hypothesis underlies even the playful tone of the early blues haiku. Read in order from the earliest pages of the book to the end, these 13 haiku reflect a view of love that gradually shifts from joy at physical and emotional intimacy to fear of bodily abuse. The first two allude simply to the pain of separation: "when we say good-bye / i want yo tongue inside my / mouth dancing hello" (16) and "you too slippery / for me. can't hold you long or / hard. not enough nites." (17). A few pages later in the book, two haiku express a desire to surrender both body and mind to the beloved—"what I need is traveling / minds talktouch kisses spittouch / you swimming upstream" (28)—and a declaration of selfless adoration: "[L]let me be yo wil / derness let me be yo wind / blow-ing you all day" (39). These almost spiritual visions of self merging with nature imply that a traditional perspective on the form guides Sanchez in the more celebratory haiku.

The next several haiku extend the traditional blues topic of romantic love by focusing on almost prosaic declarations of physical desire. Sanchez evokes the graphic sexuality found in some of Rainey's and Smith's lyrics through images of intimate contact: "i ain't yo momma / but i am this lil mama / who knows how to burn." (58), "this is not a fire / sale but i am in heat / each time i see ya" (60), and "legs wrapped around you / camera. action. tightshot. / this is not a rerun." (68). The speaker also portrays their relationship as a storybook entry into an otherwise routine life: "i wuz in Kansas / dorothy and toto wuzn't / a jacuzzi. sky. you." (62). The first signs of trouble in the trajectory of Sanchez's blues haiku appear when the speaker lightly admonishes her lover for minor trans-gressions: "am i yo philly / outpost? man when you sail in / to my house, you docked." (40) signals that she has been neglected, while a hint of gos-sip prompts the comment that "yall talking all under / my clothes bout my love bizness / friends be doin that." (59). A lover's overly possessive attitude also sends up a red flag, prompting a hint of angry self-assertion: "is there a fo rent / sign on my butt? you got no / territorial rights here" (69). As a narrative, these blues haiku depict the inevitable disintegration of romance, a trend that culminates in a desolate tone more common to blues lyrics.

The twelfth and thirteenth blues haiku in the *Like the Singing Coming Off the Drums* series both reflect a sense of loss that the speaker tempers by reevaluating her situation. The combination of these two rhetorical elements suggests that the blues provides a source of objectivity in these pieces. The second-person narration that drives much of the book also yields in the final haiku to a surrealistic image narrated in third person:

> my face is a scarred
> reminder of your easy
> comings and goings. (70)

> his face like chiseled
> china his eyes clotting
> around rubber asses. (81)

The "scarred face" in the first of these examples could refer to tear-streaks or worry-lines, but its position as precursor to the final blues haiku lends it a troubling air of more deliberate harm. In this last example, the speaker changes narrative perspective in order to present an image of the lover that objectifies his dangerous qualities even as it places the blame for the situation entirely on his shoulders. Images of "chiseled / china" and "rubber asses" evoke manmade materials, impervious to change; "his eyes clotting" suggests both death and the healing of a wound. This healing does not necessarily signal redemption, since the "rubber asses" may belong to other women, objectified or doll-like in their submission to his treatment. The blues haiku in this book in particular illustrate Sanchez's use of the haiku form to communicate compressed feminist messages inspired by blues subjects and attitudes. Her work not only participates in the literary tradition of filtering human emotion through the natural world but also complicates the views of love already established by the blues tradition. Joyce A. Joyce argues that there are "sharp similarities between the African proverb and haiku poetry," including "brevity of expression, the figurative characteristics essential to poetry, and . . . the goals of arousing emotions and/or providing insight" (144–45). The blues haiku's affinity with its African cultural roots strengthens Sanchez's definition of a specifically African-American feminism.

Regina B. Jennings labels Sanchez's combination of political statement and blues references her "blue/black poetics," a historically conscious approach to poetic composition that references both "the tragic institution of European slavery and the vital energizer that reformed the tragedy" (127). Kathleen Crown uses a similar combination of terms when she argues that Sanchez's developing feminist sensibility "merg[es]these differently gendered 'blue' (spiritual) and 'black' (political) aesthetics" ("Collector of Shouts" 36). These assessments locate her work's formal innovations at the intersection of history and political act. Her poetry's composition also grows out of a commitment to educating her audience, a characteristic that Jennings attributes to Black Arts practitioners and links to traditional African modes of communication (125). Sanchez refashions traditional poetic forms, the elegy and the haiku, as black cultural expressions, seeking out opportunities for creative expression that showcase her cross-cultural allegiances.

Haiku theorist Hiroaki Sato posits that "American haiku poets, living in a tradition that emphasizes freedom rather than conformity, show a distinct 'willingness to experiment with ever new forms'" (207). Sanchez's work displays a consistent determination to surpass the limits of both cultural ideology and poetic form. On teaching her students to first explore and then challenge poetic form, Sanchez remarks that when they finally understand the difficulty of writing free verse, "[they] really recognize what a free verse is all about. It is *not* free. It is not sprawling all over the damn page. There's a reason for having one word on one line, not just because you feel like it . . . you must begin to hear that reason, and understand that reason" (Melhem, "The Will and the Spirit" 169). Sonia Sanchez's affiliations with Black Power institutions and the Black Arts Movement, as well as her developing feminist sensibility, demonstrate that she has struggled to define a politics that can reconcile personal belief and collective consciousness. These efforts have culminated in her role as a teacher who guides others to locate social meaning in textual experiment.

TEACHING AND ACTIVISM

Sanchez has often discussed the importance she places on her teaching as well as her writing and activist work. Frenzella Elaine De Lancey calls her classroom methodology a "liberation pedagogy" that uncovers the false assumptions underlying social stereotypes ("Scientist and Poet" 31). De Lancey describes Sanchez's teaching strategies as oppositions to "mentacide," or "attempts to deconstruct embedded [Eurocentric] images" ("Cracking the Skull" 31). This painful process sometimes produces "moments of cognitive dissonance" and "transitional moments of dis/ease" (De Lancey, "Cracking the Skull" 28). Ultimately, Sanchez's classes contest discriminatory beliefs through writing, discussion, and public acts. She also encourages her students to confront the traumas that exist within every culture's histories; when students "went searching for [themselves]," she suggests, "[they] discovered other people hidden, too. . . . You couldn't teach this and stay in one place" (Feinstein, "Interview" 172). Sanchez's own struggles to define a black feminist politics help to shape the activist principles of her pedagogy.

Sanchez employs pedagogical strategies in texts for audiences of all ages. The title poem of one of her earliest books, *It's a New Day: Poems for Young Brothas and Sistuhs* (1971), reminds children of their responsibility to distinguish themselves. Here she urges boys to become political and religious leaders like Louis Farrakhan and Elijah Muhammad, while girls should look to Clotelle, the heroine of black abolitionist writer William Wells Brown's famous novel; Gwendolyn Brooks; and Fannie Lou Hamer. The poem's incantatory rhetoric suggests that Sanchez sees social activism as an appropriate subject for all her potential readers.

Sanchez often mentions her childhood introduction to the work of Langston Hughes, Gwendolyn Brooks, and black Russian poet Alexander Pushkin. An African-American librarian at a neighborhood library noticed Sanchez's voracious reading and offered her several books that gave her a new perspective on black literature (Leibowitz 362; Melhem, "Will and Spirit" 77; Tate, "Sonia Sanchez" 147; Reich 84; Kelly 680). Sanchez's frequent references to this experience demonstrate that she never forgot this librarian's insight into her particular needs, and she has continued to foster similar interactions with her own students. She first worked with children at a nursery school and then taught at the Downtown Community School, a private institution in Greenwich Village. Following her studies with Louise Bogan in New York City, Sanchez taught at San Francisco State College, the University of Pittsburgh, Rutgers University, Manhattan Community College, Amherst College, and Temple University (D. Williams 449). Before her retirement from Temple in 1999, she was the Laura H. Carnell Professor of English and chair of the Women's Studies department, the first African-American professor to hold an endowed chair at the university as well as its first Presidential Fellow (Melhem, "The Will and the Spirit" 134). Sanchez's commitment to by now thousands of students echoes her cherished exchanges with that long-ago librarian.

Sanchez's activist understanding of pedagogy also prompted her participation in the early years of African-American studies and black women's literature programs. She worked with psychologist Nathan Hare to establish San Francisco State College's black studies program, the United States' first Institute for Black Studies, in 1968 (Spady, "Consummate Teacher" 23; Gabbin, "Southern Imagination" 194). In 1969, Sanchez taught the very first college seminar on literature by African-American women writers, a course at the University of Pittsburgh entitled "The Black Woman" (Kelly 683). Both of these projects grew out of Sanchez's work in the Black Arts Movement and illustrate her commitment to education as activism. During this period, she also led a poetry workshop at the Countee Cullen Library in Harlem and a program at Philadelphia's Afro-American Historical and Cultural Museum (Thompson 169).[16] Her political involvement extended into work with MADRE, Making Our Mothers Stronger (MOMS) in Alabama, and the National Black United Front (Salaam, "Sonia Sanchez" 298). Jazz has consistently invigorated the activist themes of her poetry, serving as a vehicle for social commentary.

"[O]n seeing pharaoh sanders blowing," a poem included in *Home Coming*, provides an early example of Sanchez's pedagogical approach to poetic composition. Dedicated to "chuck," the piece opens by evoking jazz performance conventions: the subheading "set 1." This first section of the poem begins with a thrice-repeated command to "listen" to the speaker, a black man who is "staring / at your honky faces" (lines 12–13).

The speaker, presumably experimental jazz saxophonist Pharaoh Sanders himself, symbolically embodies the tension between two races in the visual contrast between his dark skin and white eyes. The speaker's deliberately aggressive stance and derisive name for his white audience suggest a submerged power. Sanchez's descriptions of Sanders's performance techniques convert this derision to outright antagonism with images that link the sounds of his music to its condemnation of social discrimination. Sanders's music manifests a direct threat to racists. Although the openly violent metaphors characteristic of Black Power's militant stance frame this menace, it also serves to illustrate the connections Sanchez habitually draws between unconventional poetic presentation and political statement. Experimental formal devices highlight the poem's critique of unjust social conditions.

Sanchez's decision to personify the United States as a female figure renders this poetic instruction particularly disturbing. Turning his attention from whites in general to American society, the speaker addresses his enemy as a white prostitute whose illegal activities endanger her life. Sanchez also juxtaposes another vision of white American femininity, "Mary Had a Little Lamb," to this metaphorical violation of the United States. Like John Coltrane, with whom Pharaoh Sanders worked for a few years, Sanchez rewrites the text of a prosaic, white-authored tune as a lesson in African-American social experience. In this speaker's mouth, the nursery rhyme assumes unfamiliar connotations that erase any innocence "mary" once had in the face of unwelcome experience; the white "little lamb" that she possesses provokes someone else to take her life. Both of these apostrophic statements equate the female with weakness, signaling an absence of the feminism that would characterize many of Sanchez's later jazz elegies and her blues haiku. Rather, her depiction of white oppression as weak and feminine recalls popular Black Arts rhetoric.

The portrait of American life that Sanchez offers in "on seeing pharaoh sanders blowing" illustrates a central tenet in her pedagogy: to pursue cultural readings that oppose meaningless standards of personal and literary decorum. The speaker ultimately delivers an aural rather than a textual message, concentrating on the graphic sounds that accompany death: throats are slit, accompanied by ambulances' sirens and the echoing peals of manic laughter. This cityscape is nightmarish rather than serene, belying conventional notions about the peaceful nature of death. Her poetic strategies illustrate the performative potential of jazz-based poetics.

In the classroom and in her poetry, Sanchez has remained an advocate of racial equality, in the spirit of her 1960s political involvement. Her experiences with the New York branch of CORE and the city's progressive Democrats influenced her early years as a teacher, for instance (Spady, "Consummate Teacher" 21). However, women's issues have increasingly dominated her politics since the 1980s. Discussing her participation in Black Arts activities, she notes that black men and women shared a "communal voice" born of similar concerns and priorities (Tate, "Sonia Sanchez" 143), yet women's attention to personal relationships created what she calls a "'secondary consciousness'" in which "black women began to look at black men secondarily during the period of [their] enslavement" (Kelly 684). This statement suggests that Sanchez's experiences with male leadership during the 1960s and 1970s prompted her to rethink her earlier notions of sexual politics. Rather than seeing race as an identity trait to which all other social concerns were subordinate, she began to consider the complex intersections of race, class, and gender. This heightened black feminist consciousness, aligned with the work of activists and theorists like Barbara Smith and Deborah K. King, resulted in her work's thematic explorations of black women's experiences and a series of formal innovations that recall both African performance elements and African-American musical experimentation. Sanchez avers that one "can teach people to be better than they are" by opposing social discrimination (Reich 92). Her post–Black Arts poetry's imbrication in black feminist thought indicates that she still sees her creative work as a tool for illustrating the politics she advocates.

The poetic devices of "Improvisation," a poem from *Wounded in the House of a Friend,* include women-centered themes and typographical elements that visually approximate vocal performance. This combination typifies the third-wave feminist work that Sanchez created in the 1990s. The piece's historical referents, coupled with unique performance elements, serve as tools for audience instruction. Here the links Sanchez draws between giving birth and surviving the Middle Passage imply that black women's experiences with social injustice have been inscribed on their bodies; the visceral nature of this violation both permeates modern birth processes and ties the burden of survival to the successful act of reproduction. A textual imitation of improvisation shapes each stanza. In the first stanza, the laughter and wordless cries of a female speaker alternate with declarations of self: "Ha ha. / oooooooooooo ai yi yi yi yi yi yi" (lines 1–2). Joyce A. Joyce points out that "repetition . . . plays a crucial role in the structure of the African oral performance," citing "Improvisation" as an apt illustration of this trait (140). This joyous celebration of the speaker's existence and reference to the form's cultural roots lessen, however, when the next stanza juxtaposes "I was" with "I am": the speaker's present state evokes both her own past and the experiences of her predecessors. Although she lives a rich life in the present day, she admits "it was the coming across the ocean that was bad" (line 17): the self-fulfillment she enjoys has come at a dear price, the capture and torture of millions of African slaves.

Like Sanchez's childhood self, this speaker stutters as she tells her tale. Repetitions-with-a-difference reflect her uncertainty about the mode of communication itself, a reaction prompted by the graphic horrors of Middle Passage practices. The three following stanzas provide the concrete evidence of suffering, repeating a list of abusive experiences that re-creates the historical moment for listeners. The list also suggests a revision of the Western epic catalogue. Sanchez repeats phrases such as "the standing on auction blocks" (line 70) and "the giving birth" (line 82) in blocks of text whose only variations come in the occasional emergence of a complete sentence from the deluge of nouns: "[I]t was the raping that was bad" and "it was the landing that was bad" (lines 36, 65), for example. These repeated words echo vocal stuttering to highlight the extreme cruelty of these human-rights abuses. Sanchez employs similar sentence structures throughout these stanzas in order to locate her performative techniques in African tribal performance while mimicking the cruel detachment with which these actions were performed on millions of African victims.

Sanchez defines feminist community in "Improvisation" as a resource that can help bring closure to the historical past. The poetic narrator interrupts repetitions of the last two Middle Passage violations of black women's bodies, "standing" and "giving birth," with a forceful reiteration of self: "don't touch me" (line 73). The ambivalence of this line—its expression of both defiance and self-deprecation—echoes in the next two lines' wordless cries and invocation of Olukun, an African god of wealth and the sea (Parrinder 82, 108). However, when the speaker reasserts her identity, as in the poem's opening, an unseen auditor replies. Her symbolic power replenishes as she temporarily casts off the shadow of Middle Passage abuses in favor of engaging in the traditional communal activity of call-and-response. After demanding "what" and "where" her audience is, she affirms that "there you are!" and states that "I'm not looking at you / You're looking at me" (lines 117, 130–31). Now the speaker assumes the role of recorder, preserving cultural history as a tool of healing for her audience. The speaker's earlier uncertainty toward historical memory and personal identity resolves in the discovery of inherited cultural knowledge. Sharing the burden of survival—assuaging the contemporary narrator's guilt over her ancestors' pain—establishes a feminist community rooted in the African past.

Sanchez's conclusion to "Improvisation" reiterates her opening condemnation of Middle Passage abuses but adds a reminder of the existing survivors who have triumphed over social oppression. "It was the raping that was bad" resolves in the last stanza to "It was / the coming that was baddddddddddddddd . . . / living dying coming coming dying living / living ing ing" (lines 163–64, 169–70). This final "stutter" sets the tone for the directive repeated through the poem's last six lines: "How to live" (lines 171–76). Kathleen Crown labels this poem's improvisatory passage through the history of African women's experiences in slavery an "ecstatic speaking of outside female and maternal consciousnesses" that reflects Sanchez's "new lyric subjectivity—dialogic, choral, . . . terrifyingly multiple" ("Collector of Shouts" 45, 31). Her feminist politics references specific historical situations and acknowledges the multiple jeopardy inherent to black women's lives. The reappearance of capital letters in the work—particularly the subjective "I"—also suggests that she has refigured her work's social perspective to include the nuances of individual identity within a collective experience. The poem's incorporation of both visual and aural elements not only reflects a continuing jazz influence over Sanchez's work, in part Coltrane's persistent presence in the poem (Feinstein, "Interview" 169), but also anticipates the improvisatory strategies and possibilities for public communication that factor into her most recent professional interest: spoken-word performances.

CONCLUSION: HIP TO THE SPOKEN WORD

In 1985, Sonia Sanchez reflected on the 1960s shift in African-American poetics to which she had contributed: "This was also when the poetry began to change and move towards Black themes much more. We're talking about '65, '66. And what that meant simply is that, for some reason, I began to understand the need to integrate the talk with the poem" (Melhem, "Will and Spirit" 78). Although she refers here to the combination of political rhetoric and nonstandard poetic form with which she and many of her fellow poets experimented during the period of Black Arts, "the need to integrate the talk with the poem" aptly describes the late-blossoming move toward performance poetics among avant-garde poets from a variety of backgrounds and "schools." Sanchez explains her poetry's reliance on a blend of live performance and textual innovations as a method of "incorporating the hipness that was in that black urban setting," comparing her use of such modern-day markers of hipness like rap to Langston Hughes's use of "the jazz idiom" (Kelly 682). Similarly, Houston Baker cites Sanchez's "efforts . . . to articulate strategies for advancing a national *sound* and *sounding* of New World experience" as evidence that she is a "Black Renaissance" writer ("Our Lady" 179; original italics). This formulation suggests that the performative qualities of her later poetry highlight the persistent relevance of historical events to experimental poetics.

Sanchez's decision to ground her poetry in history and the improvisational strategies of jazz stems from her interest in cultural performance. She and other twentieth-century black vocal artists transform performative inheritances from previous generations to articulate the social issues shaping their own times. Several writers have recognized the link between Sanchez's interest in spoken-word performance and the history that she depicts in her poetry. In an article comparing Sanchez's work with that of rapper Sister Souljah, Frenzella Elaine De Lancey argues that both artists are "'naysayers' to those cultural excesses pertinent to their time and place in history" ("Sonia Sanchez's *Blues Book*" 153); Souljah and Sanchez both advocate histories alternative to mainstream accounts. Dara Cook's article comparing Sanchez and rapper-poet Mos Def situates Sanchez within a historical continuum of avant-garde movements by making the (debatable) claim that she, like other "radical poets of yesterday," is "now firmly established in the canon of contemporary poetry" so she can help to gain public respect for the innovations of hip-hop and rap artists (24). Sanchez's own comments on her relationships with musicians like Mos Def and Tupac Shakur emphasize the historical connections between black artistic movements that explore language use. She claims that "a natural kind of continuity" exists between Harlem Renaissance writers, Black Arts Movement poets, and hip-hop artists because of their shared interest in specifically African-American linguistic inflections (Spady, "Centrality" 53; Alim 16).[17] She has passed the "jazz idiom" she learned from Hughes on to Def, as material to provoke or inspire his future experiments.

The Black Liberation Press published two of Sanchez's speeches, "The Poet as a Creator of Social Values" and "The Crisis of the Black Community," under the title of *Crisis and Culture* in 1983. In the first of these pieces, Sanchez writes that "[t]he power that the poet has to create, preserve or destroy social values, depends greatly on the quality of his/her social visibility and the functionary opportunity available to poetry to impact lives" (*Crisis and Culture* 2; original punctuation). By 1990, she asserts that "all artists, all poets are political" (Melhem, "The Will and the Spirit" 153). The hope for change that she expresses in the first article has metamorphosed into a will for change in the second. Her poetry seconds this will through its invocations of improvisatory jazz performance. Perhaps as a sign of this creative shift, her latest elegies celebrate the intrinsic abilities of her subjects, rather than using them as ideological vehicles. Two elegies for Tupac Shakur included in *Like the Singing Coming Off the Drums*, "Love Poem" and "For Tupac Amaru Shakur," acknowledge the untimely nature of Shakur's death but position the speaker's grief in relation to a community of fellow creators, past and present. Shakur's fellow participation in innovative performances, coupled with Sanchez's belief in the power of art to effect social change, inspires her new approach to the jazz elegy.

Sanchez's most recent jazz elegy, "A Poem for Ella Fitzgerald," also included in this volume, testifies to its author's apparent resolution of formerly conflicting beliefs about feminism and the blues. When Fitzgerald, an exemplar of midcentury female jazz and blues performance, appears on the stage, her fellow musicians hail her as an artist whose talent completes the band: "[S]quads of horns came out / to greet her" (lines 13–14). Lyrics from three of her best-known tunes—"Perdido," "A-Tisket, A-Tasket," and "Oh, Lady Be Good!"—are quoted in italicized fragments alongside a reference to Fitzgerald's famous talent for scat singing: "bop bop dowa / bop bop doowaaa / bop bop dooooowaaaa" (lines 93–95). Sanchez calls her "Ella, / first lady of tongues" with an "Ella-tonian voice soft / like four layers of lace." (lines 53–54, 67–68), paying homage to the improvisational music that Fitzgerald created even as she rewrites the adjective commonly used to describe Duke Ellington's playing, "Ellingtonian." The poem's narrator imagines the singer as "nut arching over us / feet and hands placed on the stage / music flowing from her breasts" (lines 83–85), in the figure of an Egyptian goddess associated with the sky and its rain (Brooks De Vita 33). These elements of African history and feminist creation culminate in the final lines of the poem, an elegiac homage to a strong woman singing the blues to celebrate life's promise rather than to bemoan its disappointments.

Sanchez's mythological invocation of Fitzgerald's talents exemplifies the feminist sensibility that underlies her jazz poetics. Such references to African heritage play a key role in the experimental work of other jazz poets like Jayne Cortez. Cortez's work complicates the feminist ethic advanced in Sanchez's poetry by introducing elements of African and African-American cultural inheritances as central components of a historically situated black feminism. For Cortez, surrealist influences, gospel music, and African mythology comprise the background to her jazz-influenced innovations in poetic form and performance. After exploring the political potential of Black Arts and adding free-jazz innovations to her compositional repertoire, she creates an international, humanistic feminism based in the traditional African practice of *nommo*.

CHAPTER 3

TALK TO ME: ECOFEMINIST DISRUPTIONS IN THE JAZZ POETRY OF JAYNE CORTEZ

RON MANN'S 1982 FILM *POETRY IN MOTION* FEATURES 24 POETS PERFORMING AND DISCUSSING THEIR WORK, sometimes accompanied by musicians whose compositions respond to the spoken word. One such musical-poetic performance takes center stage in the five-minute segment on Jayne Cortez's work. Here Cortez describes the improvisatory ethic that guides both her writing and her work with the Firespitters, the band with whom she performs her pieces:[1]

> I'm playing with the visual and the verbal connections. On paper. And then when I'm reading, then it's, you know, the verbal and the, the music coming together. It's sound, it's about sound. The sound of the poetry against the sound of the music. The way I work is, improvised or invented off of the word, it's like the call and response pattern, which is an old African pattern. I am making statements, or I'm asking questions, and the music is responding to me, and I'm responding back to them, and we're listening to each other. Making not only comments on what you're doing, but extending that, taking it out and exploring the possibilities of the poetry and the music together. (*Poetry in Motion*)

Cortez provides this analysis in voiceover as the picture cuts back and forth between a scene in which she sits on a couch with Mann and one in which she and the band react to one another midperformance.

This collage precedes the group's rendition of Cortez's poem "I See Chano Pozo." Here she wears a red-and-blue-striped dashiki with dark pants and a large silver necklace in the shape of a stylized African face. Her decisions to wear traditional African clothing and to perform this particular poem with the band demonstrate that naming takes a central place in her poetics. Like Sonia Sanchez, she depicts her performance's cultural roots as African in order to invoke a specific set of historical associations. The poem affirms Pozo, a Cuban conga player who is credited alongside trumpeter Dizzy Gillespie with introducing Afro-Cuban elements to jazz (Gioia 222–24).[2] The poem's repeated lines assert that Pozo's music motivates "Atamo," "Mpebi," "Donno," "Obonu," "Atumpan," "Mpintintoa," "Ilya Ilu," "Ntenga," "Siky Akkua," "Batá," and "Fontomfrom" (lines 13, 15, 17, 19, 21, 65, 67, 69, 71, 73, 75):[3] "various Africa drums" (Cortez, *Coagulations* 111) whose timbres resonate with music's power to articulate human emotion.[4] By repeating her affirmations of Chano Pozo and varying through vocal tone and inflection the printed versions of the poem, Cortez oversignifies the poetic form, defying the rhetorical boundaries of both print and previous performance. Her naming of Pozo's accomplishments functions as a political act that positions his work in opposition to Western methods of public communication. Her commitment to social protest through linguistic alteration roots her textual improvisations in a cultural ethic that resembles Sanchez's later strategies.

Jayne Cortez's work explodes, through hyperbolic poetic images and innovative performance strategies, the social and rhetorical structures that enable oppressive social conditions. Her poetry's themes, many of which are articulated via scatological imagery, align her work with contemporary artistic movements such as Black Arts and the early-century surrealists.[5] Franklin Rosemont describes surrealism as an "unparalleled freedom" of image and a commitment to revolution "in every aspect of life" ("Introduction" 65, 67), both elements that Cortez continues to explore. She has published work in the surrealist journal *Arsenal* and in Franklin Rosemont's 1980 collection *Surrealism and Its Popular Accomplices* (Woodson 73), though specifically African-American sources help to shape her brand of surrealism. Tony Bolden argues, for instance, that surrealism's "radical politics . . . are compatible with the ideas of Black Arts theorists" (*Afro-Blue* 121). Aldon Nielsen calls Cortez's artistic approach "a black American surrealism" drawn from "the compacted imagery of the blues" (*Black Chant* 225). D. H. Melhem uses Cortez's own term "supersurrealism" to denote the associations she creates in her poetry between graphic surrealist imagery and political offenses ("Supersurrealist" 206). She employs surrealism in order to critique modern social conditions, while her poetry's performative elements signify a rebellion against conventional methods of public expression.

Cortez crafts poetry based in conceptually difficult surrealist imagery, yet she also advocates the communal, egalitarian atmosphere of spoken-word performance. This juxtaposition, which might at first seem contradictory, illustrates her work's political resolve. Her audience cannot participate in her poem's affirmation of Chano Pozo as an innovative cultural icon without understanding the rationale behind the images—like "a very fine tube of frictional groans" (line 4)—that she uses to characterize him. The poetry occupies a narrow space on the edge of competing differences, often refusing reconciliation and synthesis even as it moves with a sense of deliberate uneasiness among oral and written traditions. The best theoretical framework for understanding these differences derives from the cultural traditions of the African-American music to which Cortez owes much of her source material. Some of her vocal performance strategies, for instance, originate in gospel music. The esoteric imagery of her surrealism also shares thematic material with the blues and artistic impulses with heavily theorized jazz traditions like the bebop and free jazz movements; several of her musician friends worked in these movements. The historically black musics of blues and jazz thus provide her with a flexible yet culturally specific language in which to voice her critiques of contemporary political situations.

Cortez offers poetic censures of many violent political situations; her social critiques also cover the exclusionary habits of artistic movements such as Black Arts. Karen Jackson Ford has interpreted Cortez's use of surrealist imagery in the context of a powerful rhetorical style as a reappropriation of certain masculinist strategies common to Black Arts poets.[6] The difference between Cortez's work and that of her contemporaries, Ford claims, lies in Cortez's use of the "Black Arts excesses" of liberatory rhetoric, highly sexualized language, and scatological imagery to address a "wider range of concerns" that included misogyny (*Poetics of Excess* 219). Her transformation of such "excesses" demonstrates one of the ways in which Cortez cultivated more accurate views of women's bodies and the environments that contain them in order to recoup popular misconceptions.

Cortez identifies this kind of revisionist work as feminist by drawing parallels in the poetry between violations of women's bodies and specific historical atrocities. The points where these abuses converge allow her to argue that women should take control over their economic, political, and physical environments. She marks this argument's contribution to specifically black creative work by referencing the cultural associations and performance practices of blues and jazz. At the same time, her live spoken-word performances revise traditional notions of women's roles in jazz. Her vocal improvisations and interactions with the other performers in her group invoke both the histories of early-century black female blues singers and the communal jazz performance ethic that dates back to the bebop era. In many of her live and recorded performances of poetry and jazz, she exploits the thematic parallels between the natural environment and women's bodies in improvisatory riffs. This strategy aligns her political agenda with that of ecofeminism.

Cortez fosters an ecofeminist critique in her poetry and performance that charges mainstream society with the responsibility for concealing crimes perpetrated against women's bodies and the land, both national and natural, in which they live. The poetry's politics is predicated on the material qualities shared by female bodies, national land, and historical texts. Members of all three of these categories have been subject to outside ownership and are vulnerable to being scarred or otherwise altered. Cortez's work interrogates the ways in which historical events have been publicly represented through textual revision, reiteration, and variation. This historical revisionism enables her to redefine the healthy, socially responsible environment as a source of autonomy in which women's bodies can achieve agency.

In their introduction to *Reweaving the World: The Emergence of Ecofeminism* (1990), a foundational text of the movement, editors Irene Diamond and Gloria Feman Orenstein describe the book's impetus as "both the diverse range of women's efforts to save the Earth and the transformations of feminism in the West that have resulted from the new view of women and nature" (ix). In her article in this collection, Charlene Spretnak uncovers the roots of ecofeminism in "radical" or "cultural" feminism, which seeks to revise the traditional gender dynamics that have enabled dominating behavior (5). Ynestra King also cautions against replicating structures of dominance, arguing instead for a combination of feminisms that grows out of "a genuinely antidualistic, or dialectical, theory and practice" (116). Lee Quinby seconds this point, defining ecofeminism's potential value as a "theory in the interrogative mode" (124). Ecofeminists interrogate the social institutions that understand both women's bodies and the environment as objects that can easily be exploited for public profit. Cortez performs similar investigations by reframing materiality as a source of agency. This poetic strategy aligns her work's social messages with the bodily politics of Sherley Anne Williams's work, though her political agenda differs from Williams's in its attention to the national ramifications of environmental abuse.

Cortez's approach to ecofeminist critique reflects the complexities of a later stage in the movement.[7] Her poetry proves to be a rich ground for ecofeminist literary analysis, which joins interpretation of a text's formal elements to considerations of its environmental and activist themes. Greta Gaard and Patrick D. Murphy's introduction to *Ecofeminist Literary Criticism: Theory, Interpretation, Pedagogy* (1998) defines ecofeminism as "a practical movement for social change arising out of the struggles of women to sustain themselves, their families, and their communities" that combats "the 'maldevelopment' and environmental degradation caused by patriarchal societies, multinational corporations, and global capitalism" (2). When these ideas are applied to literature, readers gain insight into the relationships between characters and their natural environment (Gaard and Murphy 7). Murphy points out in another essay that ecofeminism also facilitates political critique because it intersects with literature "as the influence and continuation of an activist movement" ("'The Women'" 45). In Cortez's work, for instance, she challenges the very vocabulary that dominant culture uses to define women as objects rather than subjects, through hyperbolic condemnations of physical and environmental abuse.

Cortez appraises social inequalities in her performances but also composes her poetry using a complex mix of elements: ecofeminist critique, "supersurrealist" imagery, and jazz references. Her investment in the environmental contexts of political events and her reliance upon a scatological, surrealist vocabulary allow her to conceptualize women's bodies and nationally defined environments as texts themselves, subject to violation yet capable of contributing to radical thought. Her poetry draws connections between jazz and blues references and surrealist themes; its formal imitations of jazz performance techniques recall her live-performance methods, which originate in the call-and-response patterns of gospel. Musical references in her work also help rhetorically to explode preestablished patterns of social restriction and point to the performative function of her work: acts of naming. Repeated interpellations highlight violations of women's bodies and the land, while offering a method of communication grounded in African traditions and alternative to Western cultural discourses.[8]

RADICAL MUSICAL ROOTS: *NOMMO*, GOSPEL, AND FREE JAZZ

Cortez's compositions suggest that she frames the vocal act of naming as a key force in her poetics. In her 1978 interview with fellow poet Alexis DeVeaux, she defined the process of poetic composition in terms of the phonetic and structural relationships in which words engage: "[P]oetry is a manipulation of language, the putting together of thoughts and ideas.

The relationship of word to word. A combination of phrases . . . what the Africans call *nommo*" (79). Invocations of *nommo* in her published poetry simulate the verbal activities of live performance. The term *nommo* refers to the act of naming an action, object, or concept in order to fix it in its particularity—and, in so doing, to infuse it with an authority specific to the speaker.[9] A person who possesses the ability to articulate the name that exactly suits this one object and no other, to find its *nommo*, can access the inherent potency of speech and activate a political presence. Cortez relied upon the process of *nommo* when she founded Bola Press in 1973. The press's first project was to publish her third book of poetry, *Scarifications* (1973), most of whose poems examine the historical experiences of black people in America.[10] She saw the press as an opportunity to exercise commercial and artistic control over her writing (Melhem, "Supersurrealist" 209). The name "Bola" derives from her own name in the Nigerian language Yoruba: Oyebola. "Oye" refers to "Oya," the wife of Shango, the Yoruba god of thunder associated with strong will and competitiveness (C. Ford 162–64); "bola" means successful (Melhem, "Supersurrealist" 183). Cortez's decision to mark this book with a multilayered, traditional African name links her characteristic textual innovation to mythic archetypes and non-Western discourses.

The nonverbal signification that Cortez achieves in live performances of her poetry points to her work's musical sources. Her poetry and vocal performances' interpellation strategies closely resemble gospel music's call-and-response patterns. Bernice Johnson Reagon characterizes gospel as a music both "congregational and composed": it requires the vocal participation of a large group of singers yet evolves through variations written by ministers and other music leaders (13). Gospel songs, like Cortez's pieces, exist in both oral transmission and written transcription. However, the stigma of orality prevented gospel from being recognized as "serious" music for many years (Reagon 38). Addressing this issue, Tony Bolden argues that Cortez's work "calls into question the hegemony of a script-centered poetics" by drawing on some key oral elements of gospel forms such as the riff chorus ("All the Birds" 62).[11] Don Cusic also notes that in gospel "[t]he same song is rarely ever sung the same way twice, with an emphasis on improvisation within the song causing each performance to be a wholly different experience for both singer and audience" (54). These ideas suggest that Cortez's poetry both participates in the gospel tradition and reproduces the improvisation techniques common to jazz through lines that are varied in multiple repetitions. Her work's themes evoke gospel's ability to "make the feeling of human separateness . . . bearable" by "acknowledging the burden" of human existence, "bearing witness" to it, and "finding redemption" in the shared experience of pain (Werner 28, 29). The communal existence that she invokes in her poems echoes through its jazz references as well, as her narrators pay tribute to the past, remembering the blues and gospel roots of their music, and position themselves as the next "link in the chain of tradition" (Werner 132, 135). She builds upon the historical traditions of both gospel and jazz through the juxtaposition of diverse musical elements in her work.

Cortez began cultivating her notion of the jazz impulse in her childhood. Both her education and her leisure activities taught her to appreciate a range of musical styles and to associate gospel, blues, and jazz within a network of specifically African-American cultural associations. She was born in Fort Huachuca, Arizona, on May 10, 1936. Her father was stationed at the army base there until they moved to San Diego, California, when Cortez was seven years old (Melhem, "*MELUS* Profile" 71–72). Soon after, they moved to West Los Angeles, where she attended the Thirty-sixth Street Elementary School with both African-American and Japanese-American students. Five years later, the family found a new home in Watts, South Los Angeles. Cortez was forced to go to a primarily white high school just outside Watts, where she encountered racist conditions. Later, she attended Los Angeles's Manual Arts High School, where she studied piano, bass, and cello performance as well as drawing, painting, and design (Melhem, "Supersurrealist" 197–98). She also matriculated at Compton Junior College. In addition to the classical training she received at school, she listened at home to Ella Fitzgerald, Billie Holiday, Lena Horne, Duke Ellington, Count Basie, Jimmy Lunceford, Charlie Parker, and Thelonious Monk, among others (Melhem, "*MELUS* Profile" 72; "Supersurrealist" 198).

Cortez devoted much of her time to music, but she has also noted that oral "signifying" was a daily part of life in her childhood and adolescence: "It was an everyday ritual. Oral poetry in an oral atmosphere" (Melhem, "Supersurrealist" 200). Signifying is a naming strategy. A speaker signifies in order to both establish her identity through verbal acuity and demarcate the subject of her words. Henry Louis Gates Jr. defines signifying as "a mode of formal revision" that draws on "troping," pastiche, and "repetitions of formal structures and their differences" (52). The presence of both signifying rituals and musical study in Cortez's early life indicates that naming and gospel influences are linked in her poetry.

Cortez's acts of naming were tied to jazz early in her career; she began writing poetry seriously after her personal and professional involvement with Ornette Coleman, a jazz saxophonist known for his experimentalism. In 1954, she began going to jazz clubs to hear him play.[12] After meeting Cortez, Coleman expressed his appreciation for her substantial knowledge of music, and they married a short time later. Since Cortez was only 18 years old at the time, and neither one had much money, they lived with her parents for a few months while she made all of their clothes (Litweiler 34). Two years later, their son Denardo was born (Melhem, "*MELUS* Profile" 72). Although Cortez's domestic responsibilities could have impeded her creative work, she continued to pursue experiences during this period that contributed to her poetry's later investment in live performance.

Cortez's marriage to Ornette Coleman did not last long, but his avant-garde ideas about jazz composition and performance probably contributed to her later work with the Firespitters as much as did the performative techniques of gospel. Coleman pioneered the notion of "motivic chain-associations," a technique in which other group members rewrote his solo phrases in the course of improvisation, returning them to him in a new form (Jost 59); this process resembles Cortez's own approach to live performance. She also introduced Coleman to childhood friend Don Cherry, who became famous himself as a jazz trumpeter (Litweiler 37–38).[13] Her marriage to Coleman was short-lived since their family needed a regular income, yet neither his commitment to an unprecedented musical style nor the high price his band charged for gigs enabled financial stability. She "felt that 'very little compromise' was required for Ornette to be performing regularly," but he was not willing to change his approach. They separated and then divorced in 1964 (Litweiler 45, 95). During the same year, Cortez, having studied drama at the Ebony Showcase in Los Angeles, cofounded the Watts Repertory Theatre Company, where she "directed plays, acted, and read her poetry, supporting herself meanwhile by factory and office work" (Melhem, "Supersurrealist" 182). She also began reading her poetry to the accompaniment of several Los Angeles musicians in 1964 (Cortez, *There It Is*). Jazz themes and performance techniques remained an important presence in her work from then on.

Cortez's jazz-inflected pieces gained social relevance as she worked in local political organizations. These experiences helped her to draw the connections between social experience and creative expression that form the basis of her poetry's interpellative methods. In 1963, she met James Forman, the executive secretary of the Student Nonviolent Coordinating Committee (SNCC), and Fannie Lou Hamer, landmark civil rights activist, and began volunteering in Mississippi's voter registration movement (DeVeaux 78; Melhem, "Supersurrealist" 200). She claims that her coincident work with the Watts group was "always political" and strengthened her interest in poetry as a medium of "art, craft, and discipline" (DeVeaux 78). The physical expressivity that she cultivated with her

Watts colleagues translates in her written work to embellished repetitions of personal names and historical events. These reiterations of cultural allusions, often elaborated through explanatory clauses in subsequent repetitions, mimic live improvisation and draw the reader's attention to the persistence of oppressive social practices across cultures.

One of Cortez's first uses of poetic naming as political critique can be seen in "So Many Feathers," a poem that appears in both *Mouth on Paper* (1977) and *Coagulations* (1984). This tribute to African-American dancer and singer Josephine Baker repeatedly invokes Baker's physical characteristics while attempting to understand the contradictions of her character. The speaker employs one naming technique, repetition with a difference, in order to describe a woman not only beautiful and talented but also, because she agreed to perform for members of the white upper class, indirectly complicit in the oppression of blacks in Durban, South Africa. The poem's three stanzas equate the power of Baker's physical presence with the sublime: the hyperbolic imagery used to depict her implies that she embodied both the best and the worst of humanity. In performance, she "became terror woman of all feathers / of such terrible beauty / of such fire / such flames" (lines 12–15). Her physical presence as a black female performer signified the pleasure conveyed by her unusual talents and the social injustice that her cultural ancestors and contemporaries have suffered.

Cortez repeats and improvises upon Baker's name throughout the poem, aligning her work with a community of listeners in a manner similar to the call-and-response strategies of gospel. As Sherley Anne Williams's work suggests, women's use of such strategies can strengthen community by highlighting experiences that performer and audience share. In this poem, the speaker invokes Baker's identity in order to refuse the superficial glitter of "magnetic dance" (line 1), "rhinestones and satin banana G-strings" (line 2), "pink diamond tongue" (line 4), "royal blue sequins pasted on your lips" (line 48), "fantastic legs studded with emeralds" (line 49), and "orange flint pelvis of the ruby navel" (line 61). "Josephine" repeats five times in the first stanza and nineteen times in the third, as the urgency of the speaker's interrogation of her life and work increases. The building, expressive volume that these repetitions imitate resembles the emotional climax sought in a gospel performance. Baker successfully crossed racial and economic barriers, as the speaker's praise of her "exploding red marble eyes in new york" and her "breaking color bars in miami" (lines 18, 20) demonstrates. The poem hails her as the "mother of orphans" (line 22), "legion of honor" (line 23), and "rosette of resistance" (line 24), an entertainer who improved her life by "splitting the solidarity of her beautiful feathers" (line 26). These accomplishments and titles of honor suggest that she achieved valuable goals for her social communities.

The speaker's words of praise link Baker to both Christian and military mythologies only temporarily: "mother of orphan homes" references the Virgin Mary's association with orphans, while "legion of honor" and "rosette of resistance" signify military achievement. The poem's second stanza challenges Baker's right to such validation by condemning her decision to give performances in apartheid-governed South Africa. "[W]hy split your flamingos," the speaker laments, "with the death white boers in durban south africa" (lines 31–32). Her failure to condemn the human-rights violations of apartheid, which have forever changed the South African landscape, rewrites her physical body as an instrument of persecution. Baker was blessed "with magnificent face of Ife mask" (line 33),[14] but instead of maintaining her solidarity with the people of the African diaspora, she ignored "the torture chambers / made of black flesh and feathers" (lines 39–40). The speaker draws an unmistakable link here between Baker's costume and the institutions of apartheid: the words "feather" and "feathers" appear 11 times in connection with this torture-chamber reference. Though feathers signify flight, certain vodun practices, and ceremonial garments in other contexts, Baker's decision to mark her body with feathers to enhance her appeal as an entertainer here removes her symbolic power from the realm of social signification. White desire limits her body just as the black South African population and their land have been circumscribed.

The speaker offers three hyperbolic statements in the second half of the poem as an attempt to come to terms with Baker's contradictory life. The second stanza ends with "I want to understand why dance / the dance of the honorary white / for the death white boers in durban" (lines 43–45), reproving Baker for deciding to become an "honorary white." The third stanza attests to Baker's participation in that historical moment by recalling her characteristic dress: "After all Josephine / I saw you in your turquoise headdress" (lines 46–47). A reiteration of her titles of praise—"I remember you rosette of resistance" (line 66)—and a catalogue of her physical assets reinforce the interrogation of Baker's performance persona. This final act of naming works to reconcile the magnitude of her creative presence with her apparent complicity in white South African social persecution by reiterating the word "double." The speaker describes her as

> Josephine of the double-jointed knees
> double-jointed shoulders double-jointed thighs
> double-jointed breasts double-jointed fingers

double-jointed toes double-jointed eyeballs
double-jointed hips doubling
into a double squat like a double star into a giant double snake
with the double heartbeats of a young girl
doubling into woman-hood
and grinding into an emulsified double spirit (lines 70–78)

Here the speaker imagines Josephine Baker as a woman containing her own doppelganger. The many connotations of the word "double-jointed" in this context include the physical flexibility necessary for her dances to the music of "le jazz hot," her success as a double agent in the world of entertainment who moves with ease between black and white cultures, and W. E. B. DuBois's notion of "double consciousness": "this sense of always looking at one's self through the eyes of others, of measuring one's soul by the tape of a world that looks on in amused contempt and pity" (3). Visible evidence of Baker's doubleness suggests that her audiences seek to commodify her body and voice even as her transformation "into a giant double snake" implies both power and deception.

The poem's imagery in this section points to Baker's subversive potential as well: in African mythology, snakes are associated with female creation goddesses like Mawu and Mboze and with the destructive power of Egyptian Queen of Heaven Hathor, who could take on the "deadly aspect" of "cobra goddess Ua Zit" (Brooks De Vita 56–57). However, Cortez reiterates "i remember" nine times alongside the final eleven repetitions of "Josephine" at the end of the poem to remind the reader of the complexities of Baker's life. The poem ultimately illustrates the parallels between Baker's experience and the harsh social conditions that have shaped the lives of African peoples. These parallels replace the image of selfish opportunism created earlier in the piece with a transgressive creativity. In the end, Baker appears to conform to white expectations while communicating the horrors of national and physical abuses to the witnesses who know how to read her.[15]

Cortez employs naming strategies that evoke subjects' contradictory traits through varied repetitions, as in her portrait of Josephine Baker, in several poems. These reiterations draw parallels between environmental or political violations and the abuses suffered by women. Tony Bolden defines this poetic technique as a gospel-inspired "riff chorus," a refrain varied through subsequent repetitions that is "employed in the call and response by black preachers and their congregations" (*Afro-Blue* 122). In call-and-response, also known as "raising" or "lining" a hymn, the preacher or other musical leader, often male, gives the solo "calls" and receives a group response after each line from the congregation or choir.

This structure enables flexible, dynamic musical responses, yet it preserves a hierarchy between a male leader and an often largely female choir. Although Cortez's work contains many examples of the riff chorus, the thematic focus of her variations in print as well as the improvisations of her recorded performances indicate that the egalitarian performance ethic of jazz helps to revise this hierarchical element. Her poetic treatments of women's experiences suggest that she considers gender politics as well as broader social inequalities in the context of black music. As she notes in an interview with Sascha Feinstein,

> The refrain might be expected but what the refrain is relating to is unexpected. . . . There are comings and goings. You go, you return, and in between there are internal and external changes, environmental changes, changes based on personal experience, based on information. . . . The refrain is a device to add the next layer of sound, next metaphor, next transformation. (62–63)

This definition of the riff chorus's effects highlights its potential to foster not only improvisation but also revolutionary statement.

Cortez uses the riff chorus to create a six-stanza tribute to legendary blues singer Willie Mae Thornton in "Bumblebee, You Saw Big Mama." This piece, which appears on the *Taking the Blues Back Home* album by Jayne Cortez and the Firespitters (1996) and in *Somewhere in Advance of Nowhere* (1996) and *Jazz Fan Looks Back* (2002), features what initially seems to be a basic call-and-response form.[16] As in "So Many Feathers," however, repeated responses to the speaker's "calls" vary in a manner that recalls jazz improvisation. These variations bring to mind the oral flexibility Cortez employs in her recorded performance of the piece and highlight the parallels she draws between Thornton's body and the national landscape. Each of the stanzas except the fifth begins with the phrase "You saw Big Mama"; the fifth provides a variation on this act of testimony with the assurance that "You didn't have to wonder" about her talents (line 34). All six stanzas are followed by the word "Bumblebee," the title of one of Big Mama Thornton's tunes. Assigning life via apostrophe to one of Thornton's songs suggests that her lasting reputation has surpassed her real-life hardships. Cortez's tribute to Thornton helps to efface her painful personal history and opens up space to accommodate her overwhelming musical legacy.[17]

Cortez reassigns agency to Thornton in the poem by creating a series of expansively detailed vignettes that call out the fact of her existence— "You saw Big Mama"—and respond with images of the earth as her body, implying performances so powerful that audiences can only grasp them on a planetary scale. Reiterations of Thornton's name in connection with terrestrial geography locate her power in the earth she stands on; the repetitions of "Bumblebee" suggest that the music she produced now defines her identity. In an interview, Cortez describes Thornton as "dynamic and unpredictable," "an aggressive singer and obviously an aggressive person" who controlled the direction of her professional and personal lives (Feinstein, "Returning" 64). The feminist ethic that Cortez admires in Thornton emerges in the poem's associations between socially resonant texts, women's bodies, and the environment.

Cortez's repeated interpellations both honor the poem's subject and point to the roots of Thornton's music in gospel performance. The varying repetitions of "Big Mama" and "Bumblebee" suggest that call-and-response can resonate among performance participants rather than operating only as a series of exchanges between a group and its leader. In the performance of this piece on the *Taking the Blues Back Home* album, Cortez repeats the phrase "You saw Big Mama" 11 additional times before lines describing Big Mama's cosmic activities, and she repeats "Bumblebee" three times after each stanza, rather than just once as in the printed version. Such multiplying invocations indicate that Cortez complicates gospel's riff chorus through the improvisatory strategies of bebop-era jazz performance. Her poem participates in the aesthetics of the jazz impulse, which "asks what about those parts that *don't* fit: the dreams, desires, unanswered questions" (Werner 133). Cortez tries to fill in some of those gaps for Thornton. The Firespitters' tune on this track runs underneath Cortez's spoken words, responding to the cadences of her voice and soloing between stanzas of the poem. This performance reinforces the piece's associations with jazz styles in which each player takes an equally central role in the performance and improvisation occurs on individual and collective formal levels.[18] The dialogue between Cortez's voice and her band members' instruments also pays tribute to Thornton's blues: the solo voice mimics Thornton's performance, while the calls and responses recall the blues' debt to gospel music.

Poetic images that solder the geography of Big Mama Thornton's body to national landscapes identify the piece's politics as feminist. In a manner similar to Sherley Anne Williams's poetic treatments of Bessie Smith, Cortez presents Thornton as an example of a black woman professional whose physical presence defies the repressive social structures of the United States. Thornton's experiences in the musical world are equated with fractures in American geographies to illustrate the connections between personal and national identity. Such connections also echo in the extreme portraits of loss and deprivation painted by traditional blues lyrics. Her "cocktail dresses" with "cut off boots," "cowboy hat," and "man's suit" (lines 2, 3, 4, 5) suggest that she struggled to promote herself in the largely male-dominated world of midcentury blues performance. These gestures toward cross-dressing also imply sexual ambiguity and reference black women's efforts to claim social recognition. The image of Thornton's "moaning between ritual saxes / & carrying the black water of Alabama blood / through burnt weeds & rainy ditches" (lines 29–31) not only depicts her life in blues-lyrics terms but also points to the social dangers she faced as a black female entertainer.

Cortez frames the national impact of Thornton's talent as "valley roar / of her vocal spleen" (lines 39–40), although her work must build upon the legacy of her musical precedents: she was "tamped on by the hell hounds" (line 56) left by other blues greats like Robert Johnson. Thornton's final act in the poem occurs when she "chewed off [Bumblebee's] stinger" (line 64). By mastering the complexities of her own tune, "Bumblebee," Thornton demonstrates that her legacy persists in spite of professional and social discrimination. Here Cortez privileges the hyperbolic imagery of the blues in order to highlight Thornton's lived defiance of the social roles conventionally assigned to black women. Cortez links her body to American geographies to suggest that African-American women's experiences with discrimination have shaped the character of the national landscape.

"Bumblebee, You Saw Big Mama" foregrounds the political potential latent in poetic connections between land and the body. Its repeated "calls" and graphic, surrealist imagery reflect Cortez's evolving performance strategies. Discussing her work with D. H. Melhem, Cortez commented that

> [m]ost of the musicians who've played with me have all been musicians who play jazz. They are used to inventing off of different rhythm patterns and different sounds. So they relate to what I'm doing in the same way. They interject their own sound and attitudes. And I do the same thing. . . . Working with the music has provided me with a lot of freedom. I don't feel restricted. ("Supersurrealist" 204)

The music-making that Cortez has experienced, from the classical studies and jazz records of her youth to her work with Ornette Coleman to her performances with the Firespitters, shapes the politics behind her creation and the formal qualities of her poetry. Her work cultivates a feminist ethic that grows out of the material links between the abuses perpetrated on women's bodies and violations of public landscapes. Textual imitations of collective improvisation and call-and-response emphasize her poems' graphic imagery, for which she is indebted to both blues lyrics and the early-century surrealist movement.

SURREALISM AND AFRICAN SCATOLOGY: ARTISTIC CONTEXTS

Critics such as D. H. Melhem, Alexis DeVeaux, and Aldon Nielsen have attributed the scatological discourses of Cortez's poetry to surrealist influences, assigning her work a "black surrealist" label that she herself amends to "supersurrealist" (Melhem, "Supersurrealist" 181). Accurate readings of her poems must take into account their surrealist elements in addition to the musical influences of gospel and free jazz. "Bumblebee, You Saw Big Mama" contains, for example, surrealist images like "cry laughing her eyes into / circumcision" (lines 17–18) and "the happy hour of her négritude" (line 8). In *The Black Surrealists*, Jean-Claude Michel defines négritude as "the expression of an oppressed race" and a key element of black surrealism, associated with the work of black Francophone poets Aimé Césaire, Léopold Sedar Senghor, and Léon Damas (95–99). Cortez has cited both Césaire and Damas as important influences in her poetry (Melhem, "Supersurrealist" 208–9; DeVeaux 106). Césaire's work earned a surrealist label for its "coupling of words and violence" and celebratory, hyperbolic metaphors (Michel 66). Damas, associated with surrealism for a briefer period of time, relied upon strong, repetitive rhythms as a means of communicating political ideas (Michel 117).[19] Michel hypothesizes that surrealism "only crystallized" the desire to define an independent identity that many black diasporic writers had already expressed (14). Cortez uses surrealist imagery to evoke this history and as a thematic means of textual improvisation.

Paul Garon has noted the artistic and social parallels between surrealist and blues- and jazz-influenced poetry. Both types of writing are predicated on what Garon calls "a dynamic fusion between the concept of revolt and the concept of poetry" (7), and both offer a critical analysis of mainstream culture (Rosemont, "Afterword" 220–23). Cortez's work relies upon a constellation of dynamic blues and gospel techniques. These musical devices, in combination with her work's "supersurrealist" elements, help to foreground feminist concerns that are allied with ecological issues. In her poetry, the improvisatory call-and-response techniques of jazz and blues discourse put scatological images and feminist statement into a complex dialogue that avoids the privileging of one discursive method over another.

Franklin Rosemont's analysis of André Breton's writings on surrealism confirms the presence of philosophical links between the early surrealist movement and the principles of négritude that inform Cortez's work. Rosemont notes that the surrealist project, as "a unitary project of total revolution," sought to account for both ways of knowing and ways of living, as well as opposing traditional social categories in a manner similar to négritude ("Introduction" 1, 5). It surpasses national and artistic boundaries, opting for a focus on collective struggle. In support of this idea, Rosemont quotes a letter that Black Arts poet Ted Joans sent to Breton about the potential that surrealism holds to combat "the 'abject vicissitudes' of a racist society" ("Introduction" 7). Joans's stated commitment to overcoming social inequalities and improving the quality of life for minority groups aligns radical black thought of the twentieth century with surrealist ideals. Cortez's use of surrealist imagery in conjunction with the blues and jazz influences that Garon cites suggests that her feminist politics grows out of a radical agenda similar to Breton's and Joans's.[20]

A political urgency presaging this agenda informed Cortez's early work. She arrived in New York City in 1967, attracted by the jazz musicians working there and the opportunities for creating her own performances. She divided her time between writing and earning a living, and published her first book, *Pissstained Stairs and the Monkeyman's Wares*, in 1969. Cortez dedicated this book to the Watts Repertory Theatre Company, for whom many of the poems had originally been written as performance pieces (Melhem, "*MELUS* Profile" 72). Cortez has identified the primary theme of this book as ghetto life's "parasitical affliction of capitalism, symbolized by drugs" (Melhem, "Supersurrealist" 183). Her graphic, scatological imagery evokes both the physical discomfort of day-to-day life in extreme poverty and the lingering economic and racial discrimination that produces such lives. The poems force readers to confront these uncomfortable truths by presenting arguments in favor of public policy revision.

While Cortez cultivates "supersurrealist" elements through both verbal performances and published texts, her work also betrays a debt to visual art traditions. She married sculptor Mel Edwards in 1975; he has provided woodcut illustrations for nearly every one of her books. They also collaborated on a 30-year retrospective of his work in steel sculptures, *Fragments* (1994), which includes photographs, drawings, and her poetry as illustrations (Melhem, "*MELUS* Profile" 73). The graphic images of bodily violation and the African mythological references that inflect her work mirror several of the themes that pervade Edwards's woodcuts. Cortez's work alone and in collaboration highlights the material circumstances of women's lives, marking her politics as feminist.

In "Grinding Vibrato," a poem included in both *Mouth on Paper* and *Jazz Fan Looks Back*,[21] Cortez's surrealist imagery uncovers some of the ways in which black women undergo exploitation. The "blues woman," a mythological figure modeled on African-American female blues singers, represents these women's experiences. The poem's alternating images of the blues woman's body and scenes from nature draw a clear parallel between her experiences and those of the nation—an ethical commentary on crimes committed against women.

Stanza one serves as a brief introduction to this archetype's visual characteristics, celebrating her "beaded face" (line 2), "painted lips" (line 3), and "hair smeared / in the oil of Texas" (lines 4–5) as signs of female power. The two following, much longer stanzas examine what remains of her mythic beauty in the aftermath of physical and ideological violation. Both stanzas comment that she was "looking good and sounding beautiful" (lines 6, 22) until a surreal collection of invaders stole her powers, both physical and intangible. Statements such as "the horseman wanted your thunder" (line 7), "the boa constrictor wanted your body" (line 8), and "syringes of upright hyenas / barbwired your meat to their teeth" (lines 9–10) both evoke images of intense physical trauma and point to the blues woman's origins in mythology. Horsemen symbolize divine possession in some vodun practices; hyenas are often associated with death (Parrinder 38, 40). However, images of "scabs the size of quarters / scabs the size of pennies / the size of the shape of you" (lines 14–16) undermine the potentially transgressive nature of these images. The beasts' actions result in the symbolic theft of speech, physical beauty, and personal autonomy from the blues woman. She counts the cost of these traits in the impersonal coinage of capitalism, suggesting that she has paid for both her existence within American culture and her subversion of that culture with her very flesh.

Cortez pays homage to the historical origins of the surrealist movement in the poem when she draws parallels between the fate of African-American women and the experiences of the black diaspora. The blues woman's losses leave her with "all pigeon holes and spider legs colonized woman" (line 17): her exploitation by the forces of mainstream capitalism violates her body and removes her agency. "Pigeon holes" and "spider legs" signal that her language, too, has been rewritten; these phrases reference the new languages African slaves had to learn as well as surrealists' reframing of commonplace expressions. Words that might once have evoked the special abilities of a blues singer, according to the logic of Stephen Henderson's mascon words—"funky," "blue," and "throat"—now function as signs of physical violation: "funky piece of blood flint / with blue graffitied arms / a throat of dead bees" (lines 18–20). "Funk" describes the deathlike rigidity of flint rather than a sharp scent or fluid physical movement and "blue graffiti" recalls the numbers tattooed on Jewish prisoners' arms in concentration camps. The scatological tone of these lines' surrealism indicates that the blues woman's body participates unwillingly in these repressive structures. Her only resistance—"swollen fingers that dig into a swamp of broken purrtongue" (line 21)—registers in the terms of physical disability.

In the poem's third stanza, however, Cortez offers verbal protest—another reference to the piece's roots in gospel and blues impulses—as a means of opposing physical and colonialist abuse. She reframes the piece's representative subject as "Blues song woman who was looking good and sounding beautiful" (line 31) and glosses her new "song," symbolizing African-American women's potential for creative struggle against oppression, as "those nasal love songs" (line 24), "those strident battle-cry songs" (line 25), "that copper maroon rattle resonator / shaking from your feet to your eyes" (lines 26–27), "the sound of water drum songs" (line 28), and "grinding vibrato songs to work by to make love by / to remember you by" (lines 29–30). Here the blues woman's power originates in her use of mythologically resonant drums and rattles and her own voice. Sound figuratively escapes the written text, just as the blues woman's body escapes her oppressors' grasp.

Cortez's imagery and rhetoric in this poem suggest that political action can renew the violated body of the blues by assuring black women a position from which to challenge inequality. The loss of "thunder" (line 32) and "spirit" (line 33) has produced an "uprooted woman with the embalmed face / pall bearer lips / and hair matted in the mud of Texas" (lines 36–38). However, the poem's narrator identifies a possible redemption for the blues woman in protest. "[H]ow many ounces of revolution do you need" (line 39), the speaker asks, "to fill the holes in your body" (line 40). The three unpunctuated questions left unanswered at the end of the poem urge reader-listeners to assume social responsibility—"is it too late to get back your lightning / is it too late to reconstruct your blues song sister tell me / is it too late for the mother tongue in your womanself to insurrect" (lines 42–44)—while the speaker's uncertainty forestalls the possibility of closure for the problems that face black women. Though the blues woman has already suffered violations that endanger her resources of myth and history, feminist protest can aid the struggle to find new solutions. Opal Palmer Adisa calls Cortez "[t]he poet who is most unflinching on the subject of rape, who dramatizes it and renders it in explicit war terminology." Such references to war, Adisa asserts, signify an essential resistance to the abuses that society implicitly condones (370). Cortez's ability to portray difficult subjects "unflinchingly," in the scatological language of surrealism, implies that, for her, political activity protects material selves. Her "blues woman's" experiences reflect those of African-American women.

African mythology forms more of the background to Cortez's feminist politics in "Solo," a poem from *Festivals and Funerals* (1971).

Eugene Redmond calls this book "[m]usical, daring, ambivalent, complex and technically dexterous" in its attempt to "summarize . . . the uncertain world of blacklife [*sic*]" (415). The title alludes to the jazz practice of passing solos among the members of an ensemble. This group's players include Shango (line 11); Ogun (line 12), god of iron and creation (C. Ford 165); Damballa (line 14), a Haitian vodun god associated with snakes (Brooks De Vita 56); Malcolm X (line 15); "Oshun goddess of honey hot vinegar mangos and / castor oil / queen of fire at the crossroads" (lines 22–24); and Legba (line 25), godly messenger and guardian of the crossroads between the world of humans and the spirit world (Parrinder 88). These figures represent the very gods' opposition to events such as "the / massacred sharpesville gods of flesh" (lines 16–17), a reference to the murder on March 21, 1960, of 56 blacks protesting against apartheid laws in Sharpesville, South Africa. Oshun's position as the sole goddess in this pantheon and the detailed definition of her role that Cortez provides showcase black women's particular contributions to such political statements. As a "solo" performer, Oshun functions as "holder of the past / creator of the future / and lover to the black birds building a / new world supreme" (lines 30–33). "Supreme" recalls the musical innovation and social vision of John Coltrane's album *A Love Supreme*, while "black birds" alludes to the jazz artistry of Charlie "Bird" Parker. Cortez connects a poetic discourse defined by jazz elements with jazz's African mythological heritage through the figure of Oshun. The poem's final, unpunctuated line—"Welcome"—communicates confidence that African history and African-American creativity can help to address Western crimes against blacks.

Cortez has acknowledged the pervasive influence of African history in her poetry, explaining that she draws on both "traditional African elements" and certain "details and situations of modern Africa" like socialism and neocolonialism (Melhem, "Supersurrealist" 205). Her cultivation of an Afrocentric feminist politics in poems like "Solo" and "Grinding Vibrato" suggests that her feminism responds both to the historical past and to contemporary events. She underscores the urgency of her political interventions by juxtaposing scatological and blues-based images under the rubric of surrealism.

PERFORMANCE POETRY AND POLITICAL EXPRESSION

Her poetry's consistently expressive politics enables Cortez to focus on the potential of the live spoken word in interviews and in performances with the Firespitters; she calls their work together "a collective experiment. A collective composition" (Melhem, "Supersurrealist" 204). Their collaborations do not foster competition, yet the group's combination of jazz improvisation techniques with surrealist imagery and political commentary signals their work's unique contributions to the realm of performance poetry. To date, Cortez has produced eight albums of music and spoken-word performance with this group of jazz musicians. In poems and performance pieces alike, she creates evolving lists of musical accomplishments, human-rights abuses, and disturbingly graphic bodily images in order to fix in her audience's minds the specific names of injustice and achievement. These lists communicate the urgency of African-American political intervention in order to, as she puts it, "raise consciousness, to overcome our limitations, our position in the United States" (DeVeaux 79). Her politics centers on black women's social experiences and their absence from governmental decision-making.

The particular combination of political acuity and rhetorical flexibility in Cortez's performances suggests that her aesthetic philosophy bears a close resemblance to that of slam and other types of radical performed poetry. Radical poetry possesses transgressive political and formal potentials, to which both performers and audience react. Tyler Hoffman calls slam poetry a "subaltern poetry" that presents a social viewpoint "alternative to (and subversive of) the official culture and its orderings—as it seeks to undo ethnic, racial, gender, and sexual stereotypes" (49). Hoffman draws on Mikhail Bakhtin's theory of the parodic possibilities of carnivalesque behavior: the idea that the inversion of social roles encouraged during carnival costume balls reflects working-class desires to disrupt the social order. This theory undergirds his argument that slam poetry enables radical and liberatory speech, especially for its minority performers, and offers the possibility of occupying a cultural space alternative to the mainstream (Hoffman 62). Julie Schmid also hypothesizes that "the synthesizing of literary and performance traditions . . . that goes on at any given slam venue is a necessary component in the creation of an alternative, intercultural community poetics" (640). Cortez and her fellow performers define such a poetics in their multilayered, improvisatory performances.

In an article on what she more broadly terms "dissident traditions," Maria Damon agrees with Hoffman's and Schmid's sense of the potential for radical expression afforded by performance poetry but locates its social relevance in its capacity for immediate public communication. The live, improvisatory performance of poetry includes "battles of wit and argumentation" that are "studied, celebrated, performed, and challenged in discursively productive ways" (Damon 334). Poets and audiences come together in the production of a communal art that supersedes the boundaries of the stage. Slam poets often self-publish and self-promote even after gaining a public reputation; they prefer to control the processes by which their work is disseminated (Damon 337). These qualities also define Cortez's approach to poetic performance and composition. She produced her first spoken-word recording, *Celebrations and Solitudes*, in 1975, with musical accompaniment by bassist Richard Davis (Cortez, *There It Is*). Five years later, she made her first recording with early members of the Firespitters, an album entitled *Unsubmissive Blues*. She has worked with this group in different incarnations ever since. At least three members of the Firespitters—Denardo Coleman, Bern Nix, and Al MacDowell—have also been members of Ornette Coleman's jazz ensemble, Prime Time (Chinen).

Though she notes in several interviews that she does not sing, instrumental music has shaped Cortez's live and recorded vocal improvisations since her first recordings. Her voice acts as another instrument in the ensemble, often engaging in calls and responses with other performers as well as developing and maintaining rhythmic patterns. Her vocal style incorporates improvisatory variations on repeated lines or passages as well as melismas that highlight individual words. In her recorded performances, both instrumental and vocal lines keep a rapid tempo; Cortez mirrors musical accents executed via high-hat taps or the tongued attacks of wind instruments with a precise articulation, while her chants change pitch in response to the musicians' improvisations. In the liner notes to the *Taking the Blues Back Home* album, many of the pieces' lyrics are reproduced with a deliberate use of unconventional spacing and punctuation, just as in her published books. Transcriptions of her performances like this one afford listeners a glimpse of Cortez's composition techniques and highlight her poetry's close artistic affiliation to jazz.

Cortez's live performances draw not only on jazz's performance techniques but also on its historical association with social critique, highlighting injustices through patterns of call-and-response and repetition. Her commitment to jazz-based improvisatory strategies indicates that she sees the province of the aural as a source for creative inspiration. *Taking the Blues Back Home* contains two tracks whose corresponding text was only reproduced later in a poetry collection. She describes these pieces, "Talk to Me" and "Nobody Knows a Thing," as "spontaneous fragments of words and music," apparently generated in performance or in the recording studio as successful exercises in group improvisation (*Taking the Blues*). Although spontaneous improvisations or sound-based compositions do not necessarily signify political intervention, these pieces' links to the work and life of specific musicians suggest that Cortez aligns artistic tribute with social statement.

A reading of one of these pieces illustrates the ways in which tribute to or interpellation of a subject can drive Cortez's approach to poetic improvisation. She speaks the text of "Talk to Me" (subtitled "For Don Cherry") as follows on the recording:[22]

> Like the sound
> Of the rain
> Welling up
> In the sky
> Beat it down
> To the ground
> Bring it in
> With the wind
> And the tone
> Through the zone
> Move on back
> Smear your sax
> With the stream
> Where you dream
> Send those notes
> Over here
> Speak on out
> Speak on out
>
> Speak your mind
> Trace the lines
> Pass them down
> Say it now
> Say it now
>
> Fill your horn
> With the depths
> Of the clouds
> Turning green
> Cause that's the blow
> It's all the cold
> Pepper the night
> Burst on through
> Blow on out
> Blow on out
> Talk to me
> Talk to me

This piece follows a slower tempo than most of the other pieces on the recording. Although the performance lasts less than three minutes, Cortez does not begin speaking until the first 30 seconds have passed.

The laid-back swing of the tune that carries the entire piece features a subdued electric guitar, tenor sax, and rhythmic taps on the snare drum and high hat. Once she enters the performance, Cortez picks up the rhythm and tempo established by the other band members. She delivers these lines with a precise, clear articulation, her pauses carefully timed according to the music's tempo.

In spite of the fact that Cortez generates her affirmation of Cherry's talents on the spot, the poem she creates has a fairly uniform structure. She calls out his traits in response to both his musical legacy and the rhythmically steady beat, the latter of which guides her improvisation. With the exception of three lines in the last verse, every line contains three syllables, followed by a brief pause during which the instruments continue to play. This delivery style reinforces the words' declamatory rhetoric. Several of the piece's lines begin with imperative verbs that blur the line between the invisible subject of Cortez's tribute and his abilities: she never speaks Cherry's name, but the description of his now mythic talents functions as a means of identification. Although few surrealist elements appear here, lines such as "smear your sax / with the stream / where you dream" and "fill your horn / with the depths / of the clouds / turning green" suggest that Cherry's music cannot be mistaken for anyone else's and its power exceeds the expressive limits of a more conventional vocabulary. Cortez's decision to situate this piece as the midpoint of the album, the sixth of 12 tracks, demonstrates that she values improvisation as a performance technique as much as written transcription. Though she does not invoke feminist politics, Cortez links Cherry's music to the environmental themes of her other pieces through references to "clouds" and "night." Since "Talk to Me" existed as a recorded performance before it was published in a book, it occupies a cultural space alternative to mainstream poetry; its jazz-influenced techniques define a radical edge that coincides with the ideas of Hoffman and Damon.

Such an alternative cultural space exists in the poems in which Cortez uses textual improvisation and jazz tribute to critique the social inequalities that black women have experienced. In these cases, she honors her subject's art even as she interrogates troubling social conditions that the subject may have condoned. "If the Drum Is a Woman," a poem from *Firespitter* (1982) and *Jazz Fan Looks Back*, takes its title from a 1956 Duke Ellington suite, *A Drum Is a Woman*, that contains a tune by the same name. Ellington also produced a CBS special in 1957 entitled "A Drum Is a Woman," which portrayed the history of jazz in allegorical fashion with music performed by three singers.[23] Cortez's response to Ellington's project frames the history of jazz subtly but pointedly, with the title the only clue to the poem's background source. The opening line,

"If the drum is a woman," both acknowledges Ellington's artistic heritage and casts the metaphorical premise of his piece into doubt by juxtaposing a revised version of his title to a series of violent action verbs: "pounding," "pistol whipping," and "shooting" (lines 1, 2, 3). These activities might take place in the course of a drum solo but also recall domestic abuse.[24]

Cortez's riff choruses strengthen this association between jazz performance and abuse of women when the speaker condemns the verbs "abuse," "choke," "rape," "reject," and "dominate" (lines 6, 18, 19, 29, 30) as actions that have been performed on drums. The only gender associated with the drum as object is female—the "mother," "sister," "wife," and "infant daughter" drums (lines 21, 22)—which renders the word's eventual defamiliarization through repetition all the more chilling. Cortez repeats the word "drum" 32 times in this 36-line poem, and the poem contains no visual punctuation cues except three capitalizations and a spacing variation when the phrase "don't abuse your drum" is twice repeated three times. Although much twentieth-century poetry cultivates the interpretive open-endedness associated with such a lack of punctuation, here it drives home the intensity of Cortez's message. The vertical alignment of the same word several times on the page in a series of repeated lines both forces the reader's eye to seek out the line's variants and reemphasizes the poem's angry prohibitions. Her title's link to the work of Duke Ellington serves as a reminder of the gender politics that can underlie jazz's cultural success.

After nine lines of varied repetitions exploring the abuses perpetrated on women's bodies, the poem's narrator locates some of the sources of male abuse while condemning the picture of the U.S. social climate that those violations convey. Phrases such as "displaced persons," "skins striped with flames," and "underpaid clerks" (lines 8, 9, 10) summon up images of specific moments in American history in which racial and economic injustice has sparked rage. "Displaced persons" references not only the waves of immigrants who found more pain than welcome on U.S. soil but also the African-American Great Migration during the early twentieth century and the formation of inner-city ghettos. "Skins striped with flames" could refer to any number of public uprisings in the United States in which police stepped in to quell resistance with force, while "underpaid clerks" acknowledges the chronic underemployment that many minority groups face. The central lines of the poem, "I know that this is America / and chickens are coming home to roost / on the MX missile" (16–18),[25] summarize the revolutionary unrest that peaked in the late 1960s. The surrealistic juxtaposition of "chickens" with "MX missile" recalls both the militant rhetoric of Black Power and seething Cold War tensions. Tony Bolden explains the conflict between black nationalist and domestic themes in the poem as "a study of the process whereby colonized individuals become reflections of the colonizer, and thereby reify the socio-political structure that underlies their own marginalization by victimizing others" ("All the Birds" 67). Cortez ties her censure of domestic abuse to her condemnation of crimes against nation and nature.

The relentless repetition of these "drummers'" sins names public representatives of black culture as accomplices in the degradation of women. Riffing off a simple analogy between woman and object, Cortez creates a performance piece whose music functions as a metaphor for interpersonal relationships and the ways in which those relationships articulate social inequalities. Kimberly N. Brown argues that Cortez's work "focuses on the abuses third world people face collectively: the exploitation of their labor, their bodies, and their land" (70). She links this idea of the coterminous nature of body and work to the practices of poetry itself, hypothesizing that "performance poetry can also be seen as manual work" (K. Brown 71). In her specific reading of "If the Drum Is a Woman," Brown defines Cortez's poetic labor in terms of scarification, which she understands as "theorizing from the wound, working through the scars" (67). The black women represented in this poem bear a double burden, since "the person doing the scarring wears her brother's face" (K. Brown 74). Compositions like this one allow Cortez to pursue historical accuracy and social justice through interpellation. Her poetic performances offer an opportunity to name the facts of history, the participants in unjust practices, and the ramifications that those practices have for public environments.

Cortez's teaching and activist work helped her to develop this kind of performative poetics. She taught in the English Department at Livingston College, a Rutgers University campus, from 1977 until 1983 (Melhem, "*MELUS* Profile" 76); she cites teaching as an important, albeit time-consuming, professional activity (Melhem, "Supersurrealist" 202). While she teaches and appears in the films *Poetry in Motion, Mandela Is Coming, Tribeca, Ana Mendieta: Fuego de la Tierra,* and *Yari Yari* (Meehan 59), she has also traveled to read, lecture, and participate in artistic and political communities in Brazil, Cuba, England, France, Ghana, the Ivory Coast, Martinique, Mexico, Morocco, the Netherlands, Nicaragua, Nigeria, Trinidad, West Germany, and Zimbabwe.[26] These activities illustrate her explorations of the spaces where poetry, history, and politics meet. References to Cuban history, music, and politics recur in her poetry, for instance; Aldon Nielsen labels these elements a kind of "cultural syncretism" that reflects "the long history of Latin infusions into American jazz idioms" (*Integral Music* 177). Her professional experiences and varying cultural influences define a creative aesthetic that emerges from a dynamic politics of place.

In poems that use jazz as a vehicle through which to engage this politics, Cortez creates surrealist images of the environment that highlight connections between musical performance and political critique. She interprets jazz performance in one such poem, "After Hours," as a mirror of social interaction. This strategy allows her to examine the means by which groups are categorized in economic, sexual, racial, and artistic terms. The piece advocates a feminist self-sufficiency that can oppose society's environmental crimes; its surrealist portraits of that society foreground connections between jazz's creative impetus and individual political acts.

"After Hours" opens with a denial: "I am not sucking on a form / to get drunk off of its content" (lines 1–2). This statement seems to reference Language poets' advocacy of the union of form and content while refusing to participate in the longstanding poetic traditions that dictate formal constraints. It also recalls the intoxicating political rhetoric of Black Arts writers, to which Cortez, like Sonia Sanchez, contributed at one point. Cortez undermines the legitimacy of avant-garde yet politically disengaged innovations in language to make space for her jazz-influenced discourse. Her speaker's claim that she is "not pre-booking space in / non-smoking section of the imperial pipeline to / sell used cars pussy & industrial waste" (lines 3–5) locates this discourse in the realm of public policy. She employs a familiar commercial language—"pre–booked space," "non-smoking section," "used cars," and "industrial waste"—to remind her audience that these seemingly innocuous phrases accumulate over time. Language can be a site of ideological violation and environmental pollution.

Cortez couches her critique of discursive manipulation in the poem's increasingly graphic language. Its conjunction of natural and domestic images suggests that surrealist writing can offer creative opposition to government-sanctioned doublespeak. Activities such as "watching dead moth in paprika," "inhaling graphite breeze of iodine mist," and "chewing on my warm diaper of acid rain" (lines 7, 10, 12) link consumerism to its environmental fallout while revising its familiar language. Cortez suggests that productive political intervention requires an awareness of how one's actions impact the outside world. In order to "live the routine of my routine" (line 15), the speaker must accommodate the other inhabitants of her environment: "the female porcupine chatters" and "the blue-face mandrill drills" at the same time that she "write[s] a poem" (lines 16–18). Creating a language predicated on political consciousness enables one to live "after hours," in an atmosphere akin to the creative ambiance of a jazz club late at night. When the speaker writes a poem "after hours," she does it while "taking a look at myself looking" (line 19), aware of the graphic fact of "time rotating its butt in my face" (line 21). This concrete but unsettling image serves as a reminder of the effort needed to protest social conditions, even in language. Cortez uses this scatological phrase to demonstrate that tangible rewards do not necessarily follow.

"After Hours" ends with a clear assertion of feminist politics that challenges the social roles traditionally allotted to women. The speaker's claim to "have already been / violated by survivors of the flood" (lines 23–24) complicates traditional notions of female goodness in its implicit criticism of Christian ("survivors of the flood") values. Her imperatives, "do not sweep while I'm eating / do not cover my pot with your lid" (lines 25–26), interpret conventional images of domestic life—images also often used in blues lyrics—as signs of ideological dismissal and sexual aggression. The speaker refuses these violations of her mind and body as completely as she rejected the capitalist violations that appear at the beginning of the poem. The speaker's admission that her ideas spring from fundamentally creative sources serves as a hinge between the two halves of the poem, a transition from environmental pollution to self-assertion. "I have no kiss-ass explanation for the question," she affirms, "'what is Jazz'" (lines 13–14). These surrealist images reconfigure once-familiar discourses, suggesting Cortez's unwillingness to limit the political scope of her work. Jazz's formal fluidity and creative potential serve as metaphors for the innovative feminist thought that motivates her poetry's composition.

CONCLUSION: FINDING THE EDGE

African-American poets like Langston Hughes and Sterling Brown helped to establish a long-standing practice of representing African-American dialect inflections alongside "classroom English" in poems about black culture. These juxtapositions demonstrate the essential falseness of any dichotomy between white literary and black oral traditions by illustrating the myriad sources that shape black literature. Aldon Nielsen points out that "it is commonly the case that a privileging of the oral in examinations of black writing is accompanied by a severe restricting of the registers of English considered availably 'black'" (*Black Chant* 22). This restriction indicates that common misinterpretations of African-American literature have resulted in a narrow definition of black orality, one associated almost exclusively with dialect, though Hughes's and Brown's works portray a range of powerful linguistic registers found in both black speech and black writing.

Nathaniel Mackey also opposes such reductive definitions of black language by describing the position of African-American writers as "on edge." A metaphor for both separation and penetration—being "cut off" or being "cut into"—"on edge" denotes a place "where differences intersect, where we witness and take part in a traffic of partialities" (Mackey, *Discrepant Engagement* 260). The many possible interpretations of Mackey's metaphor signal that individuals achieve this resolution only uneasily. The edge communicates a sense of periphery, but it also implies the ideas of being on the "brink" or "verge" of discovering or doing something; occupying the "threshold" of a new location; holding a position of domination or advantage; and possessing a quality of "incisiveness" or "keenness" ("Edge"). The edge is not confined to one side of an issue: it can intervene and divide a once-coherent center.

The edges in Jayne Cortez's poetry appear at the intersections of political, performative, and linguistic innovations. Her gospel and surrealist influences, her ecofeminist politics, and her live-performance practices culminate in an improvisatory poetics that owes a compositional debt to jazz. Her poems call out existing social crimes and respond with feminist condemnations of such misdeeds. She employs the hyperbolic, sometimes scatological language characteristic of both surrealism and blues lyrics in order to critique the social forces responsible for environmental violation. This critique issues from her understanding of the parallels between the state of the environment and popular social attitudes toward African-American women; ecofeminist protests motivate her poetry's rhetorical explosion of repressive linguistic structures. Cortez creates this formal strategy by exploiting language's functional elements; such attention to the meanings that form carries exists in Wanda Coleman's poetry as well. Coleman, like Cortez, acknowledges the history of Western poetics even as she establishes unique, culturally specific forms within the body of her work. She also shares Cortez's tendency to employ surrealist, often scatological imagery in the service of forceful political statements; in Coleman's case, such imagery articulates the relationships between local and transnational communities in need.

SHAPE-SHIFTING: THE URBAN GEOGRAPHIES OF WANDA COLEMAN'S JAZZ POETRY

IN AN INTERVIEW WITH TONY MAGISTRALE AND PATRICIA FERREIRA, Wanda Coleman commented on her experiences editing *Players*, a soft-core pornography magazine that published black men's writing in the 1970s: "*Players* was a job. It was a job that I came to realize was based on the importance of image. Although the magazine featured tits and ass, it was *black* tits and ass. . . . The idealization of the female form along Caucasian lines has been very detrimental to the black female" (Magistrale and Ferreira 494, 495). Coleman often pursues subjects, like the ideological implications of pornography, that many writers would not consider tackling; she does not confine her views on such topics to interviews but engages them in nonfiction, fiction, and poetry alike. As a prolific writer who has published many essays and more than fifteen books to date, including ten books of poetry, she readily expresses views that contradict popular perspectives on literature and society. Her work issues from a belief that politically committed writing can help to resist social discrimination.

Perhaps no context better illustrates this belief than Coleman's reaction to the controversy surrounding her now infamous review of *A Song Flung Up to Heaven*, Maya Angelou's 2002 autobiographical work. In the review, published in the *Los Angeles Times Book Review* (April 14, 2002), Coleman calls the book a "sloppily written fake" filled with "titillating confessions and coquettish allusions" that "shamelessly . . . cannibalizes the reputations of three major black figures: Malcolm X, James Baldwin, and King, Jr." Though Coleman takes Angelou to task for her book's poor writing, she reserves her sharpest criticism for Angelou's claim that she played a central role in 1960s black activism: "With unflinching piety," Coleman contends, she "restyles herself as a militant, fostering the illusion that she was at the core of the civil rights and black power movements" ("Coulda" 137). The public furor that ensued after this piece was published cost Coleman invitations to readings, prompted a prominent black LA bookstore to ban her, and fostered tensions within the African-American artistic community. Several letters to the editor complained about Coleman's assessment of Angelou's work, and she found herself scheduled to read opposite Angelou, in a much smaller venue, at the 2002 *Los Angeles Times* Book Festival. At the same time, she learned that many readers shared her views and were relieved that someone had dared to hold an apparently untouchable literary icon to a high set of standards. For Coleman, however, the incident reinforced several painful truths with which she had long been familiar. Her work confronts readers with the persistent social injustices of racism, sexism, homophobia, and entrenched economic disparities, yet she notes that this review, which she characterized in Ishmael Reed's *Konch* magazine as the piece for which she has "received more attention . . . than for any poem or story [she has] ever written," was "neither a scholarly treatise nor an article on racism in American Letters." "Anyone who assumes that I derive any satisfaction" from the piece's popularity among her other work, she observes, "is grossly mistaken." Instead, the review's genre and necessarily concise format, tied to a specific economic exchange, forced her to write less material and to expose herself to attack by the literary elite ("Black on Black" 151).[1] Such risk-taking continues to motivate Coleman's work, demonstrating that her fearless approach to social critique still contrasts with many contemporaries' more conservative stances.

As a poet writing out of South Los Angeles, Coleman makes it a priority to legitimize the harsh details of a geography marked by unacknowledged deprivations. To date, she has received less critical and popular recognition than this kind of work demands. Her participation in many aspects of the LA literary scene, which she describes in the Magistrale and Ferreira interview (502), also suggests that Los Angeles has evolved into a new locus for experimental poetics, though very few black writers of her generation have remained active in the area since ongoing racial discrimination limits professional and personal opportunities ("Black on Black" 141). As feminist jazz poetry expands the boundaries of a cultural tradition first defined in the early decades of the twentieth century, jazz poets like Coleman extend the genre's political relevance to include issues that arise in nonmainstream geographies. The political statements of Coleman's poetry also manifest a global scope that positions her work in the forefront of jazz poetry's—and jazz's—evolving social consciousness. She herself points out that black writers have a responsibility to further enrich black artistic traditions: "[R]elegating Jazz (and the Jazz principle) to obscurity" necessarily means that "the people who give birth to it are kept in a position of economic and cultural inferiority. . . . To recognize is to empower" ("On Theloniousism" 74). The circumstances of her writing suggest that a politically attuned jazz poetics addresses the historical exclusion of black art forms as well as the logistics of textual distribution; her work challenges conventional notions of canon formation by drawing attention to the writing's geographical locus, its contributions to ongoing arguments about social reputation, and its political agenda.

Like Harryette Mullen, another participant in LA literary activities, Coleman also uses her critical and creative writings to bring to light the work of other authors who struggle against social invisibility. For example, she conducted a radio interview for *Callaloo* with black Australian poet and activist Bobbi Sykes on Sykes's experiences with racially motivated crimes in Australia. Sykes notes that clear parallels exist between social conditions in America and those in Australia, in spite of the fact that blacks in Australia were still fighting just to obtain land claims in the mid-1980s (Coleman, "Bobbi Sykes" 294). Coleman portrays the racial hierarchies that continue to limit educational and professional opportunities for blacks in both countries through her conversation with Sykes. She similarly evaluates unjust public practices in a series of letters she exchanged with poet E. Ethelbert Miller, through which she identifies the sources of her disappointment with academia. Her lack of public recognition stems in part from an unwillingness and financial inability to limit herself to poets' usual professional pursuits: she has worked a series of jobs that includes waitress, medical transcriber and billing clerk, magazine editor, proofreader, journalist, scriptwriter, and assistant recruiter for Peace Corps / Vista. She remains unafraid of living a life on the margins even of the poetry community. Miller himself notes that he sees Coleman as a true pioneer of words, someone who might be "claiming all of Los Angeles and moving outwards to seize the imagination of what is left of the rest of America." He characterizes her as a person of "genius, anger, humor, hurt, pain, ego, and blackness" who has written "too many books for our eyes" (Coleman, "Letters" 99). His warm yet incisive assessment of her work provides one example of the accolades Coleman has received from those familiar with her writing's political directness.

In her own analyses of writing's social functions, Coleman places a high value on freedom, improvisation, and cultural knowledge.

She believes poets should choose whatever language will most effectively communicate their ideas (Juno and Vale 124); as a "Black American of slave descent, African in origin," she conceptualizes her literary ancestry as "shattered," a mix of the Western traditions taught in a particular branch of the Los Angeles school system in the mid-twentieth-century and "the Afro-American blues/jazz musical tradition" (Coleman, "What Is American"). When one's ancestry reveals breaks and absences, as this formulation suggests, the work that results might seek wholeness, consolidation, even explanations that address America's illogical history of oppression. Coleman rejects such goals, however, in favor of condemning social problems and pointing her readers toward the possibility of change. She writes in order to achieve public recognition of her work's message and worth, but on her own terms, regardless of the politics she might have to negotiate in the larger world of publicly known critics and writers. "Were I ever to achieve [literary greatness]," she notes, "I wanted it on my own very stringent terms. I wanted to earn it clean, my way, with full-and-fair recognition of my artistic work" ("Black on Black" 143). This approach both sets her apart from more conservative writers and positions her work within the tradition of the African-American autobiography, in which writers relate an individual trauma or success in order to portray the people's overall experience (O'Mara 88). Her poetry emphasizes moments when pain and alienation within particular landscapes or geographies gain one membership in a social group outside one's accustomed purview; this thematic tendency illustrates the global perspective foundational to a feminist jazz poetics of the postmodern age.

"SHE SEPARATES THE COTTON FROM THE BOLL": A POST-HISTORY OF JAZZ AND BLUES

Wanda Coleman was born on November 13, 1946, to a working-class family. Her father, an ex-boxer, worked for an advertising agency, while her mother cleaned houses and sewed (Manheim). Both of her parents encountered situations that demonstrated racism's prevalence on both individual and social levels: her father first moved to California after witnessing a lynching in Little Rock, Arkansas, while her mother worked for Ronald Reagan and Jane Wyman but quit when they would not give her a raise (Juno and Vale 118). Coleman disliked school as a child, preferring to read and write on her own, though she describes her early diaries as "bursts of *anger*—very little else." Fortunately, her parents encouraged her work; her father even taught her some elements of media production. Her first poems were published in a local newspaper when she was 13; she began reading continental philosophy in high school, which led to the realization that her school would not provide the education she needed (Juno and Vale 120). She attended California State in 1964, Los Angeles City College in 1967, and Stanford some years later but did not finish college (S. Johnson). She has taught in several institutions and continues to advocate on behalf of the socially relevant work that writers produce both within institutions and on their own.

Jazz and blues references provide formal and historical contexts for Coleman's interrogations of capitalism's transnational results in her multivolume *American Sonnets* sequence and her other poetry. Such references create a poetic discourse within the work that links political critique with musical innovation. Coleman disavows many cultural traditions; she refuses to participate, for instance, in the homage that many other African Americans readily pay to Black Arts writers (Juno and Vale 121). However, she admits to being "very much in a blues tradition," albeit "quite different from just about any black poet you can name" (Magistrale and Ferreira 499). She favors compositional and performance strategies based in improvisation, which she describes as "spontaneous infusion/renewal—not *repetition* or geometric progression/ascension." The act of improvisation itself indicates that one possesses access to a specific cultural knowledge; to truly create spontaneous work, one must write a poem (or a Thelonious Monk tune) and "continually renew it/rebirth it/present different aspects without (if you are lucky) boring listeners who see with their ears" ("On Theloniousism" 76). Coleman's creative work seeks to engage readers who hear with their eyes, invoking jazz contexts in order to call for social change.

Coleman established jazz as a central vehicle for political expression early in her career. Sascha Feinstein labels three of the poems in Coleman's 1983 collection, *Imagoes*, for instance, as jazz poems: "At the Jazz Club He Comes on a Ghost," "Blue Song Sung in Room of Torrid Goodbyes," and "Saint Theresa" (*Bibliographic Guide* 19). In these poems, jazz and blues allusions provide adjectives that briefly characterize a situation or emotions. "Saint Theresa" features a speaker who describes the title character's ultimate destination as a "bitter end / floor where old cracked wood / record player ten years of spin / groove 45 blues" (lines 2–5); the title of "At the Jazz Club" only suggests a setting for the speaker's reminiscence about a dying relationship. "Blues Song," a poem written in six sections of varying lengths, begins with a brief portrait of a "big black mama" who "wears a man's hat cocked on her head and when blue / belts out a song for all fast ladies to hear and nod / in soul felt empathy" (lines 1–3). The speaker sings a blues song whose lyrics weave through the fabric of Coleman's poem; jazz references embellish the climactic moments in her physical relationship with a lover as well as the memories of the losses she has endured. This jazz and blues language positions black creativity in the realm of the everyday, which also suffers the economic inequalities fostered by capitalism.

Coleman's jazz poems sometimes cast her critique as existential philosophy in order to convey a postmodernist disillusionment with contemporary social conditions. "The Saturday Afternoon Blues," a poem from *Imagoes* not listed in Feinstein's bibliography, complicates a traditional subject of the blues, personal hardship, by juxtaposing a traditional form to a modern perspective. The speaker describes her state of mind—"i'm a candidate for the coroner, a lyric for a song" (line 9)—and her relative loneliness since "friends are all out shopping / ain't nobody home" (lines 3–4) in the first, second, and fourth stanzas, all of which represent fairly conventional examples of blues lyrics with rough AAB form. In the speaker's claim to be "a candidate for the coroner, a lyric for a song," Coleman both identifies the depressive emotions common to the blues and gestures toward her own participation in a textual tradition that offers relief from that sadness through shared experience. The poem follows this pattern of first naming personal problems and then describing the speaker's attempts to deal with them alone until the third stanza, which differs from the others in its four-line reiteration of the poem's main theme: "[T]he man i love is a killer / the man i love is a thief / the man i love is a junky / the man i love is grief" (lines 18–21). The end rhymes of lines 19 and 21 add to the poem's song-like quality, while their content provides a solid explanation for the speaker's sorrow. Coleman continues the work of her blues predecessors by updating the lyrics' message within a conventional form. Rather than merely bemoaning her isolation, the speaker comments that the "suicide hotline is busy" (line 5) and recognizes the many reasons why her relationship is doomed. The speaker's self-conscious linking of her personal situation with the historical tradition of blues musical production—"i'm a candidate for the coroner, a lyric for a song"—indicates that a postmodern sensibility motivates the piece's revisionism.

"[D]ancer in the window," a poem from *African Sleeping Sickness: Stories and Poems* (1990), demonstrates another jazz-based compositional strategy central to Coleman's work. Here she uses the forum of blues performance to evaluate historical portrayals of women's bodies. In this case, she interprets the popular adulation of objectified physiques as evidence of the persistent effects of slavery practices. This poem paints a brief but poignant portrait of black women on display in a variety of performance situations, sporting attire such as a "halter top and second skins" (line 2) and playing roles like "the chorus girl at café society a boogie woogie at the / bucket of blood a debutante at the black Elks hall formal ball" (lines 4–5). Coleman skillfully arranges these elements of self-presentation into a progression that clarifies the associative links between feminine attire and physical threat. The same woman might perform at a café, at a bar called the "bucket of blood," or at a "formal ball" and yet confront the same faces peering in at her, a "dancer in the window," in every setting. Coleman creates a dramatic situation here that resembles Sherley Anne Williams's depiction of Bessie Smith. Like Jayne Cortez, too, Coleman chooses "josephine baker in paris hungry eyes fish nets and bananas" (line 8) as the paradigmatic example of the ways in which wealthy, male, and/or white gazes can objectify black women. The narrator offers her final analysis of this exploitative attitude toward black women's bodies in the poem's simple final line: "[S]he separates the cotton from the boll" (line 9). Although the line could certainly be interpreted as a reference to a performer's ability to shine in contrast to her less-talented peers, its American context evokes slave labor. Josephine Baker's famously exotic costumes of "fish nets and bananas" also recall images of third-world people laboring to survive by producing food destined for wealthy first-world tables. All of the fishnet stockings in the world cannot disguise the "hungry eyes" of a black woman performing for a cruelly indifferent audience, whether on stage or in the fields.

As her portrait of Josephine Baker reveals, the historical associations and performative techniques of blues and jazz provide Coleman with poetic devices that reframe economic and geographical disadvantage as a source of creative productivity. Eric Murphy Selinger characterizes her poetry in "Trash, Art, and Performance Poetry" as "unquestionably artful, well-wrought" and posits that her combination of these devices with Language-group influences and "her love of everyday black speech" results in a "'fusionist' aesthetic" (364, 367). He cites her statement in *The Best American Poetry, 1996* that jazz enables her to "'mock, meditate, imitate, and transform, using any and every literary trick and device— even clichés—at will'" as evidence that jazz remains a primary source for her linguistic creations (Selinger 367). Like the other poets in this study, Coleman employs jazz and blues themes as a means of critiquing social conditions, while the music's performative possibilities facilitate experiments with poetic form.

Coleman's explorations of the political potential of her jazz poetics have enabled her to pursue feminist commentary in particular. *African Sleeping Sickness*, for instance, contains not only the titular collection but also a revision of an earlier work, *Mad Dog Black Lady* (first published in 1979), that includes six completely new poems. These newer pieces first articulate the feminist perspective that Coleman refines over the course of her career. She notes that she never found second-wave beliefs relevant to her experiences as a black woman (Juno and Vale 123).

Instead she represents "men and women of the underclass," particularly African-American women looking for "dignity in spite of deprivation" (Magistrale 85). Her characters' narration usually appears without punctuation, this lack of syntactical or rhetorical direction highlighting black women's "corseted identities" (Magistrale 87). At the same time, however, her poetic subjects' fates often seem to suggest that they will not find a solution to their problems. Both the poems' narratives and the collections' overarching themes give voice to Coleman's own frustration at not finding "a satisfying alternative to the oppression her female protagonists must endure" (Magistrale 93).

In one of the poems added to *Mad Dog Black Lady*, "The Laying Down Blues," for instance, Coleman complicates the allusions to capitalist social crimes presented in "The Saturday Afternoon Blues" by incorporating a critique of male privilege. This poem follows the AAB blues-lyrics form also used in "The Saturday Afternoon Blues"; its structure, coupled with a feminist censure of current social conditions, recalls the efforts of early-century blues singers to define strong roles for women. In the first two stanzas, the speaker attributes her despair to outside circumstances, admitting a desire to lie down and give up. But her sense of self-preservation prevails, as she rallies her spirits and decides to "push sorrow aside, get up before / the mirrors, force a grin" (lines 7–8) in the third stanza. Though she must pretend to an optimism she does not feel, even when facing her own reflection, she perseveres in her song, narrating a life that cannot be ignored. The third and eighth stanzas of the poem each precede an indented verse that highlights the source of the speaker's blues. Both indented stanzas feature a professional man—"corporate man" in stanza four, "artist man" in stanza nine—who cannot understand the pain the speaker experiences because of his own position of authority. In both cases, the speaker figures her interaction with this man as a mere business transaction; either "he's banking body on the dotted line" (line 10) or "he's banking booty on the game of fame" (line 23). Coleman's female speaker, implicitly objectified through male business activities, comments on the gendered nature of both blues performance traditions and professionalism. These men symbolize the impersonal power that government and business hold—power responsible for the social injustices that the speaker has observed.

In addition to invoking the usual blues subjects of hardship and neglect in the poem, however, Coleman explores the options for social rehabilitation available to oppressed women. Seeking help from outside sources, the speaker expresses her desire to "lay down / all my troubles in the bed of the police" (lines 18–19) or "take it to Congress and spread it all across the land" (line 31). Rather than accepting abuse and basic inequalities as everyday conditions, she considers turning to the governing structures meant to improve her quality of life. However, the poem ends with her realization that she cannot rely upon conventional means of social and political protection, presumably because, as a woman of color, she will only survive through self-sufficiency. The repetition of "get up before the mirror. force a grin" in the poem's final line (35) signals the inevitable resumption of this cycle of need, denial, and anger; its lack of end punctuation suggests that black women must seek an as yet undiscovered solution to social inequality. Coleman's use of jazz and blues techniques and revisionist discourse in poems like this one illuminates her claim that feminism has emerged as a legitimate practice in American politics. She attributes this development in part to the methods of social organizing introduced by 1960s black nationalists, yet notes that racism remains a serious, unresolved problem (Magistrale and Ferreira 495). Her work's engagement with international human-rights concerns demonstrates that an actively political feminist jazz poetics must seek to interrogate the experiences of women living both within and beyond the boundaries of the West.

Coleman's work in *African Sleeping Sickness* also offers another perspective on the jazz elegy popularized by contemporaries like Sonia Sanchez and Cortez. As in so many examples of the form, her jazz elegies take place in an urban landscape "where nature has long been displaced by colorless buildings and asphalt streets" (Magistrale 89). Some of the darker connotations of the book's title are clarified in its third section, subtitled "the cry of forever yearning can be heard in the heart of a people." Here most of the poems deal with the AIDS epidemic ravaging black communities in the United States—a disease known to have originated in Africa and now associated for many sectors of the American public with indigent African populations. The third of the "Auguries" poems, the seventh poem in this section, invokes familiar images of jazz clubs and singers in order to draw connections between the heavy drug use of the bebop era and the AIDS-related illnesses that plague some contemporary black communities. The poem begins with an apparently serene collage of images, "reefer champagne C-notes & mellow / a dark moody round midnight / blue gardenias" (lines 1–3), that reference not only the marijuana and alcohol used to season a jazz session but also the musicians who might perform there: Thelonious Monk, who played "Round Midnight" as one of his signature tunes, and Billie Holiday, who often wore gardenias in her hair. These celebratory impressions shift subtly into scenes of music touched by tragedy, however, in "the wisdom of the alto sax fallen to temporal blues / a sultry sequined torch / burning against the abyss" (lines 4–6). Here Coleman reminds her readers of the dangers musicians face when they subsume self to music and its accompanying lifestyle. The once "wise" alto sax can express only a transient regret, while fame makes quick work of the alluring female singer—objectified here as a "sultry sequined torch."

The wordplay that Coleman creates in the associations between "torch" singer and a torch uselessly burning itself out "against the abyss" lends the poem a darkly ludic tone appropriate for the blues. She continues to experiment with words' aural and associative meanings in the following line, which suggests that, while these performers' talents temporarily saved them from succumbing to inevitable fates, such protection could not last long: "bleak bebop sheebop" (line 7). This line evokes "black sheep" as both a category of social misfits and a parody of a children's seemingly innocuous nursery rhyme; Coleman's aural anagram of the phrase recalls the techniques of bebop improvisation. She reiterates the fate that can befall such misfits in the center of the poem—"a black man puts a magnum to the head of his infant / daughter and is wasted by s. w. a. t." (lines 11–12)—before the poem concludes with the invocation of a jazz vocalist whose own life ended in the early 1980s: "johnny hartman johnny hartman" (line 20). Drawing a clear link between social violence and black creative expression, Coleman suggests that although the latter cannot prevent the former, writers have the responsibility to confront their audiences with life's most difficult realities.

CHALLENGING TRADITIONS: MAKING FORM MEAN

Coleman has built her reputation as a writer on a signature fusion of regionalist, jazz-influenced poetics with black feminist insights into the failed promises of cultural ideology. She met her first husband, an SNCC worker, right after high school; their joint involvement in groups such as US both inspired her own political commitment and showed her that she wanted to pursue social change through art instead. Like Cortez and Sanchez, she participated in Black Power and Black Arts activities, yet she expressed her dissatisfaction with some elements of the revolution from the start. With her white activist husband, who self-identified as a "redneck from Georgia" yet claimed close affiliations with Karenga and Black Panther leader Huey Newton, Coleman spent some time moving back and forth between "the world of the black militants" and "the world of the hippies" and considering the advantages of membership in the Weather Underground (Juno and Vale 120–21). After realizing that black nationalist movements did not prioritize women's concerns, she decided to focus on creating art that would draw attention to social inequalities more effectively than many 1960s and 1970s political organizations had. She gained fame for her dramatic readings and experimented with the expressive possibilities of theater and dance as well as poetry (O'Mara 84). Between 1976 and 1996 alone, she became the first African American to win an Emmy for best writing in a daytime drama, recognizing her work on *Days of Our Lives* (1976); published 11 books of poetry, fiction, and nonfiction; performed her work on at least five recorded collections; appeared in a film about her work, *Mad Dog Black Lady* (1985) (Magistrale 97); and edited a collection of Susannah Foster poems (1990).[2] Many of these creative accomplishments highlight her work's union of social theme and technical experiment.

Coleman couches some of her most innovative work in what initially appear to be conventional poetic forms. These formal constraints in fact lend her work a greater capacity for experiment, since she uses varying line lengths, social critiques, jazz and blues references, and a range of other techniques to challenge readers' expectations of poetic tradition. She first conceived of the *American Sonnets* sequence, for instance, after her oldest son died of AIDS-related complications. She notes that the work "couldn't help but reflect my angst and disappointment, my sense of failure, my sense of *being failed*—directly related to the fact that I have received relatively little reward from my years of hard work as a writer" (P. Brown 645). Perhaps because of this link to her experiences of personal and economic deprivation, the sonnets "sort of write themselves" (Levine 216), though she had set out specifically to create a new poetic form. Rather than adhering to any one of the sonnet's traditional incarnations, she decided to pioneer a jazz sonnet, in part to answer questions of structure and function: "[H]ow," she mused, "would I make it express my ethnicity different from what, maybe, Mr. Frank Lloyd Wright did?" (P. Brown 657). Her desire to innovate both form and theme, coupled with what she describes as the innately satirical nature of her poem sequences (Levine 221), has resulted in a 100-sonnet series that explores not only the troubling consequences of life as an ethnic minority in America but also the untested potential of experimental poetics. The sonnets are not collected in a single volume but appear in the collections *American Sonnets* (1994), *Bathwater Wine* (1998), and *Mercurochrome* (2001), a method that highlights their often occasional nature.

Coleman invokes the history of the sonnet form in her series while deliberately challenging the conventions that her poetic predecessors established. Most readers of poetry recognize two forms of the traditional sonnet: the Italian or Petrarchan sonnet and the English or Shakespearean sonnet. While both forms contain 14 lines and generally employ iambic pentameter, the Italian sonnet divides into an octave rhyming ABBAABBA and a sestet rhyming CDECDE or CDCCDC. The English sonnet, on the other hand, contains three quatrains that rhyme ABAB CDCD EFEF and a concluding rhymed couplet, GG. Petrarch and Shakespeare established romantic love as the most popular sonnet subject; both forms tend to portray this topic in terms of a conflict or uncertainty that resolves by the end of the poem. In the Italian form, the romantic problem is stated in the octave and resolved in the sestet, while in the English form, each of the three quatrains presents a different perspective on the situation before an epigrammatic "turn" in the couplet offers a witty resolution or piece of advice. Coleman's sonnets are usually close to 14 lines long and sometimes feature iambic or trochaic meters; however, their content does not follow the dramatic narrative set out by either of these versions. Rather, she seeks to uncover the roots of inequality through surrealistic imagery and experimental linguistic devices such as puns and wordplay. She often represents her poems' narrator as a writer, a figure lost in the center of a desolate cityscape whose words try to assuage the wounds of social neglect.

While Coleman's sonnets eschew most familiar conventions of the form, she does incorporate quotations and borrowed rhetorical gestures that point to the gap between her experiences and those of her poetic predecessors. Her Sonnet 38, for example, which is written "after William Blake," with a nod to "The Tyger," illustrates an alien urban landscape for whose representation the standard tools of poetic composition no longer suffice. The poem begins by noting that "something in here distaff flies," a phrase that evokes the witches' observation in *Macbeth* that "something wicked this way comes" (IV.i.45). While the term "distaff" can refer to the spindle on which wool is wound, it also references the female side of a family genealogy, suggesting that the piece seeks specifically to explore women's experiences. Extending the sense that ominous conditions exist, the poem's narrator protests:

> my eyes all jitters cannot see what Elohim
> imprisons me/has made condemnation of my
> sex/has made my skin my people hex[.]

Coleman teases the reader here, offering a twist on the Romantic poetic tradition by contrasting her poem's aural resonance with its appearance on the page. This excerpt of the poem approximates four lines of iambic tetrameter when read aloud (with some exceptions in the third line, which contains nine syllables and shifts from iambic to trochaic meter after the first foot), yet Coleman's effectively placed enjambments create three lines instead of four, defying both readerly expectation and the Western tradition Blake represents.

Coleman employs such formal disjunctions to underline the transformations of white literary conventions that jazz and blues techniques can achieve. The speaker reflects that Elohim, the poem's unnamed divinity, "loves to strum and 'steels' my blues / cops my licks and slays my muse / then stretches out my broken wing / and mocks the song i'm pained to sing." Questioning the efficacy of her own words, she suggests that, on the one hand, the social stigma of her race and gender undercuts her moments of creativity. On the other hand, the poetic narrator recognizes the innovative potential inherent even in these moments of destruction, now her source material for future creations. Like Blake's poem, the piece ends with a question, but one about punishment rather than creation: "[D]oth he who caged the beast cage me?" (*Bathwater* 103). Coleman repositions both Blake and Shakespeare in order to ground her poetic geographies in the everyday realities of urban experience. Her literature does not champion stories that are meant to carry universal significance; rather, she suggests that society's insidious power structures undergird even the dissemination of "classical" texts. The analogy that she draws between literary expression and social control helps to communicate the idea that "[l]iterature is not only political, it is politics supremely—at its most vicious and most vigorous, and is, therefore, to be prized—utterly" ("On Theloniousism" 79).

Sonnet 96 provides another example of Coleman's literary revisionism—a "talking-back" that resembles Harryette Mullen's conversations with Gertrude Stein (see Chapter 5)—and transformation of the sonnet form. Here she describes "the city suffer[ing] race hysteria & heavy summer" as "a kinky sequence of reflections presages its birth twixt heavy brown thighs." This new perspective on Yeats's "rough beast," about to emerge from between "slow thighs," places the allusion squarely in the context of a Los Angeles summer, when the heat contributes another ingredient to an already festering stew of public tensions. Coleman's image suggests that social conflict, which cannot be forestalled, will come from the same brown-skinned women who suffer the fallout of that "race hysteria"; an italicized line set off by white space reminds the reader that *"you are the languages you speak."* The city's ethnically inscribed inhabitants mark their cultural territory through the very languages that provoke whites' discriminatory behavior. At the same time, Coleman comments on the writer-narrator's responsibility to represent such scenes accurately, a task that depends upon her ability to use the appropriate language in order to ward off the fate that may await her. "[N]ow that the gates of hell have slammed," the poem concludes, "i am seized and surrender my terrible squawk" (*Mercurochrome* 101). In the wake of the city's destruction, the speaker cannot access Whitman's self-affirming "barbaric yawp"; rather, she must give up her power of speech.

In spite of these interactions with her precedents, however, Coleman's work manifests a desire to resituate traditional forms and themes within a specific set of concerns grounded in the LA environment. She is not the first African-American writer to turn the sonnet form to new ends. Claude McKay's "To the White Fiends" and "If We Must Die," though formally traditional, express a tightly controlled anger at ongoing evidences of racial inequality that sits at odds with the sonnet's usual topics; Alice Dunbar Nelson, Helene Johnson, Gwendolyn Brooks, Rita Dove, and Harryette Mullen have also refashioned the form to accommodate modern contexts and issues. Like McKay, Coleman rejects familiar poetic conceits in favor of shaping political critique through disquieting metaphors and other figures of speech; she channels rage into pointed appraisals of social conditions, just as McKay did (Magistrale 91). Sonnet 45's narrator, for example, uses explicit physical metaphors to frame her challenge to base inequalities: "I do deep paper poopoo," she proclaims, "rebellious bowels and / righteous stooping give me bragging rights." Like Cortez, Coleman articulates social inequalities through a surrealist language inflected by scatological references. Her speaker's matter-of-fact attitude toward the political implications of human waste filters through a familiar bluesy vocabulary. She refuses, however, to rely solely on this language's sometimes insubstantial rhetoric: "[N]o mama don't allow no saxophones / in here. no mama don't dig Harlem vamps or moonlight / slummings with downtown tramps." Rather, she argues, "it's still more about / what you suck who they own / what they will or won't politic / how long and how much you swallow" (*Bathwater* 110). Popular perceptions mistakenly attribute a superficial glitz to blues and jazz; rather, the music's value lies in its ability to expose enduring power imbalances. Her focus on the ways in which private actions have ramifications in the public world reflects a strategy common to global feminist activism: "to reveal the 'secrets' concealed in the private realm" (Basu 11). In essence, this speaker rejects the usual blues activities of "vamping" and "slumming" in order to uncover the real-life negotiations going on behind closed doors.

The diction of the *American Sonnets* sequence represents Coleman's most direct challenge to the sonnet's formal conventions and traditional themes. Her vocabulary often incorporates academic or governmental rhetoric; she also experiments with improvisatory, jazz-based constructions and archaic usages, in addition to scatological, surrealistic imagery. In Sonnet 9, for instance, the opening line, *"love people use things"* (original italics), operates as both a random collection of meaningful words and a dictum cautioning her audience to live wisely. However, the poem's central lines—"city after city, oh ruthless decay / —these skin disruptions— / the sport of confession for pay"—suggest that the urban landscape itself blights the discourse of communal support. The city's corruption manifests in physical disease as well as in commercial exploitations of individuals. The final result of this corruption, a denial of the hope with which the poem had begun (*"use people love things"*), derives from the unrewarded demands that the city places on its people (*American Sonnets* n.p.).

Coleman offers one potential resolution of this situation in Sonnet 16, which investigates a series of actions inspired by Huey Newton through a deliberately intellectualized diction. This technique, coupled with frequent brackets and slashes, serves to distance the poetic voice from the reader while underlining the poetic proposition's serious nature. Coleman also parodies standard Black Power diction by juxtaposing aurally similar but semantically unrelated words, creating jarring analogies that suggest that unnecessarily formal speech can only mask rhetorical foolishness. The speaker avers, for instance, that "specific / group resistance of rampant narco/necromania may be / manifest in periodic eruptions of spontaneous civil violence." The poem ends as do most of the sonnets, without final punctuation, though the imitation of Newton's familiar rhetoric lends the last lines a sense of threat that remains empty without the evidence to support it: "[I]t is imperative that visionaries see / war as ultimate service for resolution" (*American Sonnets* n.p.). While these statements illustrate Black Power's true commitment to black nationalist revolution, the slippages between "narco-" and "necromania" and between "resolution" and "revolution" suggest that social change will spring from action rather than rhetorical performance.

In spite of her transformations of the sonnet form, Coleman's experiments with this important branch of poetics recall the brevity and metrical patterns of other familiar American regionalist poets like Robert Frost and Emily Dickinson. Studies such as Joseph Conforti's examination of New England literary identity demonstrate that poets have been instrumental in establishing regional identity; he asserts that Frost both "reaffirmed . . . the vitality of New England culture" and "contributed to the imaginative shift of the real New England to the north country" (268). One serious consequence of this consolidation of a uniform regional identity, however, was the fact that Frost's work "virtually erased ethnics from a pastoral Yankee world" (Conforti 280). Many poets of color subsequently have redressed this absence, perhaps most noticeably in their portraits of Harlem. Peter Brooker suggests that "the dynamic physical site of Harlem itself . . . [embodied] in its spatial relations the paradox and hope of being at once black and American" (237). Langston Hughes, for example, engaged with this geography in works like *Montage of a Dream*

Deferred (1951) by "following life on the streets and in time through the passage from morning to night in an echo of the twilight areas and stark contrasts between black and white" (Brooker 243). Nevertheless, Coleman's own portraits of Los Angeles draw inspiration not from such lyrical contrasts but from the statistical realities of marginal existence. In Sonnet 10, which she wrote "after Lowell," Coleman uses Robert Lowell's high-modernist diction to highlight the injustices that persist more than a century after slavery's dissolution. Her "reluctant pilgrims stolen by Jehovah's light" seek both to "illuminate the blood-soaked steps of each / historic gain" and to "avenge the raping of the womb / from which we spring" (*American Sonnets* n.p.). This startling image points to the experiences that have long been absent from conventional American histories, suggesting that Christian rhetoric ("pilgrims," "Jehovah") justified the specific crimes of slavery. In contrast, Coleman's intervention renders this terrible period a central part of the American past. She broadens the registers of Boston Brahmin culture and Confessionalist poetry that Lowell represents to include specific human-rights abuses.

A NEIGHBORHOOD OUTSIDE: LOS ANGELES'S NEW POETIC LANDSCAPE

In Coleman's work, Los Angeles emerges as a new center of regional poetic identity, in part because of the ways in which historical inequalities continue to shape its citizens' experiences. Her portrayals of the city suggest that it has more often been a destination than a place of origin, that her own long-term residence there represents an anomaly in literary regionalism. This subject-position marks her, however, as one of a new generation of Los Angeles writers who defy the heavily East Coast-centered regionalism of many U.S. literary movements. Because of her early beliefs that creative invention cannot be divorced from social context and that social context grows in large part out of physical environments and geographies, Coleman conceived of regional identity as an integral component of her poetry from the beginning. Both Charles Bukowski and Joan Didion, well-known LA-based writers, exercised significant influence over her work. Bukowski in particular impressed Coleman with his harsh realism, narrative abilities, and prodigious output; she describes him as "the first American writer to 'tell it like it is' from the subcultural depths" (qtd. in O'Mara 84). Though she usually saw no other African Americans in the audiences at Bukowski's poetry readings, she continued to admire his work and follow his advice. His recommendation that she send a manuscript to Black Sparrow Press led to the publication of her first chapbook, *Art in the Court of the Blue Fag* (1977); she and Bukowski both maintained long-term relationships with Black Sparrow, and publisher John Martin became her mentor (O'Mara 84). In her work, regionalist themes evoke the local communities that support writing as well as the specific qualities of urban LA geographies.

While much of her work centers on the local, Coleman also depicts individuals' relationships to larger national or global communities in both aesthetic and public statements. Indeed, recent theorizations of regional identity and regionalist tropes in literature have emerged from a more complex understanding of regionalism as a simultaneously local and global phenomenon. When writers draw connections between community outreach goals and these issues' international ramifications, their work circumvents the boundaries of the nation-state, which is not by definition dependent upon the experiences of ethnic minorities, women, or the working class. The challenges that such work poses to both the status quo and conventional poetic language resonate with what Tom Lutz has characterized as the simultaneously social and aesthetic commitment of regionalist literature (12). The multiple preoccupations of modern regionalist literature like Coleman's necessarily recall the darkest chapters of U.S. history, especially through those periods' influence over modern social policies and attitudes. For many regionalist writers, particularly those living near the country's coasts and borders, immigration remains a central topic because of its prominence in national debates over policing strategies and labor. Other writers engage with controversial topics like segregation, racial discrimination, and unequal opportunities through discussions of slavery's ongoing social fallout.

Coleman, a regionalist writer concerned with just such a range of issues, frequently portrays cultural outsiders who identify patterns of social bias. In her poems, such outsiders' ability to perceive the gross inequalities that historically have characterized the U.S. social climate helps to highlight the irrationality of racial discrimination and oppressive practices. One speaker in her twenty-second *American Sonnet*, for instance, challenges the popular notion of a coherent American national identity by remarking on the complex social hierarchy that a long history of racial strife has established: "'twould be better,' said the gypsy, 'were you / from another country and not from their coal closet'" (*American Sonnets* n.p.). A gypsy, member of a transient social group that has ethnic affiliations many people do not understand and that faces repeated social censure, seems a particularly appropriate voice for this truth. Many writers of color have commented on the different public receptions that black immigrants and African Americans receive. Here the poem's speaker suggests that this circumstance arises from the fact that the latter group provides an uncomfortable reminder of slavery; blacks represent the country's "dirty secret." Sonnet 22's opening salvo resonates with the sonnet on the facing page, 23, composed "after [Anna] Akhmatova," which begins, "here's to my ruined curbless urban psyche" (*American Sonnets* n.p.). In both cases, the speaker possesses cultural roots in a particular location, yet neglect and marginalization unsettle her existence. The "coal closet" signifies both skin color and the menial labor associated with slavery and beyond, while the violated "urban psyche" lies in tatters. The gypsy's outsider status emphasizes the fact that such social issues resonate beyond national boundaries, in a manner similar to the speaker's now "curbless" sense of self. She salutes her uniquely formed persona, one shaped by not only the deprivations she has suffered but also her ability to process and transform those experiences.

As her poetic speakers' fragmented voices suggest, Coleman's poetics relies on complex formulations of both regional and national identity. Understanding the geographic region as both a local and a national or transnational construct can help to "bring . . . into view tensions between the centre [*sic*] and the periphery, the rural and the urban, the local and the cosmopolitan" (Wyile et al. xi). Strong regional identities arise in part from "a growing suspicion of institutional nationalism" and "a larger critique of cultural hegemony" (Wyile et al. xii). Thus regionalist literature often interrogates "the relation of the region to the rest of the world" (Lutz 15). Coleman grew up in the Watts neighborhood of South Los Angeles and has often commented on her decision not to move East, to an area like New York City where a large number of poets and other artists live. Always an advocate of socially invisible communities, in one instance she described her neighborhood in 1991 as "the borderline between Hancock Park . . . and a lot of drug activity," an area in which 80 different languages are spoken and residents identify with any number of nonwhite ethnic groups (Juno and Vale 124). She argues that to be an American of color is to be "bicultural"; to be a poet of color, one must write in more than one language, using multiple linguistic registers (Juno and Vale 125). Ethnic identity need not exclude national identification, but the two categories clash, often in the context of a specific region. In response to a question about how regional identity shapes her identity as a poet, Coleman herself asks, "Don't all poets belong to, originate or reside/work in, one region or another?" pointing out that "the American institutions that foster poetry favor those poets residing in the state of New York first and those poets residing in the original 13 colonies second. The rest of us aren't even a close third" ("What Is American"). This assessment of the importance of regional identity to critical acceptance suggests that Coleman also seeks to undermine popular misconceptions of a unitary Americanness.

In order to destabilize the notion that the people of the United States share common definitions of national, regional, and cultural identity, Coleman argues that American English originates in hybridity and cultural mixing. She describes the language's essential sources as "[t]he 'adolescent' or rebellious way in which Americans truncate or bastardize 'The King's English'" in service of "a fierce and idealized individualism"; the "[c]hanges wrought on the human psyche in the 20th century by accelerated technological advances"; and war ("What's American"). She also identifies the recurrent white appropriation of black cultural products, often reflected in language use, as inevitable. Either black music and art become part of the white mainstream, or, as a part of "economic slavery," the "Black artist is forced to turn his/her back on Black heritage and adapt to White tastes/sensibilities in order to make money" ("On Theloniousism" 69). These exchanges provide evidence that "we live in a nation without proper context" ("On Theloniousism" 77). Such a context necessarily entails acknowledging the roots of one's art, working to reveal and then undermine lived inequalities, and putting the same leveling principles to work in the arts that already exist in some businesses and educational institutions. The overwhelming prevalence of popular-culture products like television and music means that black and white cultural products inevitably share elements; however, the African-American roots of blue, rock, and jazz render poetry's musical and linguistic lineages especially fraught territory ("What Is American"). Politically conscious U.S. artists of color, who take on controversial subjects in innovative forms that engage diverse audiences, contribute to the continually evolving complexities of modern American English.

In spite of these efforts, Coleman notes that much American literature consistently fails to address racism, "an issue with worldwide implications, although we never hear about this on the evening news" (Magistrale and Ferreira 496). Not only does this issue play a central role in her own work, but it also resonates with her poetry's geographies. She comes from the West Coast and acknowledges "a strong Hispanic influence" in her writing; her work manifests ties to two different regional communities, as Mullen's does. When she moved to a wealthier neighborhood in the LA area, she chose a location just outside Marina del Rey, a few miles from Watts (Levine 210), and she has spent much more time working outside academia than inside it. Though her relocation may have given her a more negative and detached perspective on her roots—perhaps "augment[ing] her representations of Watts with sinister intimations of apocalypse" (Murphet 119)—her poetry and short fiction remain centered on the unacknowledged landscapes of urban Los Angeles. Ultimately, Coleman capitalizes on her own position at the literal end of the American frontier in order to draw public attention both to the geographies that continue to support inequality and to the difficulty of escaping them. She insists that no one solution can address blacks' problems, arguing that people of color need to "use different strategies in other parts of the country, particularly in the Northern cities and out West where racism wears a different face" (Juno and Vale 121). Her work offers some valuable strategies with which to examine social issues in a specific set of landscapes.

Coleman notes in a similar vein that the Los Angeles she inhabits does not exist in the American literary imagination, though her work attempts to remedy this lack. No one has yet, for instance, written "the history of Black Los Angeles," something that her own books envision (Juno and Vale 119)—though, as Tony Magistrale points out, her work manifests a "core ambivalence" toward the city (84). Although she believes that she has "a stake here," she also suggests that such social invisibility contributes to her sense that she is "trapped here the way you feel like you're trapped in any kind of ghetto, any kind of prison. You just don't have the choice [to leave]" (qtd. in Comer 88). Krista Comer, one of the few literary critics who has paid significant attention to Coleman's work, reads her poetry in the course of a larger argument about the new regionalist literature that many recent women writers have defined in the West. Possessing no affiliations with either the natural wilderness of the desert or the moneyed environs of Hollywood, such writers can focus on overlooked city spaces and marginal subject-positions. This compositional strategy yields especially rich results for black women writers, disconnected from the "wild" spaces of the conventional West, who can use city spaces as canvases for "articulating black feminist existence" (Comer 95).

Coleman imagines just such a set of urban feminist geographies in her *American Sonnets* series. Her innovations create a literary landscape alternative to the more conventional American poetic geographies of Robert Frost's New England, which Joseph Conforti characterizes as "America's first strongly imagined region" (6). The Transcendentalists and the Fireside poets laid the ground on which Frost's later efforts were built; both the South and the New York City region have also gained prominence in American literary history through the writings of the Southern Agrarian group, Langston Hughes, Hart Crane, and the New York School, among others. However, these movements have flourished primarily in the East, as Coleman points out. Her work, on the other hand, focuses on the fixed urban spaces of southern Los Angeles, rather than the more fluid and undefined wilderness of either East or West. Her *American Sonnets* describe a world in which the tightly restricted spaces of inner-city Los Angeles echo in sketches of human-rights violations that occur across the globe. These poems call American identity into question, offering the experiences of Los Angeles working-class women of color as evidence that fair social representation must transgress political boundaries. As Coleman observes in Sonnet 37, "we're estranged o'er wicked hours / clocked to seed babysitters fatten landlords / the city the country the state the flag" (*Bathwater Wine* 102). The conditions under which such women work drive them apart rather than enabling the community that they need; instead, they spend their time supporting those who monitor their time and their children's. Coleman draws an implicit analogy between the exploitation that this economic cycle enables and the governmental superstructure that emerged from America's capitalist tradition, fostering similar structures in other places. As she suggests in Sonnet 42, such long but unrewarded days of work signal "a gash in the superstructure somewhere / (surely a dream?) fiduciary waters roaring" (*Bathwater* 107). Yet the poems offer evidence time and again that no such gash exists, and the only victims of the "fiduciary waters' " flood will be people who lack the means to sustain themselves within the system.

Coleman extends her critique of capitalism's insidious presence in several additional sonnets that explore the tensions between unquestioned patriotism and individuals' social experience. In Sonnet 55, for instance, her speaker claims to "loathe indifferent flags, the blue and the gray / a nation's shelves ill-stocked rendering meager feed / reparation briefer eden than the apple-eater's breath" (*Bathwater* 120). While these "blue and gray" flags might suggest the muted tones of a watered-down patriotism, they also reference the Civil War battles that took place between blue Union uniforms and gray Confederate ones over slavery and secession. Coleman's poetic speaker condemns the "indifference" that ultimately motivates such conflicts, especially in the face of poverty, hunger, and relentless inequalities. Comparing the United States' empty promise of reparations for slavery to Eve's unenviable position as the repository of Christianity's original sin, Coleman comments on the fleeting possibility of an idealized "Eden" to which the citizens left out of nationalist equations might aspire. No alternative to their marginal lives seems to exist, as these corruptions "introduce a salacious sucking into the vox acus / divert a nation from the death of its individualism / (which, in the absence of any consciousness / certainly cannot be missed)" (Sonnet 92; *Mercurochrome* 97). Coleman describes the media as possessing a "vox acus," or needle's voice, which pierces those who dare to oppose mainstream views and promotes a dangerous conformity, as does the government. Opposing either institution engenders risk, the speaker intimates; most people yield their awareness to preserve their sense of self-protection. In poems like these, Coleman repeatedly draws her readers' attention to the large-scale social structures that support inequality, leading us to the inescapable conclusion that local transgressions carry global consequences.

Krista Comer identifies this pattern of exchange between global and local communities in Coleman's work, arguing that the poetry's geographical situations generate much of its political impact: her first-person speakers "transform the geography of Los Angeles proper by integrating a feminist Watts into Southern California urban history" (366). Coleman has failed to attract some readers because of this very transformation; her poetic themes do not confirm the literary landscapes popularly associated with Los Angeles in the work of other California writers like Didion and Raymond Chandler. She also refuses to depict what Comer terms the usual "African-American geographical imaginaries" of slavery and of jazz and blues' popular dissemination, both of which have followed primarily South–North trajectories (359–60). Coleman's gritty depictions of tumultuous relationships, firmly grounded in a seemingly inescapable tangle of slums, operate in contradiction to other Los Angeles writers' evocations of the open spaces of the West or fast-paced city life. She reads the city landscape in terms of its inhabitants' material economic hardships rather than their possible methods of escape.

Krista Comer's assessment of Coleman's place within contemporary literary studies foregrounds Coleman's regionalist sensibility and acknowledges her interest in the multiple jeopardy of black women's experiences. In her article on Coleman's receipt of the 1999 Lenore Marshall Poetry Prize, Marilyn Hacker points out that not only has Coleman produced a substantial amount of work, but "she is also, astoundingly, only the second writer of color (and the sixth woman) to receive the . . . prize in the twenty-five years of its existence" (44). Like Comer, Hacker notes that "racial and gender issues are made more complex by the particular and peculiar geography and iconography of urban Southern California" (47). Coleman locates her critique of existing social and economic circumstances in the specific experiences of black women from southern Los Angeles, offering this space as symbolic of worldwide conditions.

Coleman promotes this regionalist aesthetic in several dimensions of her professional life. She and her third husband, poet Austin Straus, whom she married in 1981, cohosted a program entitled "The Poetry Connexion" from 1981 until 1996 on Pacifica radio station KPFK. This show focused on the work of lesser-known poets from Los Angeles in particular, as well as small independent bookstores—like EsoWon, the bookstore that banned her work after the Angelou review ("Black on Black" 147). At the same time, Coleman pushed her work's performative qualities to their limit through public readings, recordings made with other poets, and collaborations with musicians like Exene Cervenka, one-time lead singer for the punk-rock band X (Manheim). Los Angeles's literary scene comprises a myriad of attitudes, experiences, and source material; Coleman addresses this complex multiplicity in her work's collage-like structures. David Ulin suggests that "as the city has developed, it has become less a place people *go to* than one they *come from*, and by now there have been several generations of Los Angeles-born writers who don't see the city as exotic and have focused less on the ephemeral and carnival-like aspects of L. A. life than on its more enduring qualities" (xvi; original italics). In other words, for authors like Coleman, Los Angeles's urban identity exists not in Hollywood's celebrity glamour but in the lived realities of everyday life.

Coleman herself continues to explore a persistent ambivalence about Los Angeles's regionalist nature in pieces like "Clocking Dollars," a prose poem from *African Sleeping Sickness*. Here she characterizes herself as a "black worker 'womon' poet angelena, disadvantaged first by skin, second by class, third by sex, fourth by craft (the MSS & juvenilia of pitiably poor poets pull down greater pissbah posthumously), fifth by regionality" (*African* 218). She both acknowledges the social drawbacks she has experienced as a member of these groups and challenges her audience to recognize the richness of the particular intersection at which she stands. In her interview with Priscilla Brown, she points out that tradition, inheritance, and modes of behavior are figured differently in the West: "In the east, your breath is just taken away by the immensity of what's monumental. Here it's in nature. . . . So how racism works here is a lot different. And I'm interested in that too, and I think that sets me apart from some of my peers from those other regions" (639). Though she aligns herself with various African-American communities, she often locates a stronger rallying point in regional identity, finding common ground with "those writers who advocated the *inclusion* of writers in the West in the American literary canon, thus encouraging the broadening of our cultural development" (P. Brown 650). Because even the writers of color in the East have received so much literary-critical attention, Coleman repeatedly urges audiences to read the work of her Western peers, including the lesser-known Beats Bob Kaufman, Clayton Eschelman, and Charles Bukowski (Murphet 111–12). Like them, she seeks to valorize the overlooked spaces within this neglected geography, focusing on the inner-city neighborhoods of Watts, for example, as a location more "real" than Hollywood or Rodeo Drive. Her need to relocate the absent does not translate into a condemnation of its uglier details, however; rather, she contrasts "the repetitive, dominated spatial practices of everyday life in the ghetto" with "evanescent strands of utopia which occasionally take root" there (Murphet 113). This realism still contains substance and hope.

Coleman's work also offers quite unexpected portraits of urban settings and details, rather than suggesting an escape to or nostalgic longing for the wilder, natural settings of the West. Sonnet 46, for instance, reminds the reader of its urban origins through a "trail pocked by steel casings, confused / by the scuffle of inquisitive sneakers and killer shoes." However, even the horror of this crime scene diminishes when juxtaposed with the beauty of "trees genuflect[ing] in the wind" and "prayers from the fearful lucky" (*Bathwater* 111). Coleman tempers the hurried movements of first murder and then investigation with moments of reflection on the environment's unchanged serenity. Her poetic characters witness both types of scenes with equanimity, accepting violence as the price one must pay for moments of sublimity in this environment. As she argues in her interview with Tony Magistrale and Patricia Ferreira, "[A]n urban environment is where you really, really know people. You know the best of humanity, and the worst, and all that's in between" (501). As a result, her work tends to disregard the usual geographic trajectories of African-American literature, particularly those works concerned with the Great Migration, in favor of challenges posed to the East from the West or a more static reliance on Western locales. This revectoring of the poetic landscape anticipates the transgression of national boundaries that global political movements advocate.

While such stasis suggests that Coleman's poetic characters possess only a limited ability to move from place to place or to reshape the space they occupy, her work resonates strongly with recent reminders of the dangerous consequences that result when governments ignore the needs of citizens already marginalized by geography and economic circumstance, as in Hurricane Katrina's 2005 devastation of New Orleans. The poems' narrative trajectories suggest, in fact, that "her poetic subjects have no choice but to remain in city spaces. Their entrapments are not the result primarily of psychic or gendered logics. . . . They instead are prisoners of poverty, and economic disability goes hand in hand with racial and gendered oppression" (Comer 95). Sonnet 5 recounts, for instance, "the spurious chain of plebeian events / . . . / which allows who to claim the largest number of homicides / the largest number of deaths by cancer the largest / number of institutionalized men the largest number of / single female heads of household the largest number of / crimes of possession the largest number of functionally / insane" (*American Sonnets* n.p.). The chant-like formal repetitions of this catalogue refuse the comfortable lure of first-person introspection in favor of impersonally recited facts; its statistics force us to remember, however, that real people suffer these tragedies. Like Mullen, Coleman transforms the convention of the poetic catalogue into a compositional device that illuminates a specific political preoccupation, finding in the lives of Los Angeles's inner-city dwellers a valid subject for creative analysis.

In Sonnet 66, Coleman ponders the peculiar conditions in which such dwellers exist; the poetic narrator observes that "i am dying in lala in a blizzard of sun where / my killers always profit from my death." California's "blizzard of sun" displaces the conventional weather patterns of both Frost's and Dickinson's New England and Hughes's Harlem. However, that sunshine does not represent the paradise for which many tourists wish; rather, its unforgiving heat produces a kind of insanity in which inhabitants reimagine "Los Angeles" as the nonsensical "lala." Here crimes go unpunished under the rays of a scorching sun—instead, the "killers" perform dangerous actions that will sustain their own profitability. Her desiccated state moves the narrator to mourn "oh. thirst. oh. pride."—two sources of personal pain—before concluding that she is indeed "dying in lala in a sunblaze in / a dream dreamt and then forsaken" (*Bathwater Wine* 131). Her version of Hughes's "dream deferred" has been transplanted from East to West, from a northern clime to a dry, unforgiving western one. The speaker of Sonnet 47 also decries the "traffic-ridden squalor / and liquor dens" of her native "plain of smokes" (*Bathwater Wine* 112): the components of this urban western scene represent very real threats, yet they are the landscape in which she feels most comfortable.

Coleman also uses the flexible structure of the *American Sonnets* as a forum in which to explore the tension between acceptance of one's disadvantages and rebellion against persistent inequalities. In Sonnet 94, the speaker mourns "the despoiled child, the deserted schoolyard," both a result of "the burst & burnings of a city." The youth damaged by poor school systems and other institutions, a common theme in Coleman's work, express their frustrations by planning the destruction of the environment that betrayed them. These passive observations yield at the end of the poem, however, to an angry admission that trusting others' empty promises never brings about any real change. *"[H]ow i committed suicide,"* the poem's final stanza concedes, was an act in three parts: "i revealed myself to you. / i trusted you. i forgot the color of my birth" (*Mercurochrome* 99). As Krista Comer points out, racial and economic status fix many Los Angeles inhabitants in place: "Segregation has the convenient consequence of granting spatial mobility rather exclusively to L. A.'s white population while disciplining black people to Watts or East L. A. where they ostensibly belong, always signifiers for an urban or social narrative, never signifiers (in *western* discourse, that is) for 'the natural'"

(Comer 88). The very history of literature itself helps to promote the fiction that African Americans can only be found in the city, and only in its ignored inner neighborhoods. To visibly occupy either natural spaces or the wealthier sections of commercial Los Angeles would signify a challenge to the history of segregation that so much American literature assumes.

Comer suggests that Wanda Coleman offers an alternative to this either-or perspective, however, in a set of "new resistance strategies" that can be "linked to asserting a black presence in representation at large and, more importantly, to claiming and naming western spaces" (92). In part, her experiences make this a necessary choice; on the other hand, however, she acknowledges the dearth of positive female representation in the history of literary and filmic Westerns: "[A]lthough city spaces may not always be enabling spaces from which Coleman articulates stories that are simultaneously black, female, and western, *rural* or *wild* spaces enable black feminist presence even less" (Comer 95; original italics). In the process of claiming the West's geographies as landscapes in which black women legitimately move, act, and create, Coleman creates a poetic ambivalence about her work's geographies that echoes the tone in which she casts her characters' economic plights. The sites of people's daily disappointments are inevitably both familiar, beloved geographies and reminders of social injustice.

The narrators of Coleman's sonnets consistently act upon an awareness of the ways in which certain geographies reinforce prejudices and inequalities. Their voices—alternately belligerent, detached, playful, angry, and tender—replace the unified lyric voice of the traditional sonnet form with a cacophony of voices speaking to a set of complicated shared experiences. Sonnet 26's speaker, for example, addresses an unseen "lovemonger" without whom "this city is a pale rude fiction," remarking on her auditor's ability to add substance and meaning to the everyday. The loved one's "womanly radiance," "sentimental shape-changer's sufferings," and "sweetsistuh goodheart" in particular inspire admiration. However, the speaker juxtaposes this acknowledgment of beauty and endurance with a raunchy admonition to "blow that escape hatch—rubyfruit" in order to be able to "flee this sham world." This image signifies doubly, referring to both violent escape and physical ecstasy—"rubyfruit" is a slang term for the vagina—in order to suggest that either pleasure or revenge might fulfill the speaker's desire. However, she must do more than marvel at her beloved; any complete catalog of her assets contains the lived realities of life "along this parched desert floor" (*Bathwater Wine* 91).

A similar sentiment prevails in Sonnet 53; here Coleman repositions familiar fairy-tale conventions in a new landscape. "[U]pon my sword," the speaker observes, "it seems i've abandoned the concrete / for the flower, the street for the tower." With a nod to Alfred, Lord Tennyson's

"The Lady of Shalott," Coleman compares the properties of life in Los Angeles to the Arthurian world in which his poetic Elaine lived. This idyllic landscape, which necessarily references the academic "ivory tower" as well, cannot accommodate the real conditions of day-to-day life. After feeling "as / if i've spent the last five hundred years / picking cotton without pay or shade," the speaker's "soul remains the / slave," tied to the inescapable history of literary tradition. She discovers that the act of writing itself, the words on the page, represents the expensive indulgences of idealism rather than a forum for political or personal change. In the end, this act turns her planned livelihood into a prison, and the speaker begins to "loathe and curse the terrible / scribe quilling this loonytoon history" (*Bathwater Wine* 118). Here Coleman concludes that the worst penalty of reassessing one's situation lies in the realization that one may not be able to compensate for history's mistakes—and, worse, that the material one has produced makes no more sense than the colorful "loonytoons" that scroll past on a screen, lulling an uninformed audience into unquestioning acceptance. The multifaceted voices of the *American Sonnets'* poetic narrators enable such sobering revelations.

Coleman's sonnets ultimately voice concerns that American mainstream society overlooks. Individuals who occupy otherwise marginalized geographies, social classes, or ethnic groups take center stage in order to reimagine the dynamics of U.S. power relations. Comer posits, in fact, that "[b]y creating new cultural spaces of black presence where none existed before, Coleman heeds bell hooks's call to make neglected or suppressed voices of American culture heard, to make difference a political virtue, instead of a stigma" (103). "[R]ejection can kill you," the fourth Sonnet notes, since "it can force you to park outside neon-lit / liquor stores and finger the steel of / your contemplation." Coleman paints a clear picture of the entrapment that missed opportunities create here, as the speaker soon turns the potential violence contained in this scene in against herself: "[I]t can even make you / rob yourself." Her only saving graces materialize in "ragged scarecrow lusts" and a lover who "has designs on my gizzard." The poem ends with the statement that "this is the city we've come to / all the lights are red all the poets are dead / and there are no norths" (*American Sonnets* n.p.). As in many of the other sonnets, each scene serves as a metaphor not only for social inequalities but also for the obstacles that writers who come from such invisible geographies face. Living in a part of Los Angeles that tourists do not visit, pursuing subjects that other writers overlook, and exploring the ideological connotations of geographies absent from popular accounts of American poetics—at the literal "end" of the United States—already condemn such writers, as readers of Coleman's essays know, to ongoing struggles for recognition.

Claiming a place at the end of the frontier, in the West, produces, as in Sonnet 5, a "spurious chain of plebeian events" that can discourage or result in tragedy. In this case, the narrator refuses to succumb to disadvantage; instead, she gleefully exploits the transgressive possibilities of language by revising a popular saying: "[S]ee you later alligator / after while crocodile / after supper muthafucka" (*American Sonnets* n.p.). In other sonnets, the speaker underlines the basic inequalities on which the American capitalist system is founded through a clever recounting of her own contradictory experiences. In Sonnet 6, for instance, she notes that in spite of the fact that "portfolio profligates of creative capitalism / proliferate," she "hit forty before i got my first credit card" and recognizes her "only credentials" in "the holes / in one's tired bend-overs" (*American Sonnets* n.p.). Coleman turns these unfair circumstances to her compositional advantage, creating a playful opposition to inequality through alliteration, assonance, Latinate constructions, and unusual imagery.

The multiply-voiced speaker of Coleman's sonnets also finds comfort and strength in the community of people who face the same challenges she does. In Sonnet 13, she reminds her audience, "i'm with you braiding hate into a rainbow" and can "already feel my soul's freedom hymns." Her metaphor suggests that productive action can arise from pain, especially by invoking the memory of a collective history. Though she does not live an ideal existence, she perseveres, still able to "navigate through the streets, my compass broken," "savor[ing] the stench of auto exhaust and unwashed bodies / sweat stinging the unhappy eyes of my region" (*American Sonnets* n.p.). Again, Coleman underlines the often ugly material properties of marginal existence, establishing these elements as worthy additions to her store of poetic material. At the same time, however, her narrator does not accept these inequalities uncomplainingly, noting in Sonnet 90, for instance, that while "widely widely i open to love," nevertheless "my country / impregnates with seed of hate." Through a disturbing series of metaphors, Coleman intimates that a scene of sexual promise may, under the pressure of failed social contracts, end up bearing unwelcome fruit. After such treatment, the narrator concludes that she is "foolish in my fantasy / that i too am cherished" (*Mercurochrome* 95). Yet a recurrent trope in these sonnets remains the sense that one's socially marginalized position can both challenge the status quo and offer a starting point for a productive community.

CONCLUSION: WRITING TRANSFORMATION

In her *American Sonnets* sequence and other jazz-influenced pieces, Wanda Coleman frames the act of writing itself as a metaphor for political action and the slowly evolving currents of social change. The poems conceptualize the feminist and other socially conscious activities of Los Angeles's neglected geographies as acts of communication that position local concerns in relation to the larger world. The statements that her poetry articulates thus function on both professional and personal levels. In the sequence's first sonnet, she critiques "socio-eco dominance" and "socio-eco disparity," yet the poem's unusual visual appearance—featuring a mathematical equation, a lettered list of statistics, and spacing variations—suggests that she also intends to mock the sometimes meaningless experimentations of many more critically acclaimed poets (*American Sonnets* n.p.). Similarly, Sonnet 7 insinuates that the act of "tak[ing] the outer skin in. rehumaniz[ing] it" may demand a terrible price: "swallowing whole the dourness of / an unremitting scorn and unstoppable cruelty." The speaker's decision to portray a realistic, unitary self prompts others' criticism. Though Coleman invokes, through the act of personifying the work itself, a line of poetic inheritance that stretches as far back as seventeenth-century author Anne Bradstreet's "The Author to Her Book," this portrait of her emancipated poetic output is much more graphically rendered than is the ragged child of Bradstreet's poem. Even as her work "reaches for its lyric," it reveals itself as "an / abandoned stillborn blued around its eyes and bodily bruised. found buried in a dumpster / beneath the rages of an unsung life" (*American Sonnets* n.p.). While this image can also be read in economic terms, Coleman creates a contrast here between the careful self-fashioning that writerly craft demands and the dangerous vulnerability that results when a writer exposes her work to critical eyes. The writer's self-revelations gamble not only with personal memories but also with her reputation.

The act of writing signifies a particular risk for authors who represent culturally unfamiliar geographies; as Julian Murphet suggests, "to stay in Los Angeles is to relinquish many reasonable ambitions of cultural respect, guild community, grants, deals with major publishers. It is virtually to disappear." Coleman herself has also commented upon the ways in which arts grants typically exclude or overlook particular ethnicities, occupations, and regions (Murphet 4). The final poem of the *American Sonnets* series, Sonnet 100, concludes an extended commentary on the consequences of regional, ethnic, economic, and professional marginalization by drawing a link between wordplay and self-preservation. The speaker characterizes her own acts as "wordsport a gangster poet's jest," noting "how black and luscious comes each double-barreled / phrase." These metaphors underline the danger implicit in writing whose textual craft can both challenge the existing system and champion an unpopular perspective. The poem ends with a direct address to the reader, whom she challenges to "slay in me the / wretchedness that names me brute. liberate my / half-dead kill. come. glory in my rebirth. / come. glory in my wonder's will." If American audiences are willing to change their perceptions of cultural identity, they must also be prepared to pay homage to new forms of artistry. The poet-narrator who articulates these imperatives engages with the political implications of such change by playing "the gentle game of maniacs & queens" even when "writerly praise is blessed / incontinence, the spillage of delight" (*Mercurochrome* 105). Here Coleman challenges the reader and poet, speaker and audience, witnesses and participants to cooperate in the shared work of rebuilding the world.

In 2003, Wanda Coleman accepted an invitation to become "the first literary fellow of the City of Los Angeles Department of Cultural Affairs" (Manheim). This position signals a small step forward toward national recognition of the diverse goals, accomplishments, problems, and resources that the United States' many cultures entail. Coleman's own experiences, personal and professional, suit her particularly well to this job; just as she repeatedly draws her readers' attention to the "conflicts between communities" that define American social relations (Juno and Vale 122), so she also names the ideological shifts that will need to occur before people can act on real solutions. By way of her relentless excursions through a geography absent from most national accounts of regional identity, Coleman creates a new poetic regionalism that can exist alongside—or even displace—older, more familiar, and less representative American literary regionalisms. Her reenvisioned sonnet form helps to enable such a radical innovation; its retooled functions and conceits more accurately address the political needs of diverse national and global literary communities. As she suggests, emerging projects in "world poetry" will be dominated by "[u]rban American voices (particularly Black and Latino)" ("What Is American"); these voices make similar use of revised forms and politically pointed critiques. Coleman's project is not yet complete, as her continuing absence from most anthologies and mainstream studies of American poetry attests; however, her work points us toward a better future for our world of letters. Her sonnet sequence and other revisions also anticipate the jazz- and blues-based linguistic manipulations of Harryette Mullen. Mullen's investment in the intersections of linguistic play and social statement as well as her explorations of a range of poetic languages help her to define a feminism that spans the boundaries between the academy and the public sphere.

CHAPTER 5

JAZZ'S WORD FOR IT: HARRYETTE MULLEN AND THE POLITICS OF INTELLECTUALISM

HARRYETTE MULLEN WORKED ON THE *BLACK PRINT* SUPPLEMENT TO THE campus newspaper while studying at the University of Texas at Austin in the early 1970s. She also wrote editorials on race issues for that paper, the *Daily Texan* (Hogue, "Interview"). Both her journalism and her experiences as an English major in a largely white department accustomed her to serving, albeit unwillingly, as a representative voice for African Americans on campus. Mullen has often recounted a story of a class with Roger Abrahams, a white professor in the anthropology department who specialized in African-American folklore, that illustrates the disparity between white expectations and her own lived experience. One day in class, she was forced to admit her lack of exposure to some traditions of black knowledge. Abrahams wrote the acronym "HNIC" on the blackboard and asked Mullen to identify the phrase it represents.[1] When she could not, he gave the answer to the class, omitting the racist epithet. Later Mullen surmised that she had embarrassed him by failing to provide the information he expected her to possess (Bedient 668; Myers). This incident suggests that Mullen occupied an unusual position as a black woman who learned several African-American oral expressions as a component of her formal education. The link between textual interpretation and cultural literacy that the interaction establishes also anticipates many of her poetry's later formal and political strategies.

Today Mullen's work complicates formal experiment with the fluid dimensions of race, gender, and social experience, elements that many critical accounts of contemporary experimental poetry fail to consider.[2]

Her work challenges the binary oppositions that some writers establish between categories like canonical and experimental, oral and written, vernacular and academic, and black and female identity politics. Rather than consolidating such reductive logic, her poetry and criticism seek out the interactions, overlaps, and doublings that recur among contrasting approaches. Many of her scholarly articles argue, for instance, that such oppositions reflect the tenor of American racial history. In "Poetry and Identity," her indictment of the critical tendency to consider social themes and experimental form as mutually exclusive, she posits that "the 'avant-garde poet of color' threatens the cohesiveness of the accompanying narratives that allow the 'mainstream' audience to recognize, comprehend, or imagine a collective identity, purpose, and aesthetics of a literary group or movement, whether it is a group 'of color' or a movement defined by its commitment to 'formal innovation'" (86). Although she often discusses the fact that African-American writing long ago founded a tradition of formal experimentation, Mullen's attention to it here highlights concerns about her own participation in the academy and the eventual canonization of her poetry. In an interview with Daniel Kane, she admits that she has been "more concerned with reaching diverse communities of writers and readers than with influencing an institutional process that remains somewhat opaque to [her]." This emphasis upon the real-world consequences that writing can produce, rather than its theoretical implications, indicates that her criticism also seeks social relevance.[3]

Mullen's poetry emerged, with the publication of her first book, *Tree Tall Woman* (1981), into an artistic climate whose writers sought to challenge time-honored arts institutions. Such challenges have been issued in part by the Language poets, a loosely defined group of writers initially based in San Francisco's Bay Area who began to articulate the political potential of extreme formal experimentation in the early 1970s. Their ambivalence toward accepted arbiters of meaning, literary and otherwise, led them to define their project at first as a Marxist critique of the usual apparatus—commercial and ideological—of poetic composition: the academy, mainstream versions of social history, large-scale publishing houses, and the lyric tradition. Alan Golding argues that canon formation takes place through a "series of conflicts" between magazines and editors, poets and critics, the academy and the general public (xvi). His theory of canonization, based upon the assumption that "poets may seek to canonize themselves and their contemporaries in various ways, but to do so successfully in their *poems* still requires institutional mediation" (57), illuminates the work of the Language poets, whom he discusses in the book's final chapter. Because poets like Lyn Hejinian, Ron Silliman, and Charles Bernstein produce not only syntactically complex and innovative poetry but also dense theoretical readings of that poetry, they successfully negotiate the divide between critique and creativity. Their articles and books openly acknowledge the academy's power to affect literary consumption and fulfill its interpretive needs (Golding 144–45).[4]

Mullen's own negotiations of critical and creative work echo some elements of Golding's assessment. She grounds her poetic exploration of the linguistic processes by which contemporary society tends to both slight and celebrate black women's work in blues and jazz references. These references serve three major functions in her work: exploring the intersections between vernacular speech and the intellectualized discourses of academia, offering revisionist versions of social history via the traditional subjects of blues lyrics, and producing social commentary through experiments with the structures and properties of language. The history specific to black women's participation in the performance culture of jazz and blues music provides a vital source for Mullen's social commentary, while her jazz-based transformations of two learned languages, African-American vernacular speech and the linguistic strategies first identified with the Language group, underline her poetry's improvisational strategies. Her revisions of traditional poetic forms also contribute new perspectives on poetic innovation to literary history. Such revisions form an important link between her textual improvisations and those of Wanda Coleman and Sonia Sanchez.

Jazz and blues references in Mullen's writing help to create a "third language," a concept she advances in a discussion of Sandra Cisneros's untranslated Spanish phrases in *Woman Hollering Creek*. Mullen claims that some works' culturally specific references foster "a new and emancipatory literacy" in readers belonging to those cultures who feel marginalized by mainstream educational, governmental, and other discourses (Mullen, "'A Silence Between Us'" 5). Allusions to jazz and blues culture, accessible only to a relatively small fan base and rooted in African-American social history, enable Mullen to create a poetic language that includes revolutionary rhetorical, historical, and formal elements. As an African-American scholar who studied the complexities of both Language-based poetries and black dialect speech at university, she articulates a new "third space" in her work that engages both theory-based poetics and political statements. She herself describes her use of language as culturally specific, continually moving "closer to what makes poetry unparaphrasable, and thus, untranslatable" ("Imagining" 201). Both formal and social factors contribute to this specificity.

Such a third space also exists at the intersections of jazz and feminist discourses, both social forums that have excluded black women from active participation at key historical moments. Critics of experimental, linguistically complex, or conceptually difficult writing have argued that unnecessary textual intricacy may confer upon the writer a position of undeserved authority (Culler and Lamb 2–4). However, such writing can manifest an avowedly political intent, as Robyn Wiegman points out, because a socially nuanced discourse like feminism "*must* interrogate the institutional forms that already inhabit it" in order to escape culpability in its own critiques (85). Discursive complexity thus may signal a vigilant attention to social systems as those impact women's personal and professional lives. Jan Montefiore suggests that "the most interesting thinking about the possibilities of radical feminist poetry has been done in the poems themselves" because literature itself functions as both "a defining context" and "an area of political and intellectual struggle" (4, 25). A poet's deployment of language itself has material consequences; the many factors that influence a text's politics often render structural and conceptual difficulty necessary.[5] Mullen's work makes a similar assumption about the specifically feminist potential of complicated language usage.

In *The Pink Guitar*, Rachel Blau DuPlessis points out that women's "differing experiences do surely produce different consciousnesses, different cultural expression, different relations to realms of symbols and symbol users" (3). DuPlessis's ideas suggest that feminists have historically perceived language as a tool for social transformation; as she puts it, "I struggle to break into the sentences that of course I am capable of writing smoothly. I want to distance. To rupture" (144). Recent texts articulate such transformations while acknowledging their debt to historical realities like the political upheavals of the 1960s. The growing popularity of poetry readings in the mid-twentieth century also helped audiences to gain political savvy through the public spectacle of performance (Whitehead 3, 9). As Mullen's work negotiates the formal space between theory and poetics, so her feminist politics traverses the boundary between idea and practice, public and private, emphasizing African-American women's social concerns.

Modern jazz history forms the broader context of Mullen's language-based feminism. The postmodernist fragmentation characteristic of late-century jazz produced a split between avant-garde and reactionary "classic jazz" advocates that echoed the patterns of racial and artistic struggle across the century (Peretti 168–69). Ted Gioia calls this fragmentation of jazz styles "a pluralism, in which 'next new things' would come and go with amazing alacrity" (313, 338), suggesting that the specific politics attached to jazz in the 1960s and later might also fluctuate with the social climate. This plurality of styles reflects jazz's increasing entrance onto a global stage as well as the sway of its conservative classicist echelon (Gioia 374, 381). Many jazz poets like Mullen create poetic themes and forms that explore the music's potential for cross-cultural relevance and hybrid perspectives.

Yet jazz's proliferating performance practices and social messages continue to raise questions about women's historical status as jazz artists. Linda Dahl has noted that women's traditional exclusion from jazz performance arenas was exacerbated for black women, who felt "heavy pressure not to compete with black men for jazz jobs" (x). Leslie Gourse also attributes jazz's "nearly insuperable barrier of male chauvinism" to musicians' habits as well as the music's traditional gender politics (7, 12). The existence of these rapidly diversifying styles and entrenched attitudes provides the performative background to Mullen's jazz-based formal innovations and lend immediacy to her feminist commentary. The contemporary discourses of both jazz and language-based feminism guide her definition of an alternative, "third language" in which to foster her poetry's innovations. She underlines the primary importance of both identity and craft in her work while remaining open to new sources of knowledge, creative expression, and political statement. These complex, shifting sources for her jazz poetry indicate that her work's contexts and composition help to create a new feminist model for women intellectuals that bridges personal, professional, and historical spheres.

BRIDGING THE GAP: LANGUAGE AND IDENTITY

Harryette Mullen was born in Florence, Alabama, on July 1, 1953, and grew up in Fort Worth, Texas. She describes her childhood as a time centered on learning: she was, like many of her contemporaries, "routinely required to memorize and recite poetry," a form of study that "went along with piano and ballet lessons, visits to museums and art galleries, and attendance at the symphony and opera." These activities derived from her family's desire to "educate, uplift, and civilize us" (Mullen, "'When he is least himself'" 277). Her college years at the University of Texas at Austin between 1971 and 1975 covered a broad range of subjects, including Spanish, African literature, Caribbean literature, Ethnic Studies, sociology, and anthropology. Her English courses included poetry by Adrienne Rich and Gertrude Stein, whose opacity frustrated her but provided sufficient impetus for her to return to the task later in her academic career. In spite of her study of unconventional women writers like Stein, Mullen felt isolated as the only black student in the English department at that time. She took Ethnic Studies courses "to get a black professor" (Hogue, "Interview") and realized that her only means of studying nonwhite texts lay outside the English department. Classes in other fields introduced her to the works of Haki Madhubuti and Audre Lorde, among others. However, she often cites Roger Abrahams's influence in interviews, crediting his classes and books with having increased her knowledge about specific elements of black culture (Hogue, "Interview"; Bedient 668; Myers). These elements contributed background material to her later combination of black vernacular and folklore traits with the linguistic strategies of the Language poets.

Deep Down in the Jungle (1970), a collection of toasts and jokes that Abrahams gathered from a community of black men in Philadelphia, contains some of the earliest sources for the cultural references in Mullen's work. Abrahams sums up his book's understanding of street philosophy as "the assumption that everyone in your network . . . is almost always trying to manipulate, coerce, or use you. Consequently, life is seen as a constant hustle, and the one who does it best is the one who manipulates most and is manipulated least" (19). His conclusion about the nature of oral performance, which he terms primarily "improvisational in character" (100), resembles some aspects of Mullen's own creative philosophy. Some of her work's later critiques, however, take on issues reflected in his text's more careless moments: his dismissive attitude toward women, his facile conclusions about cultural production, and his opinion that orality holds a central position in black literature. Mullen's critical perspective on the subjects of Abrahams's teaching signals that she took up black vernacular elements as a vehicle for serious cultural critique, pushing his findings beyond the level of mere observation in order to argue on behalf of the need for radical change.

This education in language's power as a tool for cultural commentary contributed to the agenda that Mullen identified for *Tree Tall Woman*. She first read her poetry publicly at open-mike sessions in Austin, but found longer-lived support for her work through at first the Austin group Women and Their Work and then the Texas Circuit program. When she had compiled a substantial group of poems, many of which had already been published elsewhere, she signed a contract for *Tree Tall Woman* with Energy Earth Communications, an African-American publisher. Mullen's choice of publisher indicates her attention to constructing a recognizably black style; she characterizes the book as having been "influenced by the Black Arts Movement, the idea that there was a black culture and that you could write from the position of being within a black culture" (Hogue, "Interview").

Mullen interpellates her audience in *Tree Tall Woman* using the discursive technique of "signifyin." Here the term's connotations of "black double-voicedness" are most relevant; it includes both "formal revision and an intertextual relation" as earlier texts are repeated and revised to reflect historical change (Gates 51). Mullen's repeated blues and jazz references allow her poems to signify while also positioning her work within Houston Baker's "blues matrix." Both of these elements identify a culturally specific audience for the book.

Tree Tall Woman contains a poem entitled "Heritage," a title and subject that many twentieth-century black poets employ. Although Countee Cullen's "Heritage" remains perhaps the best-known example of this tendency, Maureen Honey's anthology *Shadowed Dreams* includes two such poems by different authors, in a section by the same name. These circumstances suggest that Mullen wrote her own "Heritage" in response to that title's substantial history, in order to signify on the broader connotations of the word. Similarly, one graphic image from another *Tree Tall Woman* poem, "The Lamp Lights into Its Prey," "You siphon off the red blood / and blues of others, / vampire fish" (lines 8–10; *Blues Baby* 38),[6] at first glance seems only to draw an analogy between a lamprey eel and the vampire mythos. The addition of "blues," however, alludes to white musicians' appropriations of black music during the swing and bebop eras and, more soberingly, indicts the labor practices of slavery. Mullen's use of culture-specific references allows her to enter into a tradition of black commentary on white oppression. Mullen's wordplay through puns and "samples" from other texts provides evidence for Juliana Spahr's theory that works that draw on both formal innovation and cultural complexity understand "reading as collective and communal," a tool for multiple types of "consciousness-raising" (6). The multiple significations of her cultural allusions enable her to interrogate and respond to the problematic politics of movements like high modernism (Spahr 102–3) as well as mainstream accounts of history.

Mullen's work in *Tree Tall Woman* also builds upon her undergraduate studies in the work of experimental poets like Gertrude Stein and Jean Toomer. Several of these poems contain wordplay and thematic allusions that anticipate the topics of her later books, as does "The Lamp Lights into Its Prey." "Tent Revival" begins with a tongue-in-cheek line, "In this fly-by-day church," whose revision of the clichéd "fly-by-night" both signifies on African-American religious traditions and provides an example of the ludic phrases that pervade her later poetry collections, *Trimmings* (1991), *S*PeRM**K*T* (1992), *Muse & Drudge* (1995), and *Sleeping with the Dictionary* (2002). In "The Mother of Nightmares," the speaker characterizes herself as "the woman with the / the razor blade pussy" (lines 12–13; *Blues Baby* 43), while in "The Joy," the narrator commands her audience to "put some starch / in your chef's hat, honey, / and start cookin" (lines 5–7; *Blues Baby* 53). The sexualized sources of power referenced in these two poems—an embodiment of the mythic *vagina dentata* and an image drawn from traditional blues lyrics—look ahead to the African-American feminist politics of *Muse & Drudge*.

During the 1980s, several professional and academic experiences helped to shape Mullen's developing poetics. She worked for the Texas

Commission on the Arts (TCA) in their Arts in Education program; she was joined in this endeavor by fellow poet and cultural critic Lorenzo Thomas, with whom she first connected in the mid-1970s, during the latter period of the Black Arts Movement. Citing Thomas's experiences as a major influence on her own writing, Mullen notes that "he offered a different model than the homegrown Texas regionalists": he had worked on musical festivals, school programs, and academic conferences in addition to writing music criticism and poetry. Thomas also introduced Mullen to the Umbra group, New York School poetry, and the work of the Language group (Henning).[7] After her work for the TCA, Mullen received a fellowship from the Texas Institute of Letters that enabled her to spend six months, August 1981–January 1982, writing in isolation on the Dobie-Paisano ranch just outside Austin (Thomas, *Extraordinary* 230–31). This period of intense creative effort, as well as her 1980s Ph.D. study in the History of Consciousness program at the University of California–Santa Cruz, contributed to the formally complex and densely allusive poems of *Trimmings, S*PeRM**K*T,* and *Muse & Drudge.* Daniel Cross Turner suggests, in fact, that Mullen's poetry possesses "a notably transregional quality" that contributes to its "hybridization on the level of form" (335). Like Sherley Anne Williams and Wanda Coleman, Mullen invests poetic attention in questions of regional as well as gender and racial identity.

At Santa Cruz, Mullen's writing developed along two diverging yet complementary lines. Her coursework included classes with African-American scholars and poets Lucille Clifton, Al Young, and Nathaniel Mackey, all of whose poetry she would later teach in her own classes (Hogue, "Interview"). Lila Abu-Lughod's *Veiled Sentiments: Honor and Poetry in a Bedouin Society,* Karen McCarthy Brown's *Mama Lola: A Voudou Priestess in Brooklyn,* and Karl Marx's writings on commodity fetishism broadened her understanding of the resources on which women can draw when encountering oppressive conditions. In her dissertation, she examined the slave narratives of Frederick Douglass and Harriet Jacobs in light of the politics of control and freedom. Here Mullen's theoretical framework derived in part from the work of Jacques Lacan and Michel Foucault; these writers' focus on social constructions of the body resonates with Abu-Lughod's and Brown's work, foreshadowing both her thematic explorations of the female body and her critiques of the social practices that attempt to constrain it. In a later article, "Runaway Tongue: Resistant Orality in *Uncle Tom's Cabin, Our Nig, Incidents in the Life of a Slave Girl,* and *Beloved,*" Mullen observes that women ultimately write more subversive accounts of literacy in slave narratives than even Frederick Douglass's paradigmatic narrative. Rather than replicating the power structures—including the primacy of the written text—foundational to white patriarchal society, Mullen claims, "both oral and written narratives by women concentrate . . . on the oral expression of the fugitive thought and the resistant orality of a runaway tongue" ("Runaway Tongue" 253).[8] She further refined her investigations of language's potential to effect change by studying Gertrude Stein's poetic techniques, which she characterizes as "an elegant solution" to the problems of accurate linguistic expression (Hogue, "Interview"). Stein's language experiments and Ron Silliman's commentary on the capitalist exploitation of literature in *The New Sentence* (1987) helped Mullen to uncover the political potential of traditional poetic language and to expand the linguistic registers of her social commentary.

The formal differences between *Tree Tall Woman* and *Trimmings*, Mullen's second book, arose in part because of her exposure to the Language community during the 1980s. However, she also studied the history of innovative black poetry and made conscious decisions about the cultural work she wanted her poetry to do. In her work's union of experimental form with cultural specificity, she has produced "a reciprocal interrogation of the implicitly white status of language poetry" (Pearcy), underlining the fact that black poetries historically challenge both formal traditions and social norms. She has also noted that she understands "writing as a process that is synthetic rather than organic, artificial rather than natural, human rather than divine," something comprising the full range of languages that one speaks, reads, studies, and listens to ("Imagining" 202). Mullen learned many of the strategies exercised in contemporary innovative poetics through the mentorship of Lorenzo Thomas and gained further exposure through her study at UC–Santa Cruz with Nathaniel Mackey. She often mentions her attendance at poetry readings and workshops sponsored by poets like Lyn Hejinian (Hogue, "Interview"; Frost, "Interview" 402), although even feminist accounts of the movement reference her work only infrequently.[9] Aldon Nielsen suggests that the prose form of both *Trimmings* and *S*PeRM**T* represents several complex dimensions in Mullen's work: her deliberate participation in a tradition of African-American prose poetry often overlooked by the critical mainstream, her reworking of the prose-poetic form, her cultivation of various levels of racial and sexual signifying that challenge conventional cultural vocabularies, and her attempts to undermine "the stability of racial identities" as well as "the stabilities of lyric voice and the verse line" ("African-American" 153–54, 159, 160). Mullen herself notes that her "work comes out of a conviction that innovation is intrinsic to black cultural consciousness" (Dargan 1015). She sought out a form in which she could explore both formal innovation and the politics of identity while cultivating links to the history of radical black poetries.

In the books she published after *Tree Tall Woman,* Mullen fosters a language-derived politics that she describes as "'talk[ing] back' to texts by white men, white women, and black men in which representations of black women are absent or subordinated to other aims" ("Runaway Tongue" 259).[10] Part of the project that Mullen ascribes to *Trimmings,* for instance, is a response, a "talking-back," to some racial allusions in Gertrude Stein's *Tender Buttons.* She calls her revision of Stein's "Petticoat" poem in that volume an act of "cannibalization" that also references Édouard Manet's painting *Olympia.* In this painting, a black woman, wearing a pink dress and holding a bouquet of flowers, stands behind a nude white woman reclining on a white couch. The darkness of the servant's body ensures that she will act as both a shadow of and a foil for the beauty of the white woman's body—which, Mullen speculates, Stein celebrates in her original poem (Hogue, "Interview"). Elisabeth Frost explains this kind of revision as an attempt to "merge public speech and 'private' experience" ("Signifyin(g)"). The text of Stein's "A Petticoat" reads only "A light white, a disgrace, an ink spot, a rosy charm," yet it underscores the visual contrast between white and black, one manifested as a disgraceful "ink spot" while the other possesses a "rosy charm." Mullen's revision of this piece also "talks back" to the broader Western literary tradition from which black women historically have been excluded by "signif[ying] on the Renaissance lyric tradition of the blazon," using an analogous form in order to highlight "the artificial cultural signs structuring gender and race" (Hogue, "Harryette Mullen's" 88). One of the most significant effects of Mullen's "revision" exists in its reversal of the different colors' connotations:

> A light white disgraceful sugar looks pink, wears an air, pale compared to shadow standing by. To plump recliner, naked truth lies. Behind her shadow wears her color, arms full of flowers. A rosy charm is pink. And she is ink. The mistress wears no petticoat or leaves. The other in shadow, a large, pink dress. (*Recyclopedia* 11)[11]

Here pink and white signify something "disgraceful," while the "shadow" appears rich in tone next to a "pale" figure. The pale nude exposes "lies," rather than "naked truth"; only the so-called shadow wears a color that belongs to her. The mistress's lack of "petticoat or leaves" suggests that she lacks not only conventional attire but also the basic sense of shame that prompted Adam and Eve to cover themselves. The poem's final line reveals its central power dynamic, when the "other in shadow" must conceal her body beneath "a large, pink dress," the color of her mistress's skin. Here Mullen challenges Stein's reading of visible cultural elements, offering a reading of a common domestic scene that lays bare its implicit politics.[12]

Trimmings was published by the Tender Buttons press, "the only specialist publisher of experimental poetry by women in the United States" (Vickery 76), another fact that highlights Mullen's participation in the projects of contemporary experimental poetry. She received the Gertrude Stein Award in Innovative American Poetry for 1994–1995, after *Trimmings* and *S*PeRM**K*T* appeared. Her use of blues and jazz references, usually couched as African-American cultural allusions, serves as a culturally specific means of formal experiment in line with Stephen Henderson's mascon words. In order to gain access to the many levels of meaning in Mullen's text, the reader must consult references such as Clarence Major's dictionary *From Juba to Jive: A Dictionary of African-American Slang* (1994) or participate in the cultural practices to which she alludes. The positive reception that her culturally specific linguistic innovations have received suggests that critical notions of what constitutes "experimental poetry" are slowly transforming.

For instance, in a poem about halfway through *Trimmings* that references Stein's famous use of the color red to signify sexuality—"When a dress is red, is there a happy ending" (*Recyclopedia* 30)—Mullen expands the associative possibilities of the color to include the Little Red Riding Hood myth and African-American folklore references. As she notes in her interview with Farrah Griffin, "[O]ut for a stroll, writing wolf-tickets," the last phrase of that poem, can be read as a version of Red Riding Hood's encounter with her legendary adversary but also connects to a mascon image. While Clarence Major glosses a "wolf" as a "male on the make," he also notes that a "wolf ticket" is "an invitation to fight with fists or weapons or both" (*Juba to Jive* 513).[13] Red Riding Hood's well-known success in defeating her wolf opponent suggests that the mascon terms' connotations serve here to empower the poem's black female narrator. Such multilayered allusions, further examples of Mullen's use of a "third language," form a backdrop to the work's focus on women's bodies, clothing, and minds, what Deborah Mix calls the "contradictory pressure on women" so often seen as sexual objects (73). This backdrop highlights the social complexities that arise at the intersections of race and gender.

The prose poems of *S*PeRM**K*T* also present several instances in which musical allusion and political statement draw readers' attention to social prejudices that arise from both racial and gender difference. Mullen employs the rhetoric common to advertisements for cleaning products to evoke the work roles traditionally assigned to black women. In the twenty-first poem, for instance, vernacular speech patterns and references to black entertainers enable readers to link different types of socially exploitative labor: "Ivory says pure nuff and snowflakes be white enough to do the dirty work. Step and fetch laundry tumbles out shuffling into sorted colored stacks. That black grape of underwear fame denies paternity of claymate raisinets" (*Recyclopedia* 85). Ads for Ivory soap, Fruit of the Loom underwear, and California raisins remind the audience of their slogans' origins in black culture. The phrases "pure nuff" and "step and fetch laundry" recall the minstrel character Stepinfetchit, while the black man dressed as a bunch of grapes in the underwear ad and the California raisins' Motown-like renditions of the company's theme song underscore additional remnants of minstrel tradition in contemporary media. Mullen implicitly links black women's enforced participation in "white" cleaning processes to these exploitations of black talent and culture.

Some musical references offer a playful inversion of culturally exploitative practices through an improvisatory style reminiscent of jazz techniques. The fifteenth poem of *S*PeRM**K*T*—"Two thousand flushes drain her white porcelana, chlorinised with antistepton disinfunktant unknownabrasives, cleanliness gets next to" (*Recyclopedia* 79)—attempts to revise the troubling histories of black labor and white notions of beauty by creating a series of neologisms that, again, evoke mascon words. "Porcelana," Spanish for "porcelain" (and the brand name of a popular skin-lightening cream), and "chlorinised," a neologism suggesting antiseptic processes, are juxtaposed with two words that directly refuse the exploitative history of minstrelsy: "antistepton" and "disinfunktant." Mullen constructs phrases that recall cleaning products by using the prefixes of negation often found in the names of chemical compounds, "anti-" and "dis-." However, this generic discourse allows her to create mascon terms that both reference and refuse minstrelsy (again, "Stepinfetchit") while bringing to mind another type of African-American music, funk. Mullen's playfully political statements suggest that she expands the lexicon of Language-based poetries through such mascon transformations.

Mullen's poetry in *Trimmings* and *S*PeRM**K*T* relies heavily on paratactic sentence constructions, indicating that her work draws on at least some of the properties Ron Silliman identified in the "new sentence."[14] At certain moments, her words seem to echo the work of Language poets like Lyn Hejinian. Lines such as "A little tight, something spiked, tries on a scandal," from *Trimmings* (*Recyclopedia* 9), for example, closely resemble Hejinian's famous phrase from *My Life*, "a pause, a rose, something on paper" (7), in their short, thematically discrete phrases and lack of a unifying lyric voice. The syllogistic movement of many of Mullen's lines occurs at a broad thematic level; her paratactic sentences reference jazz's social functions and historical conditions specific to black women's fight for social parity, topics common to her body of work. The paratactic sentence also provides Mullen with one strategy by which to textually approximate jazz riffs on these subjects, as in this example from *Sleeping with the Dictionary*, "Quality of Life":

> Walk across the park from Charlie Parker. Eat sweet potato pirogies in uppity café. Look at other merchandise. A smattering of tribes. Unheard of march in which the men protest themselves. Callaloo and collards are equivalent. Or banana is the same as *plata no es*. Narrative never is mere entertainment. To entertain is knowing how to be a woman. French theories suggest the best in women's writing are the men. "These star-apple leaves along the sound of Sonny Rollins River." Tina Turner set fire to her wigs so she could wear all burnt hair. Tourists flock to Strawberry Fields. Where sheep grazed in erstwhile Seneca Village. No one gets agit-props from avant-garde. A-Train from Caffe Reggio out of postcards. Hour and a half by subway to JFK. Bumpy return to port of lax security. Once I get that zip gun your reality Czech's in the escargot. (58–59)

Even in this passage's apparent lack of narrative coherence, Mullen makes several clear political statements. Every person mentioned by name is a famous African-American musician. Both food and music denote ethnic identity, but these references also identify categories sometimes too easily appropriated by cultural outsiders, as in the idea that "callaloo," a leafy green vegetable native to Jamaica, and "collards are equivalent." The journal *Callaloo*, with whose editors Mullen has worked, also connotes some of the highest quality writing within African-American studies. Racial discrimination still occurs, regardless of one's occupation or social standing—witness the avoidance of saxophonist Charlie Parker—yet jazz demands recognition: a reference to Billy Strayhorn's "A-Train" surfaces near the end of the piece. When Tina Turner burns her own expensive accessories, she both provides evidence that fashion still demands sacrifices and comments on many black women's tendency to straighten their hair artificially. Women must also confront repeated denigration of their accomplishments, as they can demonstrate "how to be a woman" only by entertaining and might earn the negative connotations of "agit-props" (or the "props" colloquially awarded an impressive creative performance) for their "avant-garde" work. Mullen composes her prose poems by drawing abstract ideas from juxtaposed samples of various cultural products, in an approach similar to jazz improvisation. She also critiques French advocates of fluid "female" writing like Luce Irigaray and Héléne Cixous, already overtheorized by male counterparts, suggesting that she offers her own linguistic approach to feminist statement as a desirable alternative.

"A Sweet Jelly Roll like Mine":
Blues as Revisionist History

After receiving her Ph.D. from UC-Santa Cruz in 1990, Mullen spent six years teaching literature and history at Cornell University. Her success in obtaining a prestigious academic position and her burgeoning reputation as a poet allowed her the intellectual leeway necessary to reconceptualize her priorities as a writer. Reflecting back on this period, Mullen notes that she had become increasingly aware of her largely white audiences and feared that her experimental techniques and esoteric allusions would obscure her work's cultural resonance. The African-American, blues-centered feminism of *Muse & Drudge* emerged in part as a response to these concerns, as a way to unite different groups of readers (Frost, "Interview" 416–17; Bedient 664; Griffin et al.; Hogue, "Interview"). Mullen's anxiety about the relevance of her work to the complex heterogeneity of contemporary poetry audiences signals that she was unwilling to cater exclusively to the academic audiences she shared with Language writers. She turned to blues references, creating a "written performance of [her] research into her oral tradition" (Crown, "'Choice'" 231), in order to continue formal experimentation while situating her poetry's cultural roots in a wide range of lifestyles, particularly those of African-American women.

Even as she sought to interpellate a broader audience, Mullen's career diversified in the early 1990s through readings at the Nuyorican Café in New York City and Painted Bride Art Center in Philadelphia. Here she made contact with other practitioners of experimental poetics, including multimedia poet and critic Erica Hunt. At the same time, her concern about how her poetry constructed its audience prompted her to rethink the presentation of her work. Her experiences at Painted Bride introduced her to publisher Gil Ott, who solicited the manuscript that became *Muse & Drudge*. Mullen's work with Ott on her book's cover resulted in a visual artifact that purposely "hailed" a certain segment of the population. Discussing the book's musical qualities with Elisabeth Frost, Mullen labels the blues "a sort of therapeutic activity" that positioned "blues women [as] influential and admired . . . before black women were admired on their own" ("Interview" 409). Her cover's picture of a black woman with open mouth, closed eyes, and clasped hands, framed by a brilliant blue field, suggests that black women have been both "muse" and "drudge" since the source of this particular woman's emotion remains open to the reader's interpretation. She both stands in for blues women and articulates the particularity of individual experience.

In all of her books, Mullen builds upon the themes of popular blues lyrics and creates poetic subjectivities based in the stances of blues women in order to advance an alternative portrait of U.S. culture and society. She celebrates blues performance as a space for black women's creativity but also ponders their traditional exclusion from the predominately male arenas of jazz performance. In *S*PeRM**K*T,* for instance, blues references not only suggest one role to which women have been reduced—a "spermkit," or repository for male productivity—but also critique consumer culture's investment in female shopping. These musical allusions denounce socialized racial beliefs, playfully valorizing African-American cultural traditions instead, especially in relation to food. Mullen notes that her book's unusual title comes from "the word 'supermarket' with some letters missing. . . . The missing letters just happen to be U-A-R-E, so it's like 'you are what you eat'" (Griffin et al.).[15] The poems draw links between women's roles as consumers and "eating disorders and the way that we feel about the body, the way that we feel about our appearance" (E. Williams 705), extending a commentary on mainstream society's failure to nourish its less visible members.

Many references to food within *S*PeRM**K*T* allude to images commonly found in blues lyrics, casting these signifiers of cultural knowledge in a humorous light. The eighteenth poem, for example, describes a group of meat items often categorized as "soul food":

> Off the pig, ya dig? He squeals, grease the sucker. Hack that fatback, pour the pork. Pig out, rib the fellas. Ham it up, hype the tripe. Save your bacon, bring home some. Sweet dreams pigmeat. Pork belly futures, larded accounts, hog heaven. Little piggish to market. Tubs of guts hog wilding. A pig of yourself, high on swine, cries all the way home. Streak a lean gets away cleaner than Safeway chitlings. That's all, folks. (*Recyclopedia* 82)

This series of idiomatic expressions illustrates the permeation of originally black expressions into mainstream American English and references such popular blues songs as Bessie Smith's "Gimme a Pigfoot." These expressions can be grouped into two categories that both suggest a pointed critique of capitalism: the discourse of commerce and analogies between pigs' feeding habits and the behavior of greedy humans. As Deborah Mix notes, this critique bears on race and gender politics in particular by drawing readers' attention to "the realities of consumption" in several manifestations of the public sphere (78). The book's ongoing commentary on the threat of consumer "sanitation" continues in the reference to a culturally inauthentic purchase, "Safeway chitlings," and in an allusion to the media's interest in black stereotypes: Porky Pig's famous last words at the end of a Warner Brothers cartoon, "That's all, folks." Doris Witt argues that textual representations of soul food are "related to the concurrent vilifications of African-American women as castrating matriarchs" (6). Soul food's involvement in 1960s discourses of white appropriation and black authenticity points to not only "overt inscriptions of class and race" but also "covert inscriptions of sexuality and gender" (Witt 15). This interpretation of black women's relationship to the food they traditionally consume and prepare suggests that Mullen intends these improvisatory revisions of food-based expressions to offer a new perspective on social relationships. Here black women's relationship to food preparation and consumption also evokes slavery's history of "produced" and "consumed" bodies (Mix 84). Food indirectly invokes issues of bodily appearance, reminding readers of the efforts that black women blues singers like Bessie Smith and Big Mama Thornton made to maintain their expressive freedom in the face of society's attempts to censure their actions.[16]

*S*PeRM**K*T*'s shortest poem—"Toejam must cause jelly don't. Mink chocolate melts in you" (*Recyclopedia* 86)—contains an indirect allusion to a food perhaps more commonly referenced in blues lyrics than any other, the jellyroll. Requests to "bake my jellyroll" or "get some jelly-roll" function in such lyrics as code for sexual interactions.[17] The poem's first phrase evokes a set of overlapping mascon images, while the second offers a revised version of the M&M's slogan that alludes to a rich sensual texture rather than a chocolate taste. Mullen's revisions often substitute one such sensory experience for another. These references to food also highlight black women's historical roles as domestic servants, which facilitate associations between their work and the products necessary for its completion. Foods more commonly available in supermarket chains also seem to undermine the worth of traditionally black foods. Mullen interrogates social perceptions through the lens of the blues in order to revise the context of those associations. The prominent position that black women have held as performers and subjects of the blues infuses women's subject-position in *S*PeRM**K*T* with agency and highlights their roles as producers, rather than mere consumers.

Food, cooking, and processes of consumption also provide key evidence for *Muse & Drudge*'s critique of modern society. Mullen creates food images with multiple significations in order to underline the network of connections among markers of race, sexuality, and cultural literacy. In her work, such references create an "intimate space" in which speaker and audience can share common experience (Pinto 66). She couches the book's first substantial allusion to a specific food, for example, in terms of its tactile resemblance to human flesh:

> a ramble in brambles
> the blacker more sweeter juicier
> pores sweat into blackberry tangles
> going back native natural country wild briers (*Recyclopedia* 101)

The opening "ramble" here emphasizes the participant's inevitable entrapment in a social wilderness, yet suggests that the tangle will prove to be more pleasurable than not, when it results in the discovery of fruit "the blacker more sweeter juicier."[18] This metaphor equates ripeness with both darker skin tones and sexual pleasure, a group of affiliations reemphasized by the pun in "pores [pours] sweat." Mitchum Huehls suggests that Mullen employs puns in order to "give substance to the indeterminacy of the diasporic political field and to offer a picture of black cultures that resists identity-based modes of representation" (22–23). This excerpt from *Muse & Drudge* recoups the negative connotations associated with the image of "going native" by rewriting the stereotypical "jungle" as "natural country" in which the most potentially harmful inhabitant will be "wild briers" (rather than "bears" or the racist image of "Br'er Rabbit"). Cooking and food serve as proofs of or challenges to one's cultural credibility. In another example, Mullen narrates a conversation between a personified pot and kettle—"pot said kettle's mama must've / burnt them turnip greens / kettle deadpanned not missing a beat / least mine ain't no skillet blonde" (*Recyclopedia* 105)—in which specific kinds of exaggeration and wordplay derive from African-American cultural practices like the toast. In many such instances from *Muse & Drudge*, Mullen rewrites idiomatic expressions common to "mainstream" English—"the pot calling the kettle black" and "bottle blonde"—to invoke black culture instead. Here the implied triumph of "black" over "blonde" also validates the specific experiences of African-American women.

Mullen often defines sexuality and food as sources of personal empowerment for black women, in the tradition of many famous blues lyrics by singers like Gertrude "Ma" Rainey and Bessie Smith. Such popular blues tunes as Rainey's "Prove It On Me" and Smith's "Do Your Duty" endorse women's sexual prowess and identity as sources of agency. In poetic imitations of such lyrics, Mullen usually employs a lyric voice. However, her version of the lyric includes quotations from multiple speakers and a range of perspectives that she describes as "a kind of chorus, as a group of women who have something in common but who are different and who are all speaking at the same time" (Crown, "Contemporary Long Poem" 535–36). Kathleen Crown suggests that this strategy enables Mullen to evoke "repressed elements of linguistic experience to assemble new audiences who share, across their cultural differences, varying modes of access" to such perspectives; her brand of lyricism "involves mobile, shifting, and multiple voices" ("'Choice'" 223, 232). Joel Bettridge also argues that Mullen "blurs subjectivity most fundamentally in the moments when the poem deals with formations of gender and sexual desire" (218). On an early page of *Muse & Drudge*, for example, the speaker ruminates, "call me pessimistic / but I fall for sour pickles / sweets for the heat / awrr reet peteet patootie" (*Recyclopedia* 102), which suggests both an intimate playfulness and an improvisatory riffing on her subject. Later in the work, readers obtain insight into more oblique references, such as "belly to belly / iron pot and cauldron / close to home / the core was melting" (*Recyclopedia* 113), through their associations with other instances of the narrative "I." The "iron pot and cauldron" of cooking are personified through the "bellies" suggested by their shapes, while they receive additional agency through the sexual implications of "the core [that] was melting."

Elisabeth Frost notes in her study of *Muse & Drudge*, "'Ruses of the Lunatic Muse': Harryette Mullen and Lyric Hybridity," that Mullen's "depictions of black women's bodies . . . also reinvent conventional lyric tropes" (472). Her concept of "lyric hybridity" defines Mullen's ability to unite the fragmentary voices of found poetry through the consistent advocacy of a specific social agenda and "an aesthetics that acknowledges blackness in its own 'lyric' mode" (Frost, "'Ruses'" 475). This hybrid voice identifies the links between feminism and physical experience in particular; through sexual references, Mullen portrays African-American women as agents making productive decisions without recourse to stereotypes about appropriate behavior for black women.[19] *Muse & Drudge* includes an image of the legendary *vagina dentata* as one key example of powerful female sexuality: "[C]ountry clothes hung on her all and sundry / bolt of blue have mercy ink perfume / that snapping turtle pussy / won't let go until thunder comes" (*Recyclopedia* 102). Mullen glosses this stanza as an exploration of "mythic constructions of the sexual prowess of males and females" (Bedient 659). The "country clothes" (note the allusion to Shakespeare's famous phrase "country matters," from *Hamlet* III.ii.111) here both conceal and draw attention to the speaker's "all and sundry," while the "snapping turtle pussy" appears like a "bolt" out of the "blue." The phrasing suggests as well that the female subject in this scene places a high priority on sexual satisfaction; she chooses not to "let go until thunder comes."

Mullen portrays her female subjects, confident in the power of their material selves, as representative of women in general, just as blues singers spoke for their female contemporaries. The book's narrative situations derive from the assumption that the "black woman is generic of woman, and woman is generic of humanity" (Frost, "Interview" 408). References to sexual identity sometimes appear in lines that imitate blues lyrics more precisely, as in "from hunger call / on the telephone / asking my oven for / some warm jellyroll" (*Recyclopedia* 136), and "cram all you can / into jelly jam / preserve a feeling / keep it sweet" (178). In both of these instances, Mullen's hybrid lyric voice references a coalition of "allusive, de-essentialized, and fragmented" subjectivities (Huehls 36) derived from the general history of feminist blues expression. As Elisabeth Frost points out, characteristic blues expression subsumes individual personae into a collective identity ("Interview" 408). Mullen has also noted that the book seeks "to find an intersection of writing and orality and to look at the folk tradition and the oral tradition, and music—blues and jazz, gospel music and spirituals—and to try to engage the eye of the reader and the ear of the listening audience" (Crown, "Contemporary Long Poem" 530).

Sappho/Sapphire, the collectively realized blues narrator who opens and closes *Muse & Drudge,* embodies the lived experiences of black female bodies. Mullen rewrites the figure of Sapphire, a derogatory stereotype of black women that portrays them as loud, abrasive, and oversexed, to resonate with Sappho, an early Greek lyric poet who produced some of the first feminist writings. Female bodies therefore channel power and creativity in Mullen's blues "lyrics," just as they do in Sherley Anne Williams's Bessie Smith poems. On the first page of *Muse & Drudge,* "plucked eyebrows" and "bow lips and legs" continue the exploration of women's bodies that Mullen began in *Trimmings* while also bringing to mind the "plucking" and "bowing" that would allow Sappho/Sapphire to sing the blues on her lyre (*Recyclopedia* 99). Mullen consistently aligns blues performance with varying versions of feminist creativity in this book. As Allison Cummings suggests, this nexus of blues identity politics can "provid[e] a feminist counterpoint to the cultural discourses and representations that erase black women" (27). Using a version of Zora Neale Hurston's famous phrase, "black women are the mules of the world," Mullen depicts such performance as a more positive way to expend energy than the social labors traditionally assigned to women: "[M]use of the world picks / out stark melodies / her raspy fabric / tickling the ebonies" (*Recyclopedia* 115).

Mullen also employs references to blues performance in *Muse & Drudge* as a means of both celebrating jazz as a specifically black cultural tradition and, more specifically, paying homage to musicians like Wynton Marsalis, a trumpeter and composer who won a Pulitzer Prize in 1997 for his jazz oratorio *Blood on the Fields.* Such tributes enable her to remind her audience that the struggle for gender and racial equality continues within America's marginalized geographies: "[P]recious cargo up crooked alleys / mules and drugs / blood on the lilies / of the fields" (*Recyclopedia* 172). Angela Davis argues that "[t]he performances of the classic blues women . . . were one of the few cultural spaces in which a tradition of public discourse on male violence had been previously established" (25). Mullen's work contributes to this tradition through blues and jazz references that highlight the abuses women have suffered.

The hybrid lyric voice of *Muse & Drudge* aims this kind of social critique at black men as well as white, those in power as well as those below the poverty line. The poem's narrator seems to answer Louis Armstrong's signature statement in "I Got a Right to Sing the Blues," for example, with "go ahead and sing the blues / then ask for forgiveness / you can't do everything / and still be saved" (*Recylopedia* 125). Mullen's verses demand action, rather than rhetoric; her blues speakers perform concrete acts and force readers to confront the consequences of linguistic expression: "[A]ss can't cash / mere language / sings scat logic / talking shit up blues creek" (*Recyclopedia* 153). These lines might reference Armstrong again, the self-proclaimed founder of scat singing whose rise to fame unfortunately coincided with the decline in popularity of the 1920s black female blues singers, but they also highlight the damage that exclusionary social discourses can inflict. Mullen gestures, through her work's densely allusive structure, toward the liberatory possibilities of aesthetic innovation. The multiplying significations of each line create linguistic excesses that, as Mitchum Huehls has argued, may offer "metaphorical liberation" from the social constraints that cultural memories of slavery continue to impose (25, 27). The poetic speakers' collective experiences create a blues voice that refuses "authenticity" in favor of "disrupt[ing] assumed understanding" (Pinto 60). Here Mullen argues for a specifically feminist politics by evoking the complicated demands of black women's existence; she couches her message in the historically and connotatively rich discourse of the blues.

Patricia Smith, one of Mullen's contemporaries, joins her in investigating the political implications of the blues and in challenging conventional versions of social history. Her revisions of blues lyrics showcase the material effects of abuse on the individual, providing an important rhetorical counterpoint to Mullen's "generic" representations of women. In "Your Man," a poem reprinted in her 1992 volume *Big Towns, Big Talk,* she creates her own version of the raucous blues lyrics that 1920s and 1930s blues singers made famous. Like such Bessie Smith classics as "Gimme a Pigfoot," "Kitchen Man," and "Nobody in Town Can Bake a Sweet Jelly Roll Like Mine," "Your Man" features a speaker who discusses her sex life in terms of food; she enjoys a lover who "brings me sweet bread and fried corn, / feeds me like an animal from his fingers" (lines 5–6). Hyperbolic descriptions of sexual prowess give the poem's first four stanzas a tone of hedonistic pleasure and abandon: "Your man's lovin' leaves marks like drumbeats, / disturbances on brown skin stretched across a circle of bone. / I carved his coming out of a mojo moonlight, / out of what you told me / about the voodoo in his fingers" (lines 14–18). This magical physical experience gradually erodes, however, under the pressure of the lover's forceful demands. In the last stanza, the speaker summarizes her abusive boyfriend's powerful lovemaking—"he rocks the house sometimes, / he shakes it up sometimes" (lines 25–26)—but undermines the entire poem's argument in the final lines: "[H]e makes it right. All the time. / Sometimes" (lines 27–28). Here Smith substitutes sober reflection for the proud and boastful tone common to blues lyrics by allowing the downside of this sexual relationship to emerge. The poem's allusion to the all-too-frequent occurrence of relationship abuse echoes the social commentary that her predecessors in blues performance advanced.

Smith also draws analogies between sexual pleasure and physical pain as blues subjects, relying on the expressive power of blues lyrics in a manner similar to Mullen's. "In the Ultimate Blues Bar," another poem from *Big Towns, Big Talk,* describes a blues bar as a sanctuary for men with broken hearts: "When a woman rips a man open, / this is where he comes to bleed" (lines 13–14). Smith portrays such a woman, "Janet," as a material object who possesses the power to wound her former lover physically, although the narrator wryly notes that tonight "Janet will sleep curled in a bigger bed, / a deep purple gash over her eye" (lines 45–46). Smith's own authorship and the beneficent tone that permeates the poem's last two stanzas create a sense that women's strength comes from words rather than physical force. "Bless them," the narrator repeats five times, before offering the poem's startling conclusion: "[O]nly a woman / has the balls / to break them" (lines 64–66). In keeping with the historical tradition of female-authored blues lyrics, this final statement inverts stereotypical signifiers of male power in order to indicate that the written word can prevail over shallow displays of physicality.

"BLAH-BLAH": JAZZ TECHNIQUES AND SOCIAL MEANING

In addition to the creative investment in the politics of early-century blues performance that she shares with many contemporary writers, Harryette Mullen has pursued a variety of collaborative projects since her days with the TCA. In addition to her poetry readings, courses taught at Cornell and UCLA, and a rapidly growing list of publications, Mullen has attended a poets' summer camp at Colorado's Naropa University, served as a Writer-in-Residence at Morehouse College in Atlanta, and become a fellow at Cave Canem, a Virginia-based nonprofit organization that promotes contemporary African-American poetry. Her diverse range of activities also includes judging poetry contests, like the spoken-word contests conducted by Dominique Di Prima on her radio station, The Beat, and reading at various public venues, including Los Angeles's Leimert Park on the World Stage and Fifth Street Dick's, a jazz café. Her involvement in many literary enterprises outside the academy demonstrates a commitment to making poetry a part of active social discourse, a priority that echoes in the jazz-based techniques and forms of her work.

These compositional strategies persist in Mullen's latest book, *Sleeping with the Dictionary*. Though she has acknowledged that some readers interpret these poems' preoccupations as a digression from the themes and agenda of her earlier books, she asserts that the volume falls into place along "a continuum with all of [her] work," since it "returns to themes of family and community that were prominent in [her] first book" (Kane). In *Sleeping*, Mullen also investigates words' origins, "the 'unconscious' of language," and "the materiality of language itself, the physical presence of words and letters on the page" (Mullen, "Imagining" 202). Here she uses jazz references to unite social commentary with an innovative form that expands the techniques of *Trimmings* and *S*PeRM**K*T*. Mullen claims jazz discourse as a legitimate forum for black women's work by positioning jazz as a vehicle for political poetics.

Early examples of the compositional approach to social critique that characterizes Mullen's work in *Sleeping with the Dictionary* appear in the jazz-influenced poems of *Trimmings*. One of this book's shortest pieces, for example, describes "brimming over eye shades cool complexion, delicate hue, the lid on, keeps a cool head under high hat" (*Recyclopedia* 8). In this exploration of sartorial styles' potential for social commentary, the hat brim shades the eye, even as the eye brims over with tears at a tragedy. "Eye shades" signal that women hide their pain from public view and also evoke images of bebop hipsters who wore sunglasses while performing. For women, this type of shade protects the complexion—a marker both of sheltered femininity and of public status when skin tone could determine one's social acceptability. The "delicate hue" suggests that the wearer of hat and shades has indeed kept "the lid on," but the "high hat" complicates the matter. What might be interpreted first as merely a trick of fashion, shading the wearer from the sun and demonstrating its owner's style, takes on jazz connotations with the recognition of its other meaning: a set of cymbals, frequently used in jazz performance, that clap together via a foot pedal. Additionally, Mullen has identified "cool" as a mascon term: "[S]uch words—like 'blue,' 'cool,' 'funk,' or 'soul'—are frequently used to evoke collective black experience and historical consciousness" (Young et al., "What's"). The overlapping significations of the poem's phrases recall the associative development inherent to jazz performance, as one riff takes on several meanings in the contexts of new players and a fresh performance. Mullen notes that in the course of poetic composition, she "had to take things and riff on them, as a musician improvises on a melody and really creates a new song" (Hogue, "Interview"). These improvisations resonate with the collection's title, which alludes both to the pieces subtracted from fabric (or other consumable objects) and to the decorations added to a piece of clothing; the title concept also advises that "we need to learn to read differently, which means learning to see relationships and lineages that have been, for a variety of reasons, trimmed away from literary history" (Mix 85).

Mullen extends her argument about the interdependence of race and gender issues, and their imbrication in the historical dimensions of jazz performance, in the shortest poem of *Trimmings:* "Shades, cool dark lasses. Ghost of a smile" (*Recyclopedia* 58). Elisabeth Frost has illuminated the additional implications of "shades," a racist term for African Americans that here may denote "ghosts," as "invisible presences in a culture bent on cover-ups, on hiding behind its own, often rose-colored, glasses" ("Signifyin'"). The fact that these expressions are associated with "lasses"—a colloquial term for women derived from glasses, or "shades," with one letter removed—reemphasizes the idea that blues culture fosters unconventional perspectives on gender and race. Mullen also articulates issues of discrimination in both jazz and society as a whole through gender-specific clothing; one such scenario features "girls in white sat in with blues-saddened slashers" (*Recylopedia* 34). In spite of the girls' pristine outfits, "sat in" points to the lingo of jazz performance practice even as their "blues-saddened" lives evoke the traditional melancholy tone and female performers of blues lyrics. The phrase's phonetic rearrangement of a line from *The Sound of Music*'s "My Favorite Things," "girls in white dresses with blue satin sashes," also recalls John Coltrane's famous transformation of this tune in his signature "sheets of sound" performance style (Gioia 245, 303). In both of these examples, jazz references enable the subversive potential of linguistic improvisation.

Such improvisations take place on a larger scale in Mullen's work when she revises traditional poetic forms in order to challenge the broader social implications of literary tradition. In a discussion of *Trimmings*, she argues that the "little list poem, which has become a workshop cliché," evokes the "masculine tradition" of epic poetry's "catalogues (of heroes, ships, and so forth)" (Henning). Her book's associative form, on the other hand, comprises lists of clothing references whose linguistic transformations garner them a new social relevance. This approach adds a new dimension to the history of the list poem popularized by New York School poets like Frank O'Hara and John Ashbery. Emily P. Beall's linguistic analysis of one such list poem from *Sleeping with the Dictionary* argues that Mullen's multiply signifying references "reach beyond the most obvious or prototypical qualities of the signified object," often evoking a "ghost text" born of readers' prior knowledge of phrases that Mullen's lines only point to or hint at (136). Mullen calls *Trimmings* "a female version" of the epic's "set piece in which the hero is being outfitted for a particular adventure or battle with certain accoutrements" (Crown, "Contemporary Long Poem" 531). She deliberately begins *Trimmings*, for instance, with a discussion of belts' properties "since a convention of epic poetry is to begin 'in the middle'" (Henning); thus the early narrative epic serves as the book's "ghost text." The doubled connotations of these lines also demonstrate what Mitchum Huehls has called "the formal simultaneity" of her work, the suggestion that its "multiple meanings occur simultaneously" (21). Lorenzo Thomas has noted that list composition was also a "popular Beat trope" that Amiri Baraka reworked (*Extraordinary* 159); Mullen continues this work with a feminist agenda in *Trimmings, S*PeRM**K*T, Muse & Drudge,* and *Sleeping with the Dictionary.*

Although Mullen explores themes similar to those of *Tree Tall Woman* in *Sleeping with the Dictionary*, this latest work employs formal revisionist strategies that more closely resemble the techniques of her second, third, and fourth books. The book contains 57 poems, arranged in alphabetical order by title. Many pieces grow out of generative compositional methods like anagrams, aural association, puns, homonyms, and Oulipo compositional styles, though the work overall possesses a humorous tone. In spite of her misgivings about the history of the list form, Mullen finds its associative possibilities useful in creating her work's sense of playful craft. Jazz and blues references guide her specifically sound-based list poems, which often include textual imitations of the sounds of jazz music. The list poems in *Sleeping* help to revise the catalogue tradition of the epic by incorporating elements of dialogue, found poetry, repeated sentence structures, and nonsense words. In an article on the work of Lyn Hejinian and Kathy Acker, "Rules and Restraints in Women's Experimental Writing," Carla Harryman argues that in contemporary experimental feminist writing, a "rule of thought or intellectual position is . . . what allows the difficult text to come into being at all, and it is what limits its own complexity" (117). This idea illuminates the connections Mullen draws in her own work between prescribed form and the work's thematic potential. Operating under structural constraints such as Oulipo's *noun + 7* substitutions encourages juxtapositions of apparently unrelated concepts that retain a unified social purpose. The paratactic sentence's lack of syllogistic resolution produces a similar effect.[20]

Both "Blah-Blah" and "Jinglejangle," two list poems from *Sleeping with the Dictionary,* are composed of alphabetically arranged subjects, their seemingly straightforward organization echoing the book's table of contents. Upon closer examination, the lists of seemingly nonsensical syllables that make up each of these poems often resolve into specific references to jazz performances, vocal techniques, or even other experimental poets. These references ground Mullen's list poems in specific historical moments and cultural practices that complicate her pieces' relationship to the work's formal precedents. Emptying the list poem of its New York School connotations allows her to redefine it as a vehicle for feminist innovation. In "Blah-Blah," for instance, the "Ack-ack, aye-aye" of the first line metamorphoses into the punning of "is is, It'sIts" and then the echoing repetitions of "Mahi mahi, mama, Mau Mau, Mei-Mei, Mimi, Momo, murmur, my my" (*Sleeping* 12). In these riffs on the letter M, the name of a fish, a child's nickname for her mother, and the name of a Kenyan secret society committed to expelling European settlers aurally evoke Mei-Mei Berssenbrugge, a contemporary poet engaged in language experiments. Mullen combines references to politics, art, personal life, and geography in seemingly random alphabetized lists in order to mimic the deluge of sensory input that people regularly experience. These juxtapositions compel the reader to reimagine the links between poetic language and social action, while the rapid patterns of aural links give the poem an improvisatory quality that recalls the spontaneity of jazz performance.

In "Jinglejangle," a substantially longer poem, Mullen extends the associative patterns and jazz references of "Blah-Blah" into a more substantial examination of the cultural sources that go into English's various lexicons. Most readers would recognize allusions from literature, advertising, slang and vernacular speech, history and legend, and the arts, but, as in her work in *Muse & Drudge*, Mullen does not intend the piece to be completely transparent to anyone. She observes that the poem underwent several transformations after audience members contributed their ideas at readings, calling it "a demonstration of how much poetry material there is all around us and how much we are participating in the creation of something that is poetic" (Griffin et al.). Lines such as "Mingus Among Us mishmash Missy-Pissy mock croc Mod Squad mojo moldy oldy" (*Sleeping* 39) and "rat-a-tat razzle-dazzle razzmatazz real deal redhead Reese's Pieces reet pleat" (40) link jazz, idiomatic expression, pop-culture icons, and mascon words in an arrangement that points to language's intricately branching origins as well as the rich compositional potential of improvisation. Mullen also pays tribute to other writers and pokes fun at artists' general tendency to take their work too seriously: "[P]lay as it lays pocket rocket poet don't know it pogo pooper scooper pot shot pope-soap-on-a-rope" (*Sleeping* 40) and "Scrapple from the Apple screen scene screwy Louie screw you Sea & Ski" (41). Here the titles of Joan Didion's famous novel and Charlie Parker's bebop tune participate in an aurally and textually improvisatory mix that represents a new version of the list poem.

Rather than repeating syllables as in "Blah-Blah," Mullen pairs nouns, verbs, and adjectives that illustrate the poem's central thesis: creativity originates in the interrogation of difference. Her improvisatory work links the realm of aural music to that of everyday life, to indicate that jazz informs the strategies of such performative interventions in popular culture as commercial and colloquial languages.

One of the nonlist poems in *Sleeping with the Dictionary* also functions, under Mullen's title and epigraph, as an exercise in jazz-influenced improvisation in which the aural links between words play specific musical roles. As the poem's note indicates, "Music for Homemade Instruments" resulted from her "improvising with Douglas Ewart" on the initial phrase "I dug you artless" (*Sleeping* 50). Here Mullen ties the hipster phrase "I dug you" to methods for creating and evaluating art; the poem suggests that two unnamed voices participate in an act of improvisation by tossing a series of restructured phrases back and forth: "I dug you artless, I dug you out. Did you re-do? You dug me less, art. You dug, let's do art. You dug me, less art. Did you re-do? If I left art out, you dug. My artless dug-out. You dug, let art out. Did you re-do, dug-out canoe? Easy as a porkpie piper-led cinch." The phrase "Did you re-do" becomes a refrain for the poem that echoes scat phrasing and signals the poet-musicians' use of jazz improvisation's changing same. This refrain also references the fact that Ewart, a musician and instrument-builder, plays the didgeridoo, an Aborigine wind instrument. After the initial improvisation, the poem proceeds through a series of disjunctive, almost nonsensical images—"strutting dimpled low-cal strumpets" and "bamboozle flukes at Bama"—that recall the surrealist work of Jayne Cortez, yet the repetition of variations preserves the piece's coherence. The last two sentences of this prose poem, "You dug art, didn't you? Did you re-do?" ask the reader to consider the political implications of improvisation: its ability to introduce new, unconventional perspectives on art and history.

In addition to its improvisatory pieces, *Sleeping with the Dictionary* contains several poetic encomia that illustrate the newly central role that cultural homage plays in jazz poetry. Mullen's changes to the homage's historical form recall Sonia Sanchez's blues-inflected adaptation of the haiku and the 1960s evolution of the jazz elegy. Although "She Swam On from Sea to Shine" does not contain recognizable jazz themes, its revisionist tribute to the traditional toast "Shine Swam On" suggests both improvisation and respect for its textual predecessors. Roger Abrahams devotes more space to the "Shine" toast than any other in *Deep Down In the Jungle* (79–81, 100–3, 106, 108); Mullen re-creates the toast in her poem in order to pay homage to her artistic predecessors while introducing the structural and thematic differences that cultural change produces. Abrahams describes the "Shine" toast as follows:

> Shine is a black stoker working on the *Titanic* who informs the ship's captain about the holes in the hull after the ship crashes with the iceberg. The captain keeps sending him down to pump, and he keeps re-emerging, giving the captain further information on the water in the hold. Finally Shine jumps into the water and begins swimming. He is then offered three temptations from those still on board—money from the captain and sex from the captain's wife and daughter. All of these he turns down because of the practical demands of his predicament. He is then challenged by the shark and the whale but is able to out-perform them. He swims safely to shore. (Abrahams 80)

Mullen participates in black signifying traditions by creating her own version of this text, one shaped by both oral and linguistic influences.[21] Sascha Feinstein has also drawn attention to "the great many tributes that followed" the publication of Frank O'Hara's famous poem about Billie Holiday, "The Day Lady Died" (*Jazz Poetry* 144). The key differences between Mullen's homages and those Feinstein discusses, including O'Hara's, lie in the specific social messages that she evokes and her reliance upon experimental techniques as a means of paying tribute to others' skills. Mullen gives coherence to "She Swam On from Sea to Shine," a six-page prose piece comprising primarily paratactic sentences, through recurring feminine pronouns and progressing temporal markers. In contrast to the list-based, sensory impressions of O'Hara's tribute, this poem narrates a series of actions performed by a woman who "was a poem" (64) and "was always writing anyway" (65). Mullen's homage celebrates the feminist agency that an improvisatory change in the toast's subject yields, rather than a list of spectators' experiences.

Two poems in *Sleeping with the Dictionary* illustrate Mullen's evolving homage form in their tributes to other jazz poets. She structures "Ted Joans at the Café Bizarre," for instance, as an unpunctuated series of short lines, never more than seven syllables long, that offers several visions of Black Arts poet Joans and his work. Crafting her characteristic puns and jazzlike aural associations, Mullen describes him as a "surly realist," a "purrs natch," and a "contraband leader" who is "scattering scat / sporadically all over / forever diaspora" (*Sleeping* 71). Her verse likens him to an artist, a revolutionary, and a jazz singer, while the final reference to "scattering scat" recalls not only the sexual overtones of blues lyrics but also the communal identity that history has assigned African Americans, "forever diaspora." The compositional strategies of the book's second-to-last poem, "Zen Acorn," written for Bob Kaufman, resemble those of "Music for Homemade Instruments": multiplying rearrangements of a few well-chosen words. Mullen exploits the phonetic significations of words containing "a" or "z" in order to produce what Nathaniel Mackey termed in *School of Udhra* "anagrammatic / scat" (45–46). The poem's first stanza, "a frozen / indian acorn," metamorphoses into "a narco dozen / faze an african," seven stanzas later (*Sleeping* 84). Mullen repeats, breaks apart, and recombines seemingly unrelated words and phrases to create an aural improvisation that not only serves as homage to Kaufman's work but also comments on the· cultural mixing endemic to American discourses. Mullen's customary matrix of blues and jazz references enables structural play even as she uses it as a context within which to offer social critique.

Some of Mullen's contemporaries also reimagine jazz themes and techniques in order to shape new approaches to poetic tribute. Unlike Mullen, these writers unite feminist analysis with tributes to African-American musicians that implicitly endorse the more masculinist jazz elegy tradition (as I discuss in Chapter 2). At the same time, however, their work defines a perspective on black feminist creativity alternative to that of male jazz elegists like Frank O'Hara. One such example appears in *The Weather That Kills* (1995), Patricia Spears Jones's first collection of poems, which explores themes of mutability in the context of tributes to the innovations of jazz musicians. Two of the book's more overtly blues- and jazz-influenced pieces, "The Birth of Rhythm and Blues" and "The Usual Suspect," are subtitled "From The Billie Holiday Chronicles." Both poems celebrate Holiday's accomplishments as an African-American woman and a successful musician, but they also censure the inequalities that complicate black women's social and economic survival. Asked to comment on her use of Holiday as a representative figure, Spears Jones stresses the singer's symbolic power as both musical talent and self-sufficient woman:

> She was an incredible jazz singer, the fluidity of her voice is amazing, but there's also an extraordinary sense of structure, when you think of her as a musician, and not as the iconographic female victim. I think of her as having all these things that people never ascribe to her, and that's why I wanted her to be a goddess figure. She gets to be the goddess over my book. (Berman 17)

In "The Birth of Rhythm and Blues," the speaker tells the story of her parents' lives through the music they listened to and the experiences of abuse and disappointment that they shared with Billie Holiday. Spears Jones explains a line from the poem's second stanza, "A Black woman's life is like double jeopardy" (12), by providing a pertinent example in the fourth stanza: "That point where Billie hit / bottom and found the start of a global nightmare" (34–35). She presents in the figure of Billie Holiday an image of neglected or misrepresented African-American history, producing the material consequences that individuals suffer. Questioning this tradition of neglect in "Gossip," Spears Jones writes, "What is this desire to wrap the celebrity dead in paper, / blood, wings and shit. To toss them in the fire, and wait / for the ashes to mass, a stinking incense?" (5–7). Her own answer to this harshly graphic question, "What we love is the failing, the falling," (15) offers poignancy and may inspire self-reflection. The contrast between the ugliness of lived experience and the deceptive simplicity of life's end underlines Spears Jones's focus on Holiday, a black woman whose accomplishments as a feminist and cultural messenger dwarf her experiences of both living and singing the blues.

Patricia Smith's *Big Towns, Big Talk,* another text that offers a feminist jazz tribute to a specific subject, ends with "On the Street Where She Lives," an homage to jazz and blues singer Gloria Lynne. Smith's description of Lynne's abilities emphasizes the power of both her voice and the words it speaks: "She jumped right on that last note in 'On the Street / Where You Live,' and in that verb's defiant tremble / my ears lost the power to receive and translate" (1–3). As in Smith's description of the guilty lover in "Your Man," Lynne's talents resemble magic; the speaker addresses Lynne by saying, "Miss Gloria, conjurer woman, / on the street where you live, / the houses sport dips in their red brick hips / and their doors are open mouths, scatting songs / threaded with sweet sin" (17–21). This phrasing mimics jazz lyrics in its simple word choices and tight rhymes, attributing to the very landscape of the ideal world the power of skillful verbal expression. Mullen, Spears Jones, and Smith create tributes that feature imitations of jazz performance techniques, seeking to revise the traditions of established poetic forms by infusing them with feminist sensibilities rooted in the very properties of language itself.

CONCLUSION: INTELLECTUAL TRADITIONS AND THE LANGUAGES OF FEMINIST JAZZ POETRY

Harryette Mullen crafts her poetry using tools as diverse as African-American vernacular language traits, black textual strategies, and Language-group techniques like the "new sentence," resulting in a poetics founded in the political potential of letters and words. These approaches frame the thematic attention to gender, race, class, sexuality, and social roles that shape her feminist politics. Her compositional strategies also include structural gestures meant to undermine the hegemony of both "classroom" English and mainstream, often male-centered, poetic and musical traditions. Juliana Spahr calls such constellations of poetic elements "nonstandard and atypical and polylingual grammars [used] for the purposes of cultural critique and communally rooted and reformatory reading" (155). Mullen also incorporates the culturally complex discourses of jazz alongside black linguistic registers and Language-based innovations, suggesting that her work participates in intellectual traditions that value linguistic diversity. At the same time, however, she seeks to maintain space for the kind of "communal readings" Spahr describes, rather than the elitist audience that traditional views of intellectualism imply, in order to render her work socially relevant. Mullen's interest in community speaks further to her connections with women Language writers, many of whom have expressed frustration with their exclusion from male-centered writing communities by forming alternative connections (Vickery 34). She thus defines a feminist intellectualism that understands culture, community, education, and experiment as equally valid sources of insight.

This mode of poetic composition offers one way in which American women poets of color can combat professional marginalization by institutions like the academy and the popular press, both of which continue to represent canonical texts as the most valuable intellectual property of classrooms and bookstores. Recent movements in literary and cultural theory like queer and gender studies, as well as diversifying college curricula, suggest that some scholars now prioritize marginalized work, yet social stereotyping and ongoing economic and professional discrimination provide hard evidence that public perceptions of many American minority groups do not yet reflect substantial positive changes. Mullen attempts to influence such social misconceptions by putting different spheres of women's lives—personal, professional, and public—into dialogue with one another. Her concern about her audience during the publication of *Muse & Drudge,* her exploration of some traditional forms in *Sleeping with the Dictionary,* and the republication of her earliest work in *Blues Baby: Early Poems* (2002) indicate that she alters her poetry's formal presentation to argue on behalf of both artistic innovation and the public roles of poetry.

Traditional views of intellectuals, who have often been seen as too hasty to romanticize the work of marginalized groups, complicate the efforts of writers like Harryette Mullen to diminish social inequality by interpellating diverse audiences. In *No Respect: Intellectuals and Popular Culture* (1989), Andrew Ross explains intellectuals' ambivalence toward education, which confers widely recognized "authority and privileges" even as its predetermined structure and stores of information seem to operate against "the potential freedom, dignity, and self-determination" that knowledge implies (Ross 6). The power that implicitly accompanies education also carries a tinge of elitism, potentially divorcing personal identity from social positions of authority. Mullen expresses concern about this type of split in her article "Optic White," which argues that racial passing effaces ethnic origins in favor of "identifying oneself culturally and genetically with white Americans," who occupy a privileged position at "the center of American identity" (77). The third chapter of Ross's book, "Hip, and the Long Front of Color," addresses Mullen's reservations about cultural elitism and reappropriation by examining the historical relationships between black and white cultural products, particularly music. Ross posits that white fantasies about black culture have significantly affected contemporary intellectual movements. Many writers saw black women blues and soul singers as "truth tellers," for example, celebrating the reality of African-American life—in contrast to the "male blues tradition that had nurtured a music about despair and involuntary resignation" (Ross 98). "Soul" signified cultural knowledge, even if the speaker was white, and public figures interpreted the lyrics to some soul tunes as politically charged (Ross 99). Some members of the Beats and white student organizations of the 1960s and 1970s held romanticized viewpoints like these, producing serious misrepresentations of African-American values and lifestyles. In "The Bop Aesthetic and Black Intellectual Tradition," Lorenzo Thomas offers an alternative definition of bebop-era black intellectualism that revises such fallacies: "[A] creative and explicit expression of racial pride that is logically and inextricably linked to the musicians' desire for artistic recognition and economic self-determination" (117).

Mullen adds issues of gender and sexuality and their significations in language to Thomas's model of black intellectualism. This simultaneously material and representational critique defines a new role for feminist intellectuals that seeks to avoid the political irrelevancy of an exclusionary aesthetic. Part of her project originates in a response to the misogynistic behavior championed by some members of groups like the Beats, as well as the bebop-era musicians from whom the Beats drew their self-presentations. Mullen's representation of women intellectuals as speakers for marginalized groups also gains credence from Angela Davis's understanding of African-American women blues singers as vocalizers of oppression and inequality, as well as her own commitment to "pushing the boundaries of identity to create a more inclusive, heterogeneous, and interactive text" (Dargan 1016). Andrew Ross defines "new intellectuals" as those who "have fostered cultural agendas specific to the politics of gender, race, ethnicity, and sexual orientation" (229), just as Bruce Robbins admits, in the introduction to *Intellectuals: Aesthetics, Politics, Academics*

(1990), that a "demasculinizing of the discourse about intellectuals" must take place (xviii). Mullen and other feminist jazz poets extend these assessments by insisting upon the material importance of social issues in their work, representing both historical efforts to surpass oppression and marginalized voices through their work's linguistic innovations.

Mullen and her contemporaries share a common belief in the possibilities of social change; their poetry pioneers many types of formal innovation while reframing social and artistic discourses in feminist terms. Williams reenvisions the physical presence and music of classic blues singer Bessie Smith, constrained by contemporary social norms and dismissed by some Black Arts writers as overly reminiscent of slavery-era hardships, as evidence of early black feminist accomplishment. Sanchez ties her investment in black women's political needs to 1960s black nationalism and revisions of traditional poetic forms. Cortez conceptualizes environmental abuses and misogyny as parallel practices, arguing for a feminism grounded in African culture as well as the history of socially conscious, avant-garde art. In her jazz-influenced sonnet sequences, Coleman links local and global experiences of inequality and injustice, finding analogies for the obstacles that writers of color face in her poetic subjects' daily hardships. Mullen herself develops the political connotations of academic and vernacular language in her poetry even as she highlights in her articles the accomplishments of lesser-known predecessors[22] and contemporaries.[23] The contrasting feminisms that she and her fellow jazz poets explore reflect the evolution of African-American feminist politics across the second half of the twentieth century and testify to the important work that continues to be written in post-jazz languages.

Conclusion: "Too Many Books For Our Eyes"; Future Politics, Future Poetries

A FEMINIST JAZZ POETICS ADDRESSES BOTH CREATIVE AND CRITICAL practices by interrogating the ways in which contemporary social and artistic movements marginalize women's art. Women have helped to shape the histories of both jazz and American experimental poetics, yet the public imaginary often perceives their work as a sideline to men's accomplishments. Black art and popular culture occupy a similarly vexed position in relation to the white mainstream, while many national feminist movements have overlooked the politics of black women's lives. The authors in this study, who find their experimental, jazz-based poetry triply marginalized in the context of race, gender, and artistic canon, seek to carve out spaces for the voices and perspectives absent from American literary histories. Their work's imbrication in this complex set of power relationships aligns their social and aesthetic philosophies with those of global theory; by interrogating social concerns that resonate beyond American borders, this poetry demonstrates the role that art can play in crossing, challenging, and unmaking cultural divisions. The poetry's formal strategies, which refuse the traditional confines of language, structure, and poetic form, echo its themes' transnational scope.

The work of all five poets in this study seeks to increase American awareness of feminist struggle outside the country's borders by under-lining the experiences, both contemporary and historical, of women marginalized through gender, race, cultural affiliation, sexuality, regional identity, and professional status. While they each cultivate a unique approach to experimental feminist poetics, Sherley Anne Williams,

Sonia Sanchez, Jayne Cortez, Wanda Coleman, and Harryette Mullen also share several compositional elements that can be identified as key strands in the history of radical black poetry traditions. Other African-American women poets have pursued similar projects—among them, Gwendolyn Brooks, Thulani Davis, Colleen McElroy, Carolyn Rodgers, and Elizabeth Alexander. However, the writers whose work I examine here have created techniques and modes of political expression that distinguish them from most of their contemporaries. Their poetry responds directly to traditions established within the history of white Western literature while accommodating the themes and concerns that persist in a post–Civil Rights America. They contribute to the ongoing history of experimental poetics through their development of new forms like the jazz elegy, the blues haiku, the jazz sonnet, and the jazz catalogue. Yet their sometimes fraught relationships to such artistic "schools" as the Black Arts Movement and the Language group indicate that they seek to imbue poetic forms with social meaning by referencing the real lives whose stories threaten to dissolve the boundaries of aesthetic tradition. Most of these writers also work within the American academy, or have done so at some point in their careers, using higher education as a forum in which not only to make wide-ranging political statements but also to critique the inequalities that such institutions continue to support.

The five subjects of this study also recognize a common history undergirding their work. Their poetry owes creative and political debts to 1960s and 1970s Black Arts writers, while the history of 1920s classic-blues singers like Bessie Smith and Ma Rainey inspires a palette of emotional tones, provides subject matter through which to explore feminist themes, and references an artistic tradition that their readers can immediately access. The work also responds directly to contemporary developments in the history of jazz and blues music, articulating the same kinds of social and compositional concerns that have preoccupied musicians themselves. Like the history of jazz, the history that forms the background to these poems inevitably contains fissures, gaps, and other markers of incompleteness. The relatively coherent narrative of creation discussed in Chapters 1, 2, and 3, which examine 1920s blues, bebop, and free jazz as influences in the poetry, fragments in Chapters 4 and 5. This dissolution does not signal a lack of coherence; rather, it provides evidence of the post-jazz atmosphere in which these poets invent. Their poetry evolves through an ongoing incorporation of compositional techniques, tributes, and references to the conflicted history of the music's most famous and little-known performances and performers, producing a vocabulary that interpellates jazz fans, political organizers, and students of experimental poetics. This post-jazz language reframes persistent questions of racial and gender inequality in order to offer alternate ways of seeing and working in the world.

This interest in jazz performance fosters distinctive linguistic innovations in the poetry that both foreground poetry's potential for live performance and critique the restrictive conventions of mainstream communication. All five poets make regular use of the lyric voice, for instance, distinguishing their innovations' rhetorical capacity from the apolitical compositions of some late postmodernist writers, yet speakers' voices regularly fragment under the pressure of varying perspectives and social experiences. These multiply registering lyric voices gesture at the complexity of black women's lives and illustrate the contradictory subject-positions that can result from social invisibility. Innovations like these tend to emerge in creative and social contexts specific to each writer; I also discuss other poets, such as Amina Baraka, Ntozake Shange, Margaret Walker, Patricia Spears Jones, and Patricia Smith, who cultivate similar dimensions in less substantial bodies of work. In the case of Wanda Coleman, I found no other writer creating such a varied oeuvre while also experimenting with the evolution of a form over time, as in the development of the *American Sonnets* series; thus, her chapter contains no discussions of contextually similar writers.[1]

Each poet's work in this study also engages critically with the feminist movements contemporary to her writing. Here I interpret feminism as a mode of analysis relevant both to their poetry's formal jazz experiments and to their efforts in redefining jazz discourse as a valid arena for women's work. These writers' commitment to addressing social problems on both local and international levels aligns the broader scope of their work with global or transnational feminism, a politics that accommodates multiple feminisms rather than a unitary approach to social critique.[2] Their attention to a political agenda that looks outward from the local to the international identifies what I argue should be some of the future goals of this particular branch of black experimental poetics: to understand oppressive circumstances that recur in different countries as historically situated and motivated by common prejudices; to acknowledge the importance of personal experience and community in political organizing; to address the economic underpinnings of ongoing social inequalities; and to foster feminist solidarity across ethnic, cultural, and artistic boundaries. As Bonnie G. Smith has pointed out, feminists who claim distinct cultural identities have united through common experiences of sexism, racism, and exclusionary nationalism (3). While some American feminists fail to recognize the relative privilege of their positions as members of the First World / North, U.S. women of color have long sought out solidarity with women "under siege" in other countries

(Dutt 306–7). The resulting political networks draw on local community organizations as well as transnational identifications (Moghadam 196). Cortez's and Coleman's work in particular highlights, through references to global experiences of inequality, the frustrations that women face in marginalized American communities as well as the desperate need to make their situations public.

Like the poets in this study, theorists of global or transnational feminisms come from a variety of professional backgrounds, which include social activism, political theory, and literature, among others. Both groups argue that the terms of such feminisms ought to be carefully negotiated. Chandra Talpade Mohanty famously designated "feminism without borders," for example, as an appropriate conceptual phrase that acknowledges both the remnants of social control in modern societies and existing possibilities for future political autonomy; her formulation notes the real presence of borders while "envision[ing] change and social justice work across these lines of demarcation and division" (1, 2). Such feminisms, which describe the many divergences among women's experiences while "building feminist solidarities across the divisions of place, identity, class, work, belief, and so on" (Mohanty 250), support the notion of transnational work, the term that I find most useful in identifying the kinds of political practice toward which these poets point their readers. Floya Anthias usefully defines such feminist solidarity, one that black women jazz poets help to build, in terms of "translocational positionality," a political awareness influenced by "the interplay of different locations relating to gender, ethnicity, race, and class (among others), and their at times *contradictory* effects" (275–76; original italics). Elora Halim Chowdhury argues as well that "the discourse of global feminism . . . is nonetheless inadequately accountable to issues of difference and inequality among communities of women within the US border" (53). Her reservations about the history and rhetorical associations of global feminism indicate that transnational work must analyze local and international communities using the same terms and concerns. Valentine M. Moghadam defines transnational feminist networks as organizations that "unite women from three or more countries around a common agenda" (4); the politics that African-American feminist jazz poets articulate follows a similar organization.[3]

Transnational feminisms are predicated on the diverse contributions that geographically distant yet allied communities make to large-scale social change. Activist Charlotte Bunch suggests that, in order to conceptualize feminisms internationally, one must understand the problems that such movements address in terms of human rights. Arguing that "the idea that all people have fundamental human rights has become one of the most powerful concepts that disenfranchised groups have used to legitimize their struggles" (138), Bunch proposes adopting the base elements of the 1948 Universal Declaration of Human Rights as the foundation for a global feminist manifesto. This document defines human rights as inalienable, belonging to every person; universal, mandating "the incorporation of women- and gender-aware perspectives"; and indivisible, ensuring that all rights are equally important and interdependent. Bunch points out that this last element "also challenges the historic Western bias in favor of civil and political rights over social and economic rights" (139–41). Bunch's ideas suggest that transnational feminisms specifically interrogate the intersections between local and international concerns, a principle that underlies many of the poems examined in this book. Allison Weir notes, for instance, that feminists who identify with global communities practice a solidarity that grows out of social and political critiques as well as "particular identifications with each other" (115), while Elora Chowdhury advocates joining economic critiques to the discourses of sexual autonomy and gender equality already familiar to feminist activists (64). Such patterns of connection can help to draw together feminists from diverse backgrounds without erasing the complex differences among them.

Most theorists agree that transnational feminisms must address economic concerns; these poems also relate economic hardships to demonstrate the real effects that social inequalities have on women's day-to-day lives. The basic structures of international capitalism—articulated through institutions such as the World Trade Organization, "free trade" agreements like North American Free Trade Agreement (NAFTA), and the movement of goods and services through vastly different national economies—repeatedly leave women and women's work in positions of disadvantage. These conditions point to the conclusion that "capitalism is seriously incompatible with feminist visions of social and economic justice" (Mohanty 9). The mid-1980s, the period during which all five of these poets were actively publishing, witnessed at least three developments that motivated shifts in the scope and goals of transnational feminisms: the emergence of neoliberal economics, the decline in prominence of welfare states, and an increase in popular fundamentalist thought (Moghadam 6). These changes in international economic climates continue to shape feminist movements, whose members find common ground in shared economic realities. They argue that to accurately conceptualize a feminism, or feminisms, that can tackle issues of economic privilege means to look at the experiences of marginalized women in more than one national context (Mohanty 231)—a perspective that these poets pursue. Their work manifests an awareness of the bias toward First World/North experience that exists in much feminist theorization; instead, they look outward toward parallels between the experiences of marginalized American communities and those of Third World / South communities.

I identify these poets' politics as transnationally feminist because transnational feminisms pay close attention to the ways in which social, personal, professional, and political factors shape women's identities. Allison Weir suggests that such identities ought to be understood as "*ethical-political*: focused on meanings, values, and struggles for change," as well as grounded in historical patterns of change and inflected by relationships with others (118; original italics). Catherine Eschle attributes the emergence of feminist activity within developing democratic movements across the world to women's increased awareness of three conditions: a dearth of representation within the system, "the subordination of women within leftist movements supposedly offering an alternative to liberal democracy," and the internal shortcomings of feminist movements themselves (5). While Eschle acknowledges that global political movements may fall prey to ideological generalizations, she insists that a global perspective enables women to perceive the "gendered dimensions" of every aspect of society (187–89). Power is held globally but "also takes diverse forms that interact in context-specific ways" (Eschle 204). A politics of location like this one understands feminist organization as simultaneous, multiply situated, and ongoing. The regionalist themes that Williams, Sanchez, Cortez, Coleman, and Mullen explore enable them to articulate feminist concerns on several situational and ideological levels at once.

Literature that considers the economic consequences of large-scale capitalist structures as a factor in literary composition and production can highlight the potential advantages of transnational feminist consciousness for its readers. Susan Sniader Lanser argues that the discipline of comparative studies needs to examine "the relationship between the production (and reception) of literature and various forms of global power—political, linguistic, economic, cultural" (296). Literary analyses sensitive to transnational feminist concerns should take into account the ways in which "individuals [are] constituted in culture—in nation, gender, class, race, ethnicity, religion, ideology, sexuality" via a "dialectical engagement" with these categories (Lanser 298). Such a dialectic may help to represent a multiplicity of viewpoints without establishing a hierarchy among them. Regionalist themes recur in African-American women's jazz poetry in part because of the dialectic and exchange between the local and the global that transnational feminisms assume. As Chandra Mohanty points out, "the local and the global are not defined in terms of physical geography or territory but exist simultaneously and constitute each other" (242); the connections and relationships between national and cultural identities provide political substance.

Each of the poets in this study provides a unique solution to the problem of how to couch feminist statement most effectively, though the topical focuses of their work in each case highlight an issue that has been central to transnational feminisms. Sherley Anne Williams examines some of the most damaging, stereotypical representations of black female bodies in her poems about classic-blues singer Bessie Smith. Sonia Sanchez's attention to the politics of the Black Power movement, as well as her eventual repudiation of the movement's misogyny, points to her belief that work within institutions provides an ideal ground for feminist critique. Jayne Cortez employs the familiar themes of surrealism and the blues in order to argue for the relevance of environmental concerns to feminist politics. Wanda Coleman both acknowledges and condemns the global patterns of economic inequality that have shaped black women's social experience by privileging marginalized geographies, interrogating the economic conditions and urban spaces that reveal a new, if neglected, forum for poetics. Harryette Mullen takes up the complex textual techniques of Language-based poetries and African-American linguistic traditions in order to interrogate the languages that help to constitute women's positions in art and society. The sources of each poet's feminisms—the body, social institutions, environment, language, and geography—find expression in the historical associations between African-American music and the people who perform it. This work's post-jazz dimensions exist in the specific transformations of language and historical representation that jazz-inflected discourse enables; such communication tools signify a dynamic, restructured political landscape aligned with the humanist responsibilities of transnational feminisms.

These writers' investment in the intricate connotations of political and aesthetic languages also suggests that they share some social concerns with advocates of third-wave feminist thought. Barbara Arneil distinguishes the third wave of feminism from earlier movements by noting its focus on differences *among* women, its real-world location in the material experiences of women's bodies as well as their historical positions as social outsiders, and its understanding of identity categories as relational, not binary (186–87). Third-wave feminists also conceptualize knowledge, power, and identity as nonhierarchical—instead, they function within what Arneil calls "the fluid *relation* between different identities, people and spheres" (219; original italics). Williams, Sanchez, Cortez, Coleman, and Mullen invoke multiple knowledge sources and social allegiances in their writing, a strategy that illuminates the third-wave feminist belief in writing as a practice of hybridity (Arneil 216).

I conclude, therefore, that African-American women jazz poets' social arguments grow out of any number of contextual factors, filter through the multiple perspectives that hybrid texts make possible, and often—as they themselves often acknowledge—exist at odds with other interpretations. These qualities echo the notion of identity that third-wave feminists propose, one predicated on fluidity, multiple identity factors, and contradiction (Arneil 206). In this work, language, history, society, environment, and the body constitute not categories of analysis but material influences on poetic personae. A feminist jazz poetics, by nature communal and improvisatory, defies traditional conceptualizations of women as isolated participants in avant-garde literary movement. Even in the midst of the twenty-first century's technologically driven proliferation of media outlets, jazz references continue to articulate the artistic innovations and social concerns that motivate feminist poets. At the same time, the enduring yet basic inequalities that their work insists upon revealing suggest that, for the unprepared reader, there may yet be "too many books for our eyes."

Notes

INTRODUCTION

1. In his essay on jazz and gender, David Chinitz cites an unpublished poem by T. S. Eliot, "The Smoke That Gathers Blue and Sinks," from 1911 (322); however, I find Lindsay's poem more useful as a historical marker because it anticipates the cultural racism that Harlem Renaissance and Black Arts writers would challenge in the coming decades. Lindsay also published several poems in the 1920s that either used jazz as a descriptor or criticized the music (Feinstein, *Bibliographic Guide* 58).

2. Kenneth Rexroth has written insightfully about the origins of jazz poetry as a performance art. He defines it as "the reciting of suitable poetry with the music of a jazz band" in which "[t]he voice is integrally wedded to the music and, although it does not sing notes, is treated as another instrument" (69). Like many theorists of jazz-influenced literature, he argues that jazz poetry deserves serious attention from knowledgeable audiences and artists (71). Though Rexroth describes an important stage in the emergence of jazz-poetic work, my analysis in this book will not extend to the kinds of performance on which he focuses.

3. Feinstein cites Etheridge Knight, Vachel Lindsay, Arthur Guiterman, E. E. Cummings, Carl Sandburg, DuBose Heyward, Mina Loy, Hart Crane, Langston Hughes, Sterling Brown, Melvin Tolson, William Carlos Williams, the Beat poets, Amiri Baraka, William Matthews, Yusef Komunyakaa, Hayden Carruth, Michael Harper, and Al Young as the genre's major innovators and participants in many of its ideological debates.

4. Henderson discusses these elements again in a lecture published in *Callaloo* in 1982, "The Blues as Black Poetry."

5. Henderson elaborates upon this last concept in a later article, "Worrying the Line: Notes on Black American Poetry." Here he explains "worrying the line" as "essentially a kind of analytical play on words, on parts of words, on qualities of words" (69). This broader conception alludes to both the social practices this technique embodies and the vocal melismas used to "worry" a pitch in gospel or blues music. Henderson also labels the call-and-response patterns of gospel music a kind of "worrying the line" that strengthens the sense of communal interaction essential to spiritually inspired performance ("Worrying" 72).

6. Like Feinstein, Nielsen claims that innovations in black experimental poetics have often paralleled new developments in black music; today, such innovations underline the historical importance of revision and improvisation in African-American art. Nielsen also cautions that divisions between the categories of song, chant, and poetry should be avoided in favor of Amiri Baraka's notion of the "changing same": the repetition with a difference that occurs in both black experimental poetics and black musical innovation (*Black Chant* 30). Nielsen proposes Amiri Baraka, Harold Carrington, A. B. Spellman, Oliver Pitcher, Cecil Taylor, and Joseph Jarman as representative examples of the tradition of "black chant," a concept that addresses the network of connections between oral and written traditions in African-American poetry.

7. Although Mackey's list of experimental poets differs from Nielsen's and includes writers of the African diaspora—Clarence Major, Kamau Brathwaite, and Wilson Harris—he employs similar methods by which to link these poets under the rubric of "discrepant engagement."

8. Feinstein's, Mackey's, and Nielsen's works are preceded by Charles O. Hartman's more New Critical theorization in *Jazz Text: Voice and Improvisation in Poetry, Jazz, and Song* (1991) that narrative voice functions as a key formal link between jazz music and jazz-inflected texts. Although Hartman considers how both jazz performance and poetic composition enable artists to claim social authority, his ideas focus on a somewhat narrowly defined conception of voice (4). Many critics, including both Nielsen and Mackey, have cautioned against the essentialist trap of associating African-American literature exclusively with oral traditions, rather than understanding black writing as both orally and textually influenced.

9. Both Matthew B. White and Elisabeth D. Kuhn have analyzed the gender politics of blues lyrics. White argues that "[t]hrough their music, bluesmen were able to exert power and control. They could exercise the prerogatives and privileges of a man in a patriarchal society through song" (22–23), while Kuhn suggests that the largely male authors of blues lyrics could "recreate, even within the formulaic constraints of the blues form, the same strategies that are found in real-life requests" (529). This sense of unequal gender relations within traditional blues lyrics may also provide another motivation for women jazz poets' politicized messages.

10. Namely, Sascha Feinstein and Yusef Komunyakaa's *The Jazz Poetry Anthology* (1991) and *The Second Set: The Jazz Poetry Anthology Volume 2* (1996), and Art Lange and Nathaniel Mackey's *Moment's Notice: Jazz in Poetry and Prose* (1993). Jim Stephens also edited *Bright Moments: A Collection of Jazz Poetry* (1980), while Kevin Young more recently collected the work of several emerging poets and fiction writers who draw on jazz materials in *Giant Steps: The New Generation of African American Writers* (2000).

CHAPTER 1

1. Angela Davis also notes that, while "at times Bessie Smith was a victim of male violence," on the other hand "she would not hesitate to hurl violent threats—which she sometimes carried out—at the men who betrayed her" (37).

2. Writing about the poetry of Lucille Clifton, Ajuan Maria Mance argues that "African American women poets have used their representations of black women's lives as a tool for renegotiating popular assumptions about identity and race that have limited the category of woman to female subjects who are white" (123). She calls Clifton's depictions of black women in her poems moments of "excessive display" in which "she and other women poets writing against the hegemony of the mainstream highlight the role of process—of making—in those institutions and identity categories most commonly understood as absolute" (135). Williams creates similar moments in her Bessie Smith pieces; she attaches her work's social messages to a time period, the 1920s, that anticipated future feminist movements in activism and the arts.

3. See my discussion of Maulana Karenga's attitude toward the blues in Chapter 2.

4. The strength of the relationship between Williams and Brown is underscored by the warm personal tone of an article that Williams published in *Black American Literature Forum* on the occasion of Brown's death, "Remembering Prof. Sterling A. Brown, 1901–1989."

5. The fact that the Bessie Smith poems form the largest subsection of her poetic oeuvre suggests that Williams uses her voice to speak for disadvantaged women. Although Smith is less well-known for the economic peaks and declines of her personal and professional lives, these experiences shaped her life as substantially as did her musical abilities (Albertson 24).

6. This title comes from the lyrics to a traditional African-American spiritual, "O Mary Don't You Weep," the first verse of which runs as follows: "O Mary don't you weep / Tell Martha not to moan / Pharaoh's army drowned in the Red Sea / O Mary don't you weep / Tell Martha not to moan."

7. Howard Zinn cites the growing development of "black capitalism," in which formerly radical black leaders were given business loans and advantageous political positions by white corporate giants, as a factor in black women's increasingly vocal objections to patriarchy in the early 1970s. Women laboring under the triple stigma of racial, gender, and economic minority more pointedly articulated the false consciousness of black capitalism (Zinn 456–57). Williams's characterization of black female authorship suggests her ideological roots in these currents of 1970s social discourse.

8. In their introduction to *Breaking Boundaries: New Perspectives on Women's Regional Writing* (1997), Sherrie A. Inness and Diana Royer posit that

the primary value of such writing lies in its "decentered perspective of the dominant culture's values," a perspective that "highlights cultural and geographical differences and makes its readers consider how these differences have shaped their lives and the lives of others" (2). The definition of regionalism that Inness and Royer propose emphasizes both an "investment in community" and an examination of identity in terms of "sectors based on class, gender, race, politics, religion, and a myriad of other constructs" (7). I find this combination of perspectives originating in marginalized social discourses, community, and the complicated intersections of identity politics particularly well-suited to the themes and agenda of Williams's work.

9. The truck driver drove away without bothering to investigate what had happened. A doctor on his way to go fishing happened to be the next person who appeared on the scene; he examined Smith, but before she could be moved to a hospital, another car crashed into the back of the doctor's vehicle. Two ambulances were summoned; one left bearing Smith and the other the young white couple who had been the third car's passengers. Commentators disagree about whether Smith was denied admittance at a white hospital in Clarksdale before entering the town's "colored" institution (Albertson 219–23).

10. Edward Albee's *The Death of Bessie Smith* (1959), a play that takes as truth the story that Smith was denied treatment and died before reaching a hospital that would admit her, secured her place as a personality of legendary importance in white representations of race. Angela Y. Davis chose Smith as one of the three central figures in her study of classic blues singers and their later impact on black feminists, *Blues Legacies and Black Feminism*. She has also been the subject of or mentioned in more than 50 jazz poems (Feinstein, *Bibliographic Guide* 184–85).

11. The personification of food items under the rubric of a romantic tale also recalls the associations between food and sexuality that recur in the lyrics to many blues tunes.

12. The UC–San Diego Alumni Association named Williams Distinguished Professor of the Year in 1987 ("In Memoriam" 64). She received several awards for her publications, including a Caldecott Award and a Coretta Scott King Book Award for a children's book, *Working Cotton* (1992). At least two authors claim that she received an Emmy award for a performance of poems from *Some One Sweet Angel Chile* ("In Memoriam" 64; "Sherley Anne Williams"), although I have not been able to confirm this via any official Emmy publication. At a UCSD conference entitled "Black Women Writers and the 'High Art' of Afro-American Letters," she was the guest of honor as her colleagues celebrated the twelfth anniversary of the publication of her only novel, *Dessa Rose* ("In Memoriam" 64; M. Henderson 766). In addition, she attended the 1994 Furious Flower conference at James Madison University, an African-American literature conference honoring the life and work of Gwendolyn Brooks, as a distinguished poet and scholar (Gabbin, "Introduction" 2).

13. See, however, "The Lion's History: The Ghetto Writes B[l]ack," in which Williams criticizes some white critics' tendency to dominate discussions of black authorship, concluding not that black authors ought only to write about black texts, but that they should put forward their own analyses of white-authored works as well (245, 248–49). Black women writers are best suited for the creation of such new literary histories, since in their works they both "chart the journey toward wholeness" and "critique hegemonic historical and literary discourses" in order to "extend the boundaries of those discourses to include race and gender experience" (Williams, "Lion's History" 263). Williams's attention to such patriarchal power relationships suggests that she was aware of the shortcomings that exist in some male Black Arts writers' perspectives.

14. The book's conclusions about the value of such a "streetman" also perpetuate the stereotypical portrayals of African-American life that Lorenzo Thomas criticizes in *Extraordinary Measures*. He argues that rather than presenting "pimps and gamblers" as "the only glamorous models for youngsters in the black community," cultural critics should draw public attention to the accomplishments of black artists, musicians, and athletes (141). Williams's poetry does exactly that, even if her criticism betrays other biases.

15. See my discussion of Black Arts politics in Chapter 2, in the section entitled "Black Arts, Blues Feminism, and the New Haiku."

16. Smith enjoyed a long-term but tumultuous working relationship with this niece, who oversaw her business and personal life for many years.

17. In 1929, for example, back in the recording studio after a hiatus, Smith produced what Albertson labels "three of her most blatantly pornographic songs," "I'm Wild About That Thing," "You've Got to Give Me Some," and "Kitchen Man" (154). The lyrics to all three of these songs contain thinly disguised sexual metaphors; the second and third both rely for their impact on comparisons between eating and sexual behavior. The third verse of "You've Got to Give Me Some," for instance, features the lines "Sweet as candy in a candy shop, it's just your sweet, sweet lollipop" and "I love all-day suckers, you gotta gimme some" (Davis, *Blues Legacies* 358). "Kitchen Man" ends with "Oh, his baloney's really worth a try / Never fails to satisfy" (Davis, *Blues Legacies* 305). Angela Y. Davis's *Blues Legacies and Black Feminism* includes an appendix that is the only complete source of the lyrics to all songs recorded by these three singers.

18. Williams uses this strategy again in another of the Bessie Smith poems whose source can be traced to Albertson's book. "[A]fter a visit to jack," the eighth of these poems, captures the singer's thoughts as she walks home from the hospital where she has presumably been visiting her second husband, Jack Gee. Albertson describes Bessie meeting Gee, then a night watchman in Philadelphia, in 1922, and then preparing to go to dinner with him. Gee became involved in a "shooting incident" on their date, and Bessie spent the next five weeks visiting him at the hospital before moving in with him (Albertson 40).

CHAPTER 2

1. In this section and the following one, I am conceptualizing the Black Power and Black Arts movements as ideologically interrelated but methodologically separate undertakings. Eugene Perkins, in his article for Floyd Barbour's anthology *The Black Seventies,* states that black "art can be kept relatively sovereign from subversion if we keep in mind its relationship to the Black Power Concept" (95). Addison Gayle's introduction to *The Black Aesthetic* argues in part that "[t]he serious black artist of today is at war with the American society" because he/she needs to define a national identity separate from that assigned by the United States (xvii, xxii). What is at stake in a black social movement like Black Arts is not the aesthetic value of a piece of art, but "how much more beautiful has the poem, melody, play, or novel made the life of a single black man?" (Gayle xxiii). In spite of Gayle's reductive gender politics, he makes the important point that Black Arts participants and theorists understood the movement's affiliations with Black Power organizations like the Black Panther Party and the Nation of Islam as essential to the movement's unity. See also Maulana Karenga's famous essay in *The Black Aesthetic,* "Black Cultural Nationalism" (32–38). However, I argue that Sanchez's participation in Black Power groups and Black Arts activities reflects two different stages in her professional development as an experimental poet and black feminist.

2. James G. Spady provides the text of Sanchez's earliest published poem, "Life Is Not a Dream," in his article, "Black Jazz Daughter When She Is Singing: The Historical Blues Journey of a Sonia Sanchez" (18). Written while she was studying under Louise Bogan, the poem does not feature her later formal innovations but its rhetoric suggests a developing political consciousness: "Life is a face, your face / Scabbed by white air" (lines 8–9).

3. While describing this process in 1985, Sanchez adopts a popular catchphrase of the 1970s women's movement: the specifically feminist ethic of her poetry developed more slowly than its broader activist slant, and this phrase suggests that her feminism emerged more publicly after the decline of Black Power. Elaine Brown, onetime chair of the Black Panther Party, describes her own adoption of feminist principles as a relatively late development in her political life. She had dismissed feminism as "an idea reserved for white women" until her confrontations with misogynistic practices in the Party spurred a realization of black women's particular need for self-actualization (367–68).

4. In *Placing Sorrow: A Study of the Pastoral Elegy Convention from Theocritus to Milton* (1976), Ellen Zetzel Lambert states that the traditional elegy provides not a "*solution* to the questions raised by death but rather a *setting* in which those questions may be posed, or better, 'placed'" (xiii; original italics). Poets do not conceive of such a setting as imaginary but rather as "real because it can contain pain and suffering" (Lambert xv).

Grief's natural setting also signals that it is both universal and concrete (Lambert xvii). Celeste Marguerite Schenck, writing in a similar vein, calls the elegy "a gesture toward the past" (7) and a means of reversing "the course of loss by ensuring the corpse's resuscitation" in a healthily formalized memorial or tribute (11). Schenck also conceptualizes the elegy landscape as "barren" or "deserted," reflecting nature's absorption in the work of mourning (14). Many twentieth-century elegies, particularly those that mourn specific historical moments, do not fit the traditional pastoral mold.

5. Sanchez frequently incorporates slash marks within the lines of her poems, calling them moments of "emphasis" or "stoppage" (Melhem, "Will and Spirit" 86). When I quote lines that contain slash marks, I will indicate that they are intrinsic to the piece by eliminating the space that usually precedes a slash mark dividing two lines of poetry. I have also preserved periods that appear in the poems.

6. "Liberation Poem" appears in two publications: a broadside with cover illustration by Shirley Woodson and Sanchez's second collection of poetry, *We a BaddDDD People*, with cover illustration by Ademola Olugebefola. Both versions were published in 1970 by Dudley Randall's Broadside Press. Although small formal differences exist between the two versions, every word is the same. My references come from the second version.

7. By 1970, Sanchez would also have been familiar with Amiri Baraka's *Blues People* (1963). She greatly admires Baraka's work, which she mentions in several interviews. In contrast to Karenga, Baraka notes, "I cite the beginning of blues as one beginning of American Negroes" (xii). He interprets the blues as a tool for defining black people as Americans, not slavery-era "immigrants."

8. See also the third section of "Memorial," a poem from *Home Coming*. This piece is addressed to "rev pimps" and begins with a command to the speaker's "Sisters" to stop giving up their bodies to their male revolutionary counterparts. Sanchez draws attention here to the willingness of some women—white and black—to sleep with Black Power leaders during the 1960s and 1970s as part of their "responsibility" to the movement. She shares a feminist condemnation of this practice with other black feminist writers of the period, including Michele Wallace in *Black Macho and the Myth of the Superwoman* and Elaine Brown in *A Taste of Power: A Black Woman's Story*. Frenzella Elaine De Lancey also reads this poem in terms of Sanchez's developing feminism, citing it as an example of the way in which she "refused to turn away from the contradiction inherent in the exploitation of women within a movement based on the liberation of Black people" ("Sonia Sanchez's *Blues Book*" 166).

9. In *Taste of Power*, Elaine Brown provides an autobiographical account of the events leading up to her assumption of the chairmanship of the Black Panther Party after minister of defense Huey P. Newton was forced into exile. The Black Power movement gave Brown a strong sense of

identity and political purpose, but she repeatedly confronted examples of women's subordination to men. At the first meeting of Karenga's US Organization that she attended, she was told that women ate only after all the male "warriors" had been fed (109), and both male and female leaders stated that women's abilities as seductresses and mothers would likely be required by the revolution (136–37; 189). However, at an early Black Power event in 1967, Brown read a poem deriding the common practice of men coaxing women into their beds with an invocation of their "revolutionary duty" (123). After the Black Panther Party split into factions loyal to Eldridge Cleaver, former minister of information, and Huey Newton, she remained by Newton's side, labeling Cleaver a mere rapist (225). Sanchez herself, asked to review Cleaver's memoir *Soul on Ice* for *Negro World* after he got out of prison in 1969, dismissed him as a rapist and "hustler" and never saw her article in print (Reich 81).

10. Hundreds of Coltrane poems exist. Some of the most shattering examples include Amiri Baraka's "AM/TRAK;" Jayne Cortez's "How Long Has Trane Been Gone?;" Michael Harper's "Dear John, Dear Coltrane" and "Here Where Coltrane Is;" Nathaniel Mackey's "John Coltrane Arrived with an Egyptian Lady;" Haki Madhubuti's "Don't Cry, Scream;" William Matthews's "Blues for John Coltrane, Dead at 41;" and A. B. Spellman's "John Coltrane: An Impartial Review" and "Did John's Music Kill Him?" For a comprehensive list of Coltrane poems published through 1997, see Feinstein's *A Bibliographic Guide to Jazz Poetry*, pp. 115–20.

11. Some jazz elegies, such as Michael Harper's "Dear John, Dear Coltrane," also describe specific details of the loved one's life leading up to the death.

12. According to Kimberly Benston, Sanchez wrote "a/coltrane/poem" after "witnessing a particularly moving performance of 'My Favorite Things' by Alice and John Coltrane near the end of his life" (157). The poem has retained an aura of revelation; the first time Sanchez read it in public, she was surprised by the lasting, transformative effect the piece had on her overall performance style (Benston 158).

13. Coltrane preferred discussing abstract concepts of truth and spirituality over current political issues with interviewers. These conversations imply that he conceived of jazz as a positive, albeit vaguely defined, social force. With August Blume, he stated that "[w]hen I saw there were so many religions and kind of opposed somewhere to the next and so forth . . . it screwed up my head . . . I just couldn't believe that just one guy could be right." As far as his music was concerned, he commented to Blume that "[a]ll musicians are striving to get as near perfection as they can get. That's truth there, you know" (qtd. in Porter 258, 259). Kofsky assigns political immediacy to Coltrane's work by pointing to the links between Coltrane and Malcolm X: "The very fact that the musician and the agitator . . . alike became folk-heroes to younger black-nationalist radicals (and not a few whites as well) suggests that profound similarities may

lie concealed beneath undeniable, but perhaps superficial, differences" (431). Coltrane also told Kofsky, "I want to be the force which is truly for good" (451).

14. Some of the earliest broadsides published in the United States were elegies; colonists often posted poetic tributes to deceased loved ones in public spaces (Sullivan 14). This fact draws a surprising connection between Sanchez's own evolving "literary activism" and the country's first examples of creative publication.

15. Julius E. Thompson notes in *Dudley Randall, Broadside Press, and the Black Arts Movement in Detroit, 1960–1995* (1999) that Sanchez was one of only six black women poets who was featured in *Black Poetry: A Supplement to Anthologies Which Exclude Black Poets*, which Randall edited in 1969 (45). Broadside Press played a significant role in promoting Sanchez's career, along with those of Haki Madhubuti, Nikki Giovanni, and Etheridge Knight (Thompson 163).

16. In recognition of her work as teacher, activist, and writer, Sanchez has received honors that include a PEN Writing Award (1969), a National Endowment for the Arts Award (1978–1979), Smith College's Tribute to Black Women Award (1982), the Lucretia Mott Award of the Academy of Arts and Letters (1984), the Pennsylvania Governor's Award in the humanities (1989), and the Peace and Freedom Award from the Women International League for Peace and Freedom (1988) (Salaam, "Sonia Sanchez" 306; Thompson 200).

17. See, for example, Alim's description of her experiences at the 1999 Hip Hop Week Cipher in Philadelphia. After participating in the celebratory verbal performances, Sanchez commented on her relationship with the event's younger artists: "And it reminded me a great deal of when we also got up on the stages. I was one of the first poets who got up on the stage with a lot of men. And you had to hold your own. . . . And so when I see those young Sistas holding their own, you know, I smiiile" (20).

CHAPTER 3

1. The Firespitters' membership has varied over the years. In this performance, Cortez is accompanied by a drummer, a guitarist, and an electric bassist. On the basis of other accounts of the band, I assume that the drummer is Cortez's son Denardo Coleman, the guitarist is Bern Nix, and the bass player is Al MacDowell.

2. Cortez saw Chano Pozo and Dizzy Gillespie's band playing a gig at Los Angeles's Wrigley Field in 1948 (Nielsen, *Integral Music* 177). She first wrote her poetic tribute to Pozo for the 1980 Chano Pozo Music Festival at Dartmouth (Nielsen, *Integral Music* 180). Though her poem suggests a far-reaching network of musical affiliations and overlapping references, connections between artists also occurred quite close to home.

3. "I See Chano Pozo" appears in three of Cortez's poetry collections: *Firespitter* (1982), *Coagulations: New and Selected Poems* (1984), and *Jazz Fan Looks Back* (2002). My references come from the most recent version.

4. Three of Cortez's books of poetry—*Coagulations, Poetic Magnetic* (1991), and *Somewhere in Advance of Nowhere* (1996)—contain glossaries in which she defines non-English expressions and historical references used in the poems.

5. The term "scatology" refers to a personal or textual fixation on the processes of bodily excretion. For discussions of its use in literature, see, for example, Jeff Persels and Russell Ganim's *Fecal Matters in Early Modern Literature and Art: Studies in Scatology* (Aldershot, UK: Ashgate, 2004); Reinhold Kramer's *Scatology and Civility in the English-Canadian Novel* (Toronto and Buffalo: University of Toronto Press, 1997); and Michael West's *Scatology and Eschatology: The Heroic Dimensions of Thoreau's Wordplay* (Baltimore: Modern Language Association of American, 1974).

6. Some readers have commented on the homophobic tone of "Race," a poem in Cortez's first book, *Pissstained Stairs and the Monkeyman's Wares* (1969). In her first interview with D. H. Melhem, Cortez explains that she wrote the poem specifically for a gay friend and later had second thoughts about some of its implications ("Supersurrealist" 206–7). This example points to Cortez's continually shifting political and aesthetic approaches.

7. Her position as a black woman addressing environmental issues in the context of crimes against women naturally raises questions about the relevance of ecofeminist theory to the work of black feminists. How should women whose bodies are multiply delimited by race, class, sexuality, and gender pose an ecofeminist challenge to dominant paradigms? Gaard and Murphy assert that ecofeminism is inspired by "class exploitation, racism, colonialism, and neocolonialism" as well as by the exploitation of women and nature (3). Glynis Carr claims in her introduction to *New Essays in Ecofeminist Literary Criticism* (2000) that one of her anthology's "major axioms" is that "ecocriticism must practice multiculturalism" if it is to represent political concerns accurately (20). In his introduction to *The Greening of Literary Scholarship: Literature, Theory, and the Environment* (2002), editor Steven Rosendale argues that ecocriticism offers a theoretical space in which humans' relationships with one another and their environment can be changed. These changes take place through studying history, the production of texts, their consumption, and the ways in which theory itself is written and disseminated (Rosendale xxvii–xxviii). Although none of these ecofeminist texts focus on the intersecting categories of race, class, and economic situation, their references to the particular needs of minority women suggest that ecofeminist literary criticism has already begun to diversify its theoretical approach.

8. I derive my understanding of the term "interpellation" from Louis Althusser's ideas in *Lenin and Philosophy and Other Essays* (1971). In his famous essay "Ideology and Ideological State Apparatuses," Althusser posits that "ideology 'acts' or 'functions' in such a way that it 'recruits' subjects among the individuals (it recruits them all), or 'transforms' the individuals into subjects (it transforms them all) by that very precise operation which I have called *interpellation* or hailing" (174; original italics). I use "interpellation" to designate a process in which Cortez uses repeated historical and cultural references as a means of "recruiting" her audience to a more educated perspective on social conditions. Her inter-pellations extend the boundaries of reader-listeners' experience rather than reinforcing state-sanctioned beliefs.

9. In *The Drama of Nommo* (1972), Paul Carter Harrison defines *nommo* as "the power of the Word—spoken or gesticulated—which activates all forces from their frozen state in a manner that establishes concreteness of expression" by "fusing the material with the spiritual" (xx). Molefi Kete Asante also describes *nommo*, a concept that forms the basis of his study *The Afrocentric Idea* (1987), as "the generative and productive power of the spoken word" (17).

10. Under the rubric of "scarification"—a term that can refer to breaking up soil, making shallow cosmetic or medical cuts in the skin, or sharply criticizing someone ("Scarify")—this work compares contemporary social conditions unfavorably to African mythic discourses.

11. Mark C. Gridley defines a "riff" in *Jazz Studies: History and Analysis* (2000) as "short phrases" that are varied in repetition (44). In the course of the same discussion, he comments on the differences between West African call-and-response patterns and European performance strategies: "[O]ften the sound of the call is still in the air when the response begins. The two parts overlap. And sometimes the call begins again before the response is done, thereby overlapping once more. . . . It is the promi-nence of *overlapping* call and response, not merely call and response, that distinguishes West African and African American music from music elsewhere" (Gridley 48; original italics). Tony Bolden uses the term "riff chorus" to reference the repeated lines in this kind of dynamic, improvi-satory exchange.

12. Coleman's musical eclecticism sets him apart even among jazz musi-cians; he originated the "harmolodic" approach to jazz composition and became one of the progenitors of "free jazz." Don Cherry has defined harmolodics as "a profound system based on developing your ear along with your technical proficiency on your instrument" so that every note has the potential to become the tonic, the home key of the tune (qtd. in Litweiler 131). Ekkehard Jost describes free jazz as an illustration of "how tight the links between social *and* musical factors are" (9); its impetus comes from equally weighted "interaction between *all* the musicians in a group" (16; original italics). He also points out that "visual components have such a direct bearing on the music that the acoustical result on a

record . . . can reproduce only a part" of the original experience (14). These characteristics suggest one source for Cortez's later innovations in textual form and live performance.

13. Peter Niklas Wilson comments that Don Cherry considered Cortez a "musically sophisticated woman" (14). Wilson's biography of Coleman contains a full-length photograph of Cortez reading from her sixth published book, *Firespitter*. However, the caption reads only "Jayne Cortez, Ornette's wife, London 1986" (15), though this scene took place 22 years after they divorced.

14. Geoffrey Parrinder defines "Ife" in *African Mythology* (1982) as "wide," a word later joined with "Ile," "house," to designate "the most sacred city of the Yoruba people" (22).

15. One of the poems in Harryette Mullen's *Trimmings* also looks at the "feathers" and "bananas" of Baker's self-presentation, although Mullen contrasts her "intelligent body" with a "savage art" and a "primitive stage" only briefly (*Recyclopedia* 43).

16. My references come from the most recent published version, in *Jazz Fan*.

17. Thornton became an alcoholic and died in poverty after finding commercial success limited by her gender and race. Her two most popular songs, "Hound Dog" and "Ball and Chain," are now better known through covers performed by Elvis Presley and Janis Joplin (Dahl 178–79).

18. The members of the Firespitters for this recording include Al MacDowell on bass, guitarist Bern Nix, alto sax player Talib Kibwe, tenor sax player Frank Lowe, harmonica player Billy Branch, guitarist Carl Weathersby, Sarjo Kutayeh and Salieu Suso on kora, and Abdoulaye Epizo Bangoura and Denardo Coleman on drums.

19. "At a Certain Moment in History," a poem from *Somewhere in Advance of Nowhere*, portrays Aimé Césaire as a radical opposing colonialism through his poetry. Léon Damas and Léopold Sedar Senghor also appear as members of "the African rhythm section" (line 19).

20. In *What Is Surrealism?*, Breton explains several additional activities of surrealism: perceiving "interior reality and exterior reality as two elements in process of unification" (116), cultivating thought processes that occur outside of conscious reasoning (122), revealing the inherent falseness of cultural precepts (129), and grappling with *"the problem of human expression in all its forms"* (131; original italics).

21. There are only minor differences between the two published versions of "Grinding Vibrato." In the second, Cortez has substituted "woman" where "lady" appeared in the original, capitalized "Texas," added a few connecting words, and deleted two adjectives from line 21. All references to the poem will come from the second version because I assume that it represents Cortez's most recent vision of the piece.

22. Cortez included this piece in *Jazz Fan Looks Back*.

23. Tony Bolden provides a useful reading of the album's cover: "[A] voluptuous (white) woman appears as the central image of the photograph. Sitting with her back turned between two larger drums, her arms raised and her head tilted back, the woman's curvaceous body is an extension of the drum" ("All the Birds" 66–67). Reactions to both the album and the television show were varied. James Lincoln Collier dismissed the music in *Duke Ellington* (1987) as "pedestrian" (285), while in *Beyond Category: The Life and Genius of Duke Ellington* (1993) John Edward Hasse character- izes it as a "concept album" that displayed "humor and wit" (330, 333). Although A. H. Lawrence does not pass judgment on *Drum* in *Duke Ellington and His World* (2001), he notes that Ellington felt the work represented a major accomplishment (345). The story behind Ellington's "concept" was simple: "Madame Zajj" is "born on a Caribbean isle, goes (in the second part) to New Orleans, journeys (in the third) to New York, and finally, in a fanciful projection in the future, travels to the moon. In each location, Zajj meets a man named Joe, whom she affects, and then leaves him behind for the next man named Joe" (Hasse 330).

24. My references come from the second printed version of the poem, in *Jazz Fan Looks Back*. The only difference between the two is that lines 32 and 33 in the first version appear on the same line in the second.

25. The phrase "the chickens come home to roost" is popularly associated with Stokely Carmichael's speeches on Black Power. Malcolm X used these words during the question-and-answer portion of his December 1963 speech entitled "God's Judgment on White America" to explain the assassination of John F. Kennedy, Jr. This piece is included in his collection *The End of White World Supremacy: Four Speeches*, edited and introduced by Benjamin Goodman (New York: Merlin House, 1971). See also Sonia Sanchez's "right on: wite america," a poem from *We a BaddDDD People* that includes the lines "and chickens do / come home to roost" (lines 26–27).

26. Cortez has received the Before Columbus Foundation American Book Award (1980); two Creative Artists Public Service Awards (1973, 1981); two National Endowment for the Arts fellowships (1980, 1986); and a New York Foundation for the Arts award (1987). She has also served on advisory boards for PEN, the Poetry Society of America, the Coordinating Council of Literary Magazines, and New York City's Poets House. In this last venue, Cortez delivered a poetic tribute to Nicolas Guillén, Cuba's national poet, one year after he died (Melhem, "Supersurrealist" 182). Political commitments have included "her presidency of the Organization of Women Writers of Africa, her coordination of the Yari Yari International Conference of Women Writers of African Descent, NYU, the direction of the film *Yari Yari*, her organization of the 1999 international symposium 'Slave Routes: The Long Memory,' and her participation in the Round Table: Dialogue Among Civilizations at the United Nations Millennium Summit 2000" ("Jayne Cortez's Biography").

CHAPTER 4

1. Coleman experienced a similar controversy in 1997, when she reviewed Audre Lorde's collected works, noting some problematic aspects of the writing, and found herself boycotted by a group of black immigrant writers. However, far fewer readers reacted unfavorably to this review; she summarizes Lorde in her analysis as "flawed but still the genuine article" ("Black on Black" 148).

2. She notes, however, that after her staff won the Emmy, they all lost their jobs. She did not stay in touch with her former colleagues, deciding instead to pursue "literary" writing rather than popular-culture jobs (Juno and Vale 123). Since then, she has won critical recognitions of her work that include membership in the Open Door Program Hall of Fame (1975), a National Endowment for the Arts grant (1981–1982), a Guggenheim Fellowship for poetry (1984), the Harriette Simpson Arrow Prize for fiction (1990), and the Lenore Marshall Poetry Prize from the Academy of American Poets (1999). Her ninth book of poetry, *Mercurochrome*, was a finalist for the National Book Award for Poetry in 2001 (O'Mara 84; "Wanda Coleman"; Manheim). She wryly comments that this last experience in particular demonstrated the ideological disjunction that exists between working-class poets of color and the literary elite. On the stage at the NBA ceremony, she notes, "it felt strange to hear my name (I was a poetry finalist) called out from the podium by Steve Martin—a Hollywood celebrity, a comic actor. How ironic. . . . I had devoted my best writing life to the financial wasteland of poetry, working pink-collar jobs to feed my children, partly because there was no place in the Hollywood of the last thirty years of the twentieth century for me" ("Black on Black" 141).

CHAPTER 5

1. "Head Nigger In Charge."
2. See, for example, Bob Perelman's *The Marginalization of Poetry: Language Writing and Literary History* (Princeton, NJ: Princeton University Press, 1996). Alan Golding also admits that race and gender do not play significant roles in his study of institutional influences on canon formation in American poetry, *From Outlaw to Classic: Canons in American Poetry* (xvii). These omissions point to the uncoupling of poetics and politics that characterizes many critical discussions of twentieth-century experimental poetry.
3. Like Mullen, many critics identify an urgent need to recognize the long-standing tradition of experimental African-American poetry, which joins formal innovations with social critique. See, for instance, Allison Cummings's "Public Subjects" (3–4), Deborah Mix's "Tender Revisions" (65), and Aldon Nielsen's "African-American Prose Poems" (151).

4. See Ron Silliman's *The New Sentence* (1987) and *The L=A=N=G=U=A=G=E Book* (1984), edited by Bruce Andrews and Charles Bernstein, for two of the most prominent examples of this poet-critic duality.

5. My discussion of feminism and language does not include the political organizing growing out of a shared commitment to poetic composition that Alicia Suskin Ostriker examines in *Stealing the Language: The Emergence of Women's Poetry in America* (1986), or Luce Irigaray's notion of *l'écriture féminine*, which Montefiore describes as "women's fluidity and plurality of speech" (152). My interest here lies in the potential that linguistic structures hold for material critiques of women's social roles.

6. Mullen republished the poems from *Tree Tall Woman* as part of her 2002 collection *Blues Baby: Early Poems*. My references come from the later book.

7. Thomas has demonstrated a healthy respect for Mullen's work in his turn. In a *Callaloo* interview with Hermine Pinson, he admits that he "think[s] of her work in much the same way that I think of music." Her language experiments, which he describes as an evolution over the course of her books, have resulted in "a type of poem that not only presents the colloquial surface, but also demonstrates the process by which the colloquial language generates these phrases, which, in fact, represent points of view, ways of seeing" (Pinson 299). Thomas's critical work *Extraordinary Measures: Afrocentric Modernism and Twentieth-Century American Poetry* (2000) begins with a comparison between Mullen and Phillis Wheatley as an example of "the African presence still felt by an African American poet" (3). His chapter on contemporary work presents Mullen as an important experimental poet who combines historical tradition with a specifically African-American social perspective and improvisatory structural techniques (233–34).

8. Mullen describes one type of resistant orality as "sass," which she defines as "a form of signification, or verbal self-defense," often used by black women as a means of defusing potentially dangerous situations ("Runaway Tongue" 255).

9. Megan Simpson makes no mention at all of Mullen's work in *Poetic Epistemologies: Gender and Knowing in Women's Language-Oriented Writing* (2000), while Ann Vickery's *Leaving Lines of Gender: A Feminist Genealogy of Language Writing* (2000) alludes to Mullen only in passing. Although Vickery comments that "Mullen engaged with Language writing in the mid-eighties, just as it began attracting institutional attention," this aside appears alongside a nod to "identity politics and difference feminism" as represented in the work of Gloria Anzaldúa (9). Vickery acknowledges that considering form and cultural identity as discrete poetic categories presents theoretical problems; however, she does not extend her analysis to include the impact of race or sexuality on women's writing (8). Simpson presents an even briefer acknowledgment of the multiple social factors that shape women's experience, noting that

some critics have neglected "the historically specific social implications of race and sexuality" (5).

10. Articles and anthologies that investigate work by groups "on the margins" of even experimental American poetry movements have addressed some of these issues. One such anthology, *We Who Love to Be Astonished: Experimental Women's Writing and Performance Poetics* (2002), edited by Laura Hinton and Cynthia Hogue, begins by acknowledging the fundamental limitations of Language-inspired work that operates without reference to socially defined categories like race, gender, and sexuality. Their collection attempts to join in dialogue "critical essays on works by diverse, and diversely experimental, American women writers" (Hinton and Hogue 4).

11. *Trimmings, S*PeRM**K*T*, and *Muse & Drudge* have been collected in the volume *Recyclopedia* (2006). All subsequent references to the three books come from this volume.

12. Several critics discuss the racial politics of this poem. See also Elisabeth Frost's "Signifyin(g) on Stein" (n.p.), Cynthia Hogue's "Harryette Mullen's Revisionary Border Work" (88), Deborah Mix's "Tender Revisions" (66–68), and Juliana Spahr's *Everybody's Autonomy* (104–8).

13. The noun "stroll" in this phrase also carries multiple connotations: it can refer to a "light 'gig,'" a "task not requiring much effort," or, "in jazz, to rest while someone is doing a solo; to pause so two other instruments can work out a theme" (Major, *Juba to Jive* 453).

14. Silliman argues that sentences, as "units of writing" that articulate use-value and exchange-value, measure economic relations within society (78–79). The "new sentence," defined in contrast with hypotactic sentences, relies on grammar and punctuation as units of meter (88), functions within a paragraph as a line does within a poetic stanza, and is syntactically complete only with reference to itself (89). Syllogistic movement—drawing conceptual conclusions based on the content of preceding material—occurs only in relation to "preceding and following sentences," or to the level of the paragraph, not to a coherent linear narrative (Silliman 91).

15. Mullen employs a similar strategy in the organization of *Sleeping with the Dictionary*, which, as Jessica Lewis Luck points out, contains no poems whose titles begin with the letters I, U, and Y, though the alphabetically ordered table of contents lists at least one title beginning with each of the other letters in the alphabet. One of the book's poems, "Why You and I," explains the omission by suggesting that the book's themes disrupt the reader's usual notions of identity (Luck 357).

16. See also Quandra Prettyman's "Come Eat at My Table: Lives with Recipes," in which she uses her reading of cookbooks by African-American women to claim that "[t]he 'black intelligent woman' may conceal herself to avoid '[catching] hell,' but her subject is not the preparation of a meal but the racialized politics of food" (133). Rafia Zafar argues similarly in "Cooking Up a Past: Two Black Culinary Narratives"

that food writing highlights both "personal or communal identity" and "the twinned issues of black stereotyping and class" (74). Zafar also draws an explicit link between regional food consumption and colonialism in her reading of two eighteenth-century nationalist ballads, "The Proof of the Pudding: Of Haggis, Hasty Pudding, and Transatlantic Influence" (134–36). Both of these authors see food narratives as inherently political texts rather than as examples of cultural reportage.

17. In his *Dictionary of Afro-American Slang*, Clarence Major defines "jellyroll" as "one's lover, spouse" (a definition common to the 1890s–1900s) or "a term for the vagina" (1920s–40s). On the same page, he gives a definition for "jam": "to make exciting music; to have a good time socially; to 'party'" (70). The first half of my title for this section comes from the title of a Bessie Smith song, "Nobody in Town Can Bake a Sweet Jelly Roll Like Mine," written by Clarence Williams and Spencer Williams (Davis 321).

18. Mullen notes that her poetic style has been influenced by the complex wordplay and satirical humor of Fran Ross's 1974 novel *Oreo* (Myers). Oreo's mother uses this figure of speech, common elsewhere as well, to describe her wedding-night experience with her husband (F. Ross 12).

19. For a discussion of these stereotypes, see Hazel Carby's "Policing the Black Woman's Body in an Urban Context."

20. In an interview with Christopher Myers, Mullen admits to some early doubts about the public reception of this book's heavy reliance on wordplay: "[Since the publication of *Muse & Drudge*,] these audiences now all of a sudden are sitting in the same room, which was not happening before. That kind of changes things. So what I'm doing now is going to be weird and strange and I think some people may not like it. It's prose poems again. Most of them are based on word games. I don't know if I like some of them myself. And the voice, I don't know who it is. It's not me necessarily" (Myers).

21. Geneva Smitherman's *Talkin and Testifyin: The Language of Black America* (1977) discusses the toast as an example of language practices that can aid in expanding students' cultural literacy. She provides a lengthy version performed by a student on pages 224–27.

22. She discusses Melvin Tolson and comments on Nielsen's project in *Black Chant* in the interview with Farrah Griffin et al., and references Bob Kaufman, Lucille Clifton, Al Young, Melvin Tolson, and Jean Toomer in the interview with Cynthia Hogue, for example.

23. She focuses in particular on the work of Erica Hunt and Will Alexander, both contemporary experimental poets of color. See her "Hauling Up Gold from the Abyss: An Interview with Will Alexander" and "'A Collective Force of Burning Ink': Will Alexander's *Asia & Haiti*," both part of the issue of *Callaloo* featuring Will Alexander that Mullen edited. Her article on Hunt and Alexander, "'Incessant Elusives': The Oppositional Poetics of Erica Hunt and Will Alexander," argues that "both poets exist on the boundaries of mainstream aesthetics, black

aesthetics, and the aesthetics of a restless avant-garde, and they both engage each of these aesthetic formations and their respective writing practices with what Hunt has called 'oppositional poetics'" (207).

CONCLUSION

1. Nathaniel Mackey has also created substantial examples of a "form over time" that incorporates both experimental poetics traditions and specific cultural histories. He continues to write several ongoing series, including *Song of the Andoumboulou* (collected in *Eroding Witness* [1985], *School of Udhra* [1993], *Whatsaid Serif* [1998], and *Splay Anthem* [2006]) and *From a Broken Bottle Traces of Perfume Still Emanate* (collected in *Bedouin Hornbook* [1986], *Djbot Baghostus's Run* [1993], and *Atet A. D.* [2001]). These two series alone have developed over more than 20 years and incorporate African Dogon mythology alongside aesthetic philosophy and radical experiments in textual improvisation. The poetry's political agenda, although incisive, does not engage feminist concerns.

2. Valentine Moghadam makes the important point that transnational feminists critique neoliberal capitalism in the context of globalization movements, yet they do not necessarily oppose globalization. Rather, they seek to "reorient it from a *project of markets* to a *project of peoples*" (199; original italics). I do not reject "global" as a term that identifies specific kinds of feminist analysis, but I find that "transnational" more accurately describes the direct political contact that many writers and activists, including these poets, seek out.

3. Lisa G. Materson notes that African-American women historically have worked to foster transnational communities that support their movements to eradicate social inequalities. The International Council of Women of the Darker Races (ICWDR), for instance, linked black American women's experiences to those of colonized women across the globe, creating "pan-Africanist critiques about the relationship between racism and imperialism" (Materson 36). The black press also pursued this line of reasoning during World War II; several articles denounced the Allies' decision to fight on behalf of other countries' independence while black Americans were forced to live under discriminatory conditions (Materson 41).

BIBLIOGRAPHY

Abrahams, Roger. *Deep Down in the Jungle: Negro Narrative Folklore from the Streets of Philadelphia.* 1st rev. ed. Chicago: Aldine Publishing Company, 1970.

Adisa, Opal Palmer. "Undeclared War: African-American Women Explicating Rape." *Women's Studies International Forum* 15.3 (1992): 363–74.

Akmakjian, Hiag. *Snow Falling from a Bamboo Leaf: The Art of Haiku.* Santa Barbara, CA: Capra Press, 1979.

Albee, Edward. *The Zoo Story; The Death of Bessie Smith; The Sandbox:* Three plays, introduced by the author. New York: Coward-McCann, 1960.

Albertson, Chris. *Bessie.* New York: Stein and Day Publishers, 1972.

Alim, H. Samy. "360 Degreez of Black Arts Comin at You: Sista Sonia Sanchez and the Dimensions of a Black Arts Continuum." *BMA: The Sonia Sanchez Literary Review* 6.1 (Fall 2000): 15–33.

Althusser, Louis. *Lenin and Philosophy and Other Essays.* Trans. Ben Brewster. New York: Monthly Review Press, 1971.

Anderson, Trela. "Sherley Anne Williams." *Contemporary African-American Novelists: A Bio-Bibliographical Critical Sourcebook.* Ed. Emmanuel S. Nelson. Westport, CT: Greenwood Press, 1999. 491–94.

Andrews, Bruce, and Charles Bernstein, eds. *The L=A=N=G=U=A=G=E Book.* Carbondale: Southern Illinois University Press, 1984.

Antelyes, Peter. "Red Hot Mamas: Bessie Smith, Sophie Tucker, and the Ethnic Maternal Voice in American Popular Song." *Embodied Voices: Representing Female Vocality in Western Culture.* Ed. Leslie C. Dunn and Nancy A. Jones. Cambridge: Cambridge University Press, 1994. 212–29.

Anthias, Floya. "Beyond Feminism and Multiculturalism: Locating Difference and the Politics of Location." *Women's Studies International Forum* 25.3 (2002): 275–86.

Arneil, Barbara. *Politics and Feminism.* Oxford and Malden, MA: Blackwell Publishers, Ltd., 1999.

Asante, Molefi Kete. *The Afrocentric Idea.* Philadelphia: Temple University Press, 1987.

Baker, Houston, A. *Blues, Ideology, and Afro-American Literature: A Vernacular Theory.* Chicago: University of Chicago Press, 1984.

———. "Our Lady: Sonia Sanchez and the Writing of a Black Renaissance." *Studies in Black American Literature, Volume III: Black Feminist Criticism and*

Critical Theory. Ed. Joe Weixlmann and Houston A. Baker Jr. Greenwood, FL: Penkevill Publishing Company, 1988. 169–202.

Baraka, Amina, and Amiri Baraka. *The Music: Reflections on Jazz and Blues.* New York: William Morrow Press, 1987.

Baraka, Amiri. *Blues People.* New York: William Morrow and Company, Inc., 1963.

Barbour, Floyd. "The Need for a Dirt Path." Foreword. *The Black Seventies.* Ed. Floyd Barbour. Boston: Porter Sargent Publisher, 1970. v–x.

Basu, Amrita. "Introduction." *The Challenge of Local Feminisms: Women's Movements in Global Perspective.* Ed. Amrita Basu. Boulder, CO: Westview Press, 1995. 1–21.

Beall, Emily P. "'As Reading As If': Harryette Mullen's 'Cognitive Similes.'" *Journal of Literary Semantics* 34.2 (2005): 125–37.

Bedient, Calvin. "The Solo Mysterioso Blues: An Interview with Harryette Mullen." *Callaloo* 19.3 (Summer 1996): 651–69.

Benston, Kimberly W. *Performing Blackness: Enactments of African-American Modernism.* London and New York: Routledge, 2000.

Berman, Jenifer. "Patricia Spears Jones." *BOMB* 52 (Summer 1995): 16–18.

Bettridge, Joel. "'Whose Lives Are Lonely Too': Harryette Mullen Reading Us into Contingency." *Mandorla* 7 (Spring 2004): 212–26.

Boggs, James. "The Revolutionary Struggle for Black Power." *The Black Seventies.* Ed. Floyd Barbour. Boston: Porter Sargent Publisher, 1970. 33–48.

Bolden, Tony. *Afro-Blue: Improvisations in African American Poetry and Culture.* Urbana and Chicago: University of Illinois Press, 2004.

———. "All the Birds Sing Bass: The Revolutionary Blues of Jayne Cortez." *African American Review* 35.1 (Spring 2001): 61–71.

Breton, André. *What Is Surrealism?* Ed. and introd. Franklin Rosemont. New York: Pathfinder, 1978.

Brewer, Rose M. "Theorizing Race, Class, and Gender: The New Scholarship of Black Feminist Intellectuals and Black Women's Labor." *Materialist Feminism: A Reader in Class, Difference, and Women's Lives.* Ed. Rosemary Hennessy and Chrys Ingraham. New York and London: Routledge, 1997. 236–47.

Brooker, Peter. "Modernism Deferred: Langston Hughes, Harlem, and Jazz Montage." *Locations of Literary Modernism: Region and Nation in British and American Modernist Poetry.* Ed. Alex Davis and Lee M. Jenkins. Cambridge: Cambridge University Press, 2000. 231–47.

Brooks De Vita, Alexis. *Mythatypes: Signatures and Signs of African/Diaspora and Black Goddesses.* Contributions in Afro-American and African Studies 198. Westport, CT, and London: Greenwood Press, 2000.

Brown, Elaine. *A Taste of Power: A Black Woman's Story.* New York: Random House, 1992.

Brown, Kimberly N. "Of Poststructuralist Fallout, Scarification, and Blood Poems: The Revolutionary Ideology behind the Poetry of Jayne Cortez." *Other Sisterhoods: Literary Theory and U. S. Women of Color.* Ed. Sandra Kumamoto Stanley. Urbana and Chicago: University of Illinois Press, 1998. 63–85.

Brown, Priscilla Ann. "What Saves Us: An Interview with Wanda Coleman." *Callaloo* 26.3 (2003): 635–61.

Bunch, Charlotte. "Women's Human Rights: The Challenges of Global Feminism and Diversity." *Feminist Locations: Global and Local, Theory and Practice.* Ed. and introd. Marianne DeKoven. New Brunswick, NJ: Rutgers University Press, 2001. 129–46.

Carby, Hazel V. "It Jus Be's Dat Way Sometime: The Sexual Politics of Women's Blues." *Gender and Discourse: The Power of Talk.* Ed. Alexandra Dundas Todd and Sue Fisher. Advances in Discourse Processes Ser. 30. Norwood, NJ: Ablex Publishing Corporation, 1988. 227–42.

———. "Policing the Black Woman's Body in an Urban Context." *Critical Inquiry* 18.4 (Summer 1992): 738–53.

Carmichael, Stokely, and Charles V. Hamilton. *Black Power: The Politics of Liberation in America.* New York: Vintage Books, 1967.

Carr, Glynis. "Introduction." *New Essays in Ecofeminist Literary Criticism.* Ed. Glynis Carr. London and Toronto: Associated University Presses, 2000. 15–25.

Carter Harrison, Paul. *The Drama of Nommo.* New York: Grove Press, Inc., 1972.

Chancy, Myriam J. A. "The Black Female Body as Popular Icon." *Essays on Transgressive Readings: Reading Over the Lines.* Ed. Georgia Johnston. Lewiston, NY: Mellen, 1997. 95–117.

Chinen, Nate. "Jayne Cortez & the Firespitters." *Philadelphia citypaper.net,* 15–22 February 2001. Web. 8 Dec. 2002.

Chinitz, David. "'Dance, Little Lady': Poets, Flappers, and the Gendering of Jazz." *Modernism, Gender, and Culture: A Cultural Studies Approach.* Ed. and introd. Lisa Rado. New York: Garland Publishing, Inc., 1997. 319–35.

Chowdhury, Elora Halim. "Locating Global Feminisms Elsewhere: Braiding US Women of Color and Transnational Feminisms." *Cultural Dynamics* 21.1 (2009): 51–78.

Clarke, Sebastian. "Woman of the Times: Sonia Sanchez and Her Work." *Black World* 2 (June 1971): 44–48, 96–98.

Coleman, Wanda. *African Sleeping Sickness: Stories and Poems.* Santa Rosa, CA: Black Sparrow Press, 1990.

———. *American Sonnets.* Milwaukee, WI, and Kenosha, WI: Woodland Pattern Book Center and Light and Dust Books, 1994.

———. *Bathwater Wine.* Santa Rosa, CA: Black Sparrow Press, 1998.

———. "Black on Black: Fear & Reviewing in Los Angeles." *The Riot Inside Me: More Trials & Tremors.* Boston: Black Sparrow Books, 2005. 140–51.

———. "Bobbi Sykes: An Interview." *Callaloo* 8.2 (Spring–Summer 1985): 294–303.

———. "Coulda Shoulda Woulda: 'A Song Flung Up to Heaven,' by Maya Angelou." *The Riot Inside Me: More Trials & Tremors.* Boston: Black Sparrow Books, 2005. 136–39.

———. *Imagoes.* Santa Barbara: Black Sparrow Press, 1983.

———. "Letters to E. Ethelbert Miller." *Callaloo* 22.1 (1999): 99–106.

———. *Mad Dog Black Lady.* Santa Barbara: Black Sparrow Press, 1979.

———. *Mercurochrome: New Poems.* Santa Rosa, CA: Black Sparrow Press, 2001.

———. "On Theloniousism." *Caliban* 4 (1988): 67–79.

————. "What Is American about American Poetry?" *Poetry Society of America*, November 1999. Web. 23 July 2009.

Collier, James Lincoln. *Duke Ellington*. New York and Oxford: Oxford University Press, 1987.

Collins, Patricia Hill. *Black Feminist Thought: Knowledge, Consciousness, and the Politics of Empowerment*. New York and London: Routledge, 1990.

Comer, Krista. *Landscapes of the New West: Gender and Geography in Contemporary Women's Writing*. Chapel Hill: University of North Carolina Press, 1999.

Cone, James H. *The Spirituals and the Blues: An Interpretation*. Maryknoll, NY: Orbis Books, 1991.

Conforti, Joseph A. *Imagining New England: Explorations of Regional Identity from the Pilgrims to the Mid-Twentieth Century*. Chapel Hill and London: University of North Carolina Press, 2001.

Cook, Dara. "The Aesthetics of Rap." *Black Issues Book Review* 2.2 (March–April 2000): 22–27.

Cook, William W. "The Black Arts Poets." *The Columbia History of American Poetry*. Ed. Jay Parini and Brett C. Millier. New York: Columbia University Press, 1993. 674–706.

Cornwell, Anita. "Attuned to the Energy: Sonia Sanchez." *Essence* 10 (July 1979): 10–11.

Cortez, Jayne. *Coagulations: New and Selected Poems*. New York: Thunder's Mouth Press, 1984.

————. *Festivals and Funerals*. Illus. Mel Edwards. New York: Bola Press, 1971.

————. *Firespitter*. New York: Bola Press, 1982.

————. *Jazz Fan Looks Back*. Brooklyn: Hanging Loose Press, 2002.

————. Liner notes. *Taking the Blues Back Home*. Harmolodic, 1996.

————. Liner notes. *There It Is*. Bola Press, 1982.

————. *Mouth on Paper*. New York: Bola Press, 1977.

————. *Pissstained Stairs and the Monkeyman's Wares*. New York: Phrase Text, 1969.

————. *Poetic Magnetic*. New York: Bola Press, 1991.

————. *Scarifications*. New York: Bola Press, 1973.

————. *Somewhere in Advance of Nowhere*. New York: Serpent's Tail, 1996.

————. "Talk to Me." *Taking the Blues Back Home*. Harmolodic, 1996.

Cortez, Jayne, and the Firespitters. *Taking the Blues Back Home*. Harmolodic, 1996.

————. *Unsubmissive Blues*. Harmolodic, 1980.

Crown, Kathleen. "'Choice Voice Noise': Soundings in Innovative African-American Poetry." *Assembling Alternatives: Reading Postmodern Poetries Transnationally*. Ed. Romana Huk. Middletown, CT: Wesleyan University Press, 2003. 219–45.

————. "A Collector of Shouts: Black Spirit, Black Arts, and the Poetry of Sonia Sanchez." *BMA: The Sonia Sanchez Literary Review* 3.2 (Spring 1998): 25–60.

————. "The Contemporary Long Poem: Feminist Intersections and Experiments: A Roundtable Conversation." *Women's Studies* 27 (1998): 507–36.

Culler, Jonathan, and Kevin Lamb. "Introduction." *Just Being Difficult? Academic Writing in the Public Arena*. Ed. Jonathan Culler and Kevin Lamb. Stanford, CA: Stanford University Press, 2003. 1–12.

Cummings, Allison. "Public Subjects: Race and the Critical Reception of Gwendolyn Brooks, Erica Hunt, and Harryette Mullen." *Frontiers* 26.2 (2005): 3–36.

Cusic, Don. "The Development of Gospel Music." *The Cambridge Companion to Blues and Gospel Music*. Ed. Allan Moore. Cambridge: Cambridge University Press, 2002. 44–60.

Dahl, Linda. *Stormy Weather: The Music and Lives of a Century of Jazzwomen*. New York: Limelight Editions, 1984.

Damon, Maria. "Was That 'Different,' 'Dissident' or 'Dissonant'? Poetry (n) the Public Spear: Slams, Open Readings, and Dissident Traditions." *Close Listening: Poetry and the Performed Word*. Ed. Charles Bernstein. New York and Oxford: Oxford University Press, 1998. 324–42.

Dargan, Kyle G. "Everything We Can Imagine: An Interview with Harryette Mullen." *Callaloo* 30.4 (2007): 1014–16.

Davis, Angela Y. *Blues Legacies and Black Feminism: Gertrude "Ma" Rainey, Bessie Smith, and Billie Holiday*. New York: Vintage Books, 1998.

De Lancey, Frenzella Elaine. "Cracking the Skull, Mending the Soul: Sonia Sanchez's Role as Teacher/Healer/Poet." *Wings of Gauze: Women of Color and the Experience of Health and Illness*. Ed. Barbara Blair and Susan E. Cayleff. Detroit: Wayne State University Press, 1993. 26–40.

———. "Refusing to Be Boxed In: Sonia Sanchez's Transformation of the Haiku Form." *Language and Literature in the African American Imagination*. Ed. Carol Aisha Blackshire-Belay. Westport, CT: Greenwood Press, 1992. 21–36.

———. "Scientist and Poet: The Ausetian Paradigm." *BMA: The Sonia Sanchez Literary Review* 1.2 (Spring 1996): 13–40.

———. "Sonia Sanchez's *Blues Book for Blue Black Magical Women* and Sister Souljah's *The Coldest Winter Ever*: Progressive Phases Amid Modernist Shadows & Postmodernist Acts." *BMA: The Sonia Sanchez Literary Review* 6.1 (Fall 2000): 147–79.

Desmond, Jane. "Mapping Identity onto the Body." *Women and Performance* 6.2 (1993): 103–26.

DeVeaux, Alexis. "A Poet's World: Jayne Cortez Discusses Her Life and Her Work." *Essence* 8 (March 1978): 76–79, 106, 109.

Diamond, Irene, and Gloria Feman Orenstein. "Introduction." *Reweaving the World: The Emergence of Ecofeminism*. Ed. Irene Diamond and Gloria Feman Orenstein. San Francisco: Sierra Club Books, 1990. ix–xv.

DuBois, W. E. B. *The Souls of Black Folk: Essays and Sketches*. 1903. New York: Bantam Classic, 1989.

Dunn, Leslie C., and Nancy A. Jones. "Introduction." *Embodied Voices: Representing Female Vocality in Western Culture*. Ed. Leslie C. Dunn and Nancy A. Jones. Cambridge: Cambridge University Press, 1994. 1–13.

DuPlessis, Rachel Blau. *The Pink Guitar: Writing as Feminist Practice*. New York: Routledge, 1990.

Dutt, Mallika. "Some Reflections on United States Women of Color and the United Nations Fourth World Conference on Women and NGO Forum in Beijing, China." *Global Feminisms Since 1945: Rewriting Histories.* Ed. Bonnie G. Smith. London and New York: Routledge, 2000. 305–13.

Early, Gerald. "Ode to John Coltrane: A Jazz Musician's Influence on African American Culture." *Antioch Review* 57.3 (Summer 1999): 371–85.

Easton, Alison. "The Body as History and 'Writing the Body': The Example of Grace Nichols." *Journal of Gender Studies* 3.1 (1994): 55–67.

"Edge." *Roget's II: The New Thesaurus.* 3rd ed. 1995.

Eschle, Catherine. *Global Democracy, Social Movements, and Feminism* (Feminist Theory and Politics) Ser. 8. Boulder, CO: Westview Press, 2001.

Feinstein, Sascha. *A Bibliographic Guide to Jazz Poetry.* Westport, CT: Greenwood Press, 1998.

———. "An Interview with Sonia Sanchez." *Conversations with Sonia Sanchez.* Ed. Joyce A. Joyce. Jackson: University Press of Mississippi, 2007. 155–76.

———. *Jazz Poetry: From the 1920s to the Present.* Westport, CT: Greenwood Press, 1997.

———. "Returning to Go Someplace Else: An Interview with Jayne Cortez." *Brilliant Corners* 3.1 (Winter 1998): 53–71.

Feinstein, Sascha, and Yusef Komunyakaa, eds. *The Jazz Poetry Anthology.* Bloomington and Indianapolis: Indiana University Press, 1991.

———, eds. *The Second Set: The Jazz Poetry Anthology Volume 2.* Bloomington and Indianapolis: Indiana University Press, 1996.

Ferree, Myra Marx. "Globalization and Feminism: Opportunities and Obstacles for Activism in the Global Arena." *Global Feminism: Transnational Women's Activism, Organizing, and Human Rights.* Ed. Myra Marx Ferree and Aili Mari Tripp. New York and London: New York University Press, 2006. 3–23.

Finch, Annie. "Form and Spirit: A Conversation with Sonia Sanchez." *Conversations with Sonia Sanchez.* Ed. Joyce A. Joyce. Jackson: University Press of Mississippi, 2007. 27–46.

Forché, Carolyn. "Introduction." *Against Forgetting: Twentieth-Century Poetry of Witness.* Ed. Carolyn Forché. New York and London: W. W. Norton & Company, 1993. 29–47.

Ford, Clyde W. *The Hero with an African Face: Mythic Wisdom of Traditional Africa.* New York: Bantam Books, 1999.

Ford, Karen Jackson. *Gender and the Poetics of Excess: Moments of Brocade.* Jackson: University Press of Mississippi, 1997.

———. "These Old Writing Paper Blues: The Blues Stanza and Literary Poetry." *College Literature* 24.3 (October 1997): 84–103.

Foucault, Michel. *Discipline and Punish: The Birth of the Prison.* 1975. Trans. Alan Sheridan. New York: Vintage Books, 1995.

Frost, Elisabeth A. *The Feminist Avant-Garde in American Poetry.* Iowa City: University of Iowa Press, 2003.

———. "An Interview with Harryette Mullen." *Contemporary Literature* 41.1 (Spring 2000): 397–421.

————. "'Ruses of the Lunatic Muse': Harryette Mullen and Lyric Hybridity." *Women's Studies* 27 (1998): 465–81.

————. "Signifyin(g) on Stein: The Revisionist Poetics of Harryette Mullen and Leslie Scalapino." *Postmodern Culture* 5.3 (May 1995): n. pag. Web. 4 February 2002.

Gaard, Greta, and Patrick D. Murphy. "Introduction." *Ecofeminist Literary Criticism: Theory, Interpretation, Pedagogy.* Ed. Greta Gaard and Patrick D. Murphy. Urbana and Chicago: University of Illinois Press, 1998. 1–13.

Gabbin, Joanne V. "Introduction." *The Furious Flowering of African-American Poetry.* Ed. Joanne V. Gabbin. Charlottesville: University Press of Virginia, 1999. 1–14.

————. "Sonia Sanchez." *The History of Southern Women's Literature.* Ed. Carolyn Perry and Mary Louise Weaks. Baton Rouge: Louisiana State University Press, 2002. 535–40.

————. "The Southern Imagination of Sonia Sanchez." *Southern Women Writers: The New Generation.* Ed. Tonette Bond Inge. Tuscaloosa and London: University of Alabama Press, 1990. 180–203.

Garon, Paul. *Blues and the Poetic Spirit.* San Francisco: City Lights Books, 1996.

Gates, Henry Louis, Jr. *The Signifying Monkey: A Theory of Afro-American Literary Criticism.* New York: Oxford University Press, 1988.

Gayle, Addison, Jr. "Introduction." *The Black Aesthetic.* Ed. Addison Gayle Jr. Garden City, NY: Anchor Books, Doubleday & Company, Inc., 1972. xv–xxiv.

Gersch, Beate. "Jazz—The Evolution of an Image in African-American Literature." *The Image of America in Literature, Media, and Society: Selected Papers, 1999 Conference, Society for the Interdisciplinary Study of Social Imagery, March 11–13, 1999.* Pueblo: University of Southern Colorado, 1999. 46–52.

Giddings, Paula. *When and Where I Enter: The Impact of Black Women on Race and Sex in America.* New York: William Morrow and Company, Inc., 1984.

Gilbert, Sandra M. "'Rats' Alley': The Great War, Modernism, and the (Anti)Pastoral Elegy." *New Literary History* 30.1 (1999): 179–201.

Gilman, Sander L. "Black Bodies, White Bodies: Toward an Iconography of Female Sexuality in Late Nineteenth-Century Art, Medicine, and Literature." *"Race," Writing, and Difference.* Ed. Henry Louis Gates Jr. Chicago and London: University of Chicago Press, 1986. 223–61.

Gioia, Ted. *The History of Jazz.* New York: Oxford University Press, 1997.

Giroux, Joan. *The Haiku Form.* Rutland, VT, and Tokyo: Charles E. Tuttle Company, 1974.

Golding, Alan. *From Outlaw to Classic: Canons in American Poetry.* Madison: University of Wisconsin Press, 1995.

Gourse, Leslie. *Madame Jazz: Contemporary Women Instrumentalists.* New York: Oxford University Press, 1995.

Gridley, Mark C. *Jazz Styles: History and Analysis.* 7th ed. Upper Saddle River, NJ: Prentice Hall, 2000.

Griffin, Farrah, Michael Magee, and Kristen Gallagher. "A Conversation with Harryette Mullen." *The University at Buffalo Electronic Poetry Center* (1997): n. pag. Web. 30 November 2001.

Hacker, Marilyn. "1999 Lenore Marshall Poetry Prize." *Nation* 269.19 (6 Dec. 1999): 44–45, 47.

Harryman, Carla. "Rules and Restraints in Women's Experimental Writing." *We Who Love to Be Astonished: Women's Experimental Writing and Performance Poetics.* Ed. Laura Hinton and Cynthia Hogue. Tuscaloosa: University of Alabama Press, 2002. 116–24.

Hartman, Charles O. *Jazz Text: Voice and Improvisation in Poetry, Jazz, and Song.* Princeton, NJ: Princeton University Press, 1991.

Hasse, John Edward. *Beyond Category: The Life and Genius of Duke Ellington.* New York: Simon & Schuster, 1993.

Hejinian, Lyn. *My Life.* Los Angeles: Sun & Moon Press, 1987.

Henderson, Mae Gwendolyn. "In Memory of Sherley Anne Williams: 'Some One Sweet Angel Chile,' 1944–1999." *Callaloo* 22.4 (1999): 763–67.

Henderson, Stephen. "The Blues as Black Poetry." *Callaloo* 5.3 (October 1982): 22–30.

———. "Introduction." *Understanding the New Black Poetry: Black Speech and Black Music as Poetic References.* Ed. Stephen Henderson. New York: William Morrow and Company, Inc., 1973. 3–69.

———. "Worrying the Line: Notes on Black American Poetry." *The Line in Postmodern Poetry.* Ed. Robert Frank and Henry Sayre. Chicago: University of Illinois Press, 1988. 60–82.

Henning, Barbara. "An Interview with Harryette Mullen." *Poetry Project Newsletter* (1996): n. pag. Web. 30 November 2001.

Herron, Carolivia. "Early African American Poetry." *The Columbia History of American Poetry.* Ed. Jay Parini and Brett C. Millier. New York: Columbia University Press, 1993. 16–32.

Higginson, William J. *The Haiku Seasons: Poetry of the Natural World.* Tokyo and New York: Kodansha International, 1996.

Hine, Darlene Clark, and Kathleen Thompson. *A Shining Thread of Hope: The History of Black Women in America.* New York: Broadway Books, 1998.

Hinton, Laura, and Cynthia Hogue. "Introduction: Oppositions and Astonishing Contiguities." *We Who Love to Be Astonished: Experimental Women's Writing and Performance Poetics.* Ed. Laura Hinton and Cynthia Hogue. Tuscaloosa: University of Alabama Press, 2002. 1–12.

Hoffman, Tyler. "Treacherous Laughter: The Poetry Slam, Slam Poetry, and the Politics of Resistance." *Studies in American Humor* 3.8 (2001): 49–64.

Hogue, Cynthia. "Harryette Mullen's Revisionary Border Work." *We Who Love to Be Astonished: Experimental Women's Writing and Performance Poetics.* Ed. Laura Hinton and Cynthia Hogue. Tuscaloosa and London: University of Alabama Press, 2002. 81–89.

———. "Interview with Harryette Mullen." *Postmodern Culture* 9.2 (January 1999): n. pag. Web. 1 May 2001.

Honey, Maureen, ed. *Shadowed Dreams: Women's Poetry of the Harlem Renaissance.* New Brunswick, NJ: Rutgers University Press, 1999.

hooks, bell. "Selling Hot Pussy: Representations of Black Female Sexuality in the Cultural Marketplace." *Writing on the Body: Female Embodiment and Feminist Theory.* Ed. Katie Conboy, Nadia Medina, and Sarah Stanbury. New York: Columbia University Press, 1997. 113–28.

Howard, Lillie P. "Sherley Anne Williams." *Afro-American Poets Since 1955.* Ed. Trudier Harris and Thadious M. Davis. Detroit: Gale Research, 1985. 343–50.

Huehls, Mitchum. "Spun Puns (and Anagrams): Exchange Economies, Subjectivity, and History in Harryette Mullen's *Muse & Drudge*." *Contemporary Literature* 44.1 (Spring 2003): 19–46.

"In Memoriam: Sherley Anne Williams, 1944–1999." *The Black Scholar* 29.2–3 (Summer 1999): 64–65.

Inness, Sherrie A., and Diana Royer. "Introduction." *Breaking Boundaries: New Perspectives on Women's Regional Writing.* Ed. Sherrie A. Inness and Diana Royer. Iowa City: University of Iowa Press, 1997. 1–10.

Jacobs, Harriet. *Incidents in the Life of a Slave Girl.* 1861. *The Classic Slave Narratives.* Ed. Henry Louis Gates Jr. New York: Mentor/Penguin Books, 1987. 333–515.

"Jayne Cortez's Biography." *Jayne Cortez.com*, 2002. Web. 8 Dec. 2002.

Jennings, Regina B. "The Blue/Black Poetics of Sonia Sanchez." *Language and Literature in the African American Imagination.* Ed. Carol Aisha Blackshire-Belay. Westport, CT: Greenwood Press, 1992. 119–32.

Johnson, Sheila Golburgh. "Wanda Coleman." *Cyclopedia of World Authors.* Literary Reference Center, 2004. Web. 15 July 2009.

Jones, Meta Du Ewa. "Jazz Prosodies: Orality and Textuality." *Callaloo* 25.1 (Winter 2002): 66–91.

Jost, Ekkehard. *Free Jazz.* Vienna: Universal Edition A. G., 1975.

Joyce, Joyce A. *Ijala: Sonia Sanchez and the African Poetic Tradition.* Chicago: Third World Press, 1996.

Juno, Andrea, and V. Vale. "Wanda Coleman." *Angry Women: Re/Search* 13 (1991): 118–26.

Kane, Daniel. "Interview with Harryette Mullen." *Poets Chat* (April–May 2002): n. pag. Web. 9 September 2002.

Karenga, Maulana. "Black Cultural Nationalism." *The Black Aesthetic.* Ed. Addison Gayle. Garden City, NY: Doubleday & Company, Inc., 1971. 32–38.

Kelly, Susan. "Discipline and Craft: An Interview with Sonia Sanchez." *African American Review* 34.4 (2000): 679–87.

King, Deborah K. "Multiple Jeopardy, Multiple Consciousness: The Context of Black Feminist Ideology." *Words of Fire: An Anthology of African-American Feminist Thought.* Ed. Beverly Guy-Sheftall. New York: New Press, 1995. 294–317.

King, Ynestra. "Healing the Wounds: Feminism, Ecology, and the Nature/ Culture Dualism." *Reweaving the World: The Emergence of Ecofeminism.*

Ed. Irene Diamond and Gloria Feman Orenstein. San Francisco: Sierra Club Books, 1990. 106–21.

Kofsky, Frank. *John Coltrane and the Jazz Revolution of the 1960s*. New York: Pathfinder, 1998.

Kuenz, Jane. "The Bluest Eye: Notes on History, Community, and Black Female Subjectivity." *African American Review* 27.3 (1993): 421–31.

Kuhn, Elisabeth D. "'I Just Want to Make Love to You': Seductive Strategies in Blues Lyrics." *Journal of Pragmatics* 31 (1999): 525–34.

Lambert, Ellen Zetzel. *Placing Sorrow: A Study of the Pastoral Elegy Convention from Theocritus to Milton*. Chapel Hill: University of North Carolina Press, 1976.

Lange, Art, and Nathaniel Mackey, eds. *Moment's Notice: Jazz in Poetry and Prose*. Minneapolis, MN: Coffee House Press, 1993.

Lanser, Susan Sniader. "Compared to What? Global Feminism, Comparatism, and the Master's Tools." *Borderwork: Feminist Engagements with Comparative Literature*. Ed. Margaret R. Higonnet. Ithaca, NY, and London: Cornell University Press, 1994. 280–300.

Lawrence, A. H. *Duke Ellington and His World: A Biography*. New York and London: Routledge, 2001.

Leibowitz, Herbert. "Exploding Myths: An Interview with Sonia Sanchez." *Parnassus* 12–13(2–1) (Spring–Winter 1985): 357–68.

Levine, Rachel. "Wanda Coleman: A Conversation." *Another Chicago Magazine* 35 (1999): 210–35.

Litweiler, John. *Ornette Coleman: The Harmolodic Life*. London: Quartet Books Limited, 1992.

Luck, Jessica Lewis. "Entries on a Post-Language Poetics in Harryette Mullen's *Dictionary*." *Contemporary Literature* 49.3 (2008): 357–82.

Lutz, Tom. *Cosmopolitan Vistas: American Regionalism and Literary Value*. Ithaca, NY, and London: Cornell University Press, 2004.

Mackey, Nathaniel. *Atet A. D.* San Francisco: City Lights Publishers, 2001.

———. *Bedouin Hornbook*. Los Angeles: Sun & Moon Press, 1986.

———. *Discrepant Engagement: Dissonance, Cross-Culturality, and Experimental Writing*. Cambridge Studies in Amer. Lit. and Culture 71. Cambridge and New York: Cambridge University Press, 1993.

———. *Djbot Baghostus's Run*. Los Angeles: Sun & Moon Press, 1993.

———. *Eroding Witness*. Urbana: University of Illinois Press, 1985.

———. *School of Udhra*. San Francisco: City Lights Publishers, 1993.

———. *Splay Anthem*. New York: New Directions, 2006.

———. *Whatsaid Serif*. San Francisco: City Lights Publishers, 1998.

Madhubuti, Haki. "Introduction." *Home Coming*. By Sonia Sanchez. Detroit: Broadside Press, 1969. 6–8.

———. "Sonia Sanchez: The Bringer of Memories." *Black Women Writers (1950–1980): A Critical Evaluation*. Ed. Mari Evans. Garden City, NY: Anchor Press, 1984. 419–32.

Magistrale, Tony. "Wanda Coleman, 1946– " *American Writers: A Collection of Literary Biographies*. Supplement. New York: Charles Scribner's Sons, 2002. 83–98.

Magistrale, Tony, and Patricia Ferreira. "Sweet Mama Wanda Tells Fortunes: An Interview with Wanda Coleman." *Black American Literature Forum* 24.3 (Fall 1990): 491–507.

Major, Clarence. *Dictionary of Afro-American Slang.* New York: International Publishers, 1970.

———. *Juba to Jive: A Dictionary of African-American Slang.* New York: Penguin Books, 1994.

Mance, Ajuan Maria. "Re-Locating the Black Female Subject: The Landscape of the Body in the Poems of Lucille Clifton." *Recovering the Black Female Body: Self-Representations by African American Women.* Ed. Michael Bennett and Vanessa D. Dickerson. New Brunswick, NJ, and London: Rutgers University Press, 2001. 123–40.

Manheim, James M. "Wanda Coleman Biography." *Biography.jrank.org,* 2009. Web. 23 July 2009.

Marable, Manning. *Race, Reform, and Rebellion: The Second Reconstruction in Black America, 1945–1990.* Rev. 2nd ed. Jackson and London: University Press of Mississippi, 1991.

Materson, Lisa G. "African American Women's Global Journeys and the Construction of Cross-Ethnic Racial Identity." *Women's Studies International Forum* 32 (2009): 35–42.

Mayfield, Julian. "You Touch My Black Aesthetic and I'll Touch Yours." *The Black Aesthetic.* Ed. Addison Gayle. Garden City, NY: Doubleday & Company, Inc., 1971. 24–31.

Meehan, Kevin. "Brilliant Episodes of Invention: Jayne Cortez in Poetic Dialogue with John La Rose." *Wasfiri* 21.3 (November 2006): 59–64.

Melhem, D. H. "A *MELUS* Profile and Interview: Jayne Cortez." *MELUS* 21.1 (Spring 1996): 71–79.

———. "Jayne Cortez: Supersurrealist Vision." *Heroism in the New Black Poetry: Introductions and Interviews.* By D. H. Melhem. Lexington: University Press of Kentucky, 1990. 181–212.

———. "Sonia Sanchez: Will and Spirit." *MELUS* 12.3 (Fall 1985): 73–98.

———. "Sonia Sanchez: The Will and the Spirit." *Heroism in the New Black Poetry: Introductions and Interviews.* By D. H. Melhem. Lexington: The University Press of Kentucky, 1990. 132–79.

Michel, Jean-Claude. *The Black Surrealists.* Francophone Cultures and Literatures Ser. 29. New York: Peter Lang Publishing, Inc., 2000.

Mix, Deborah. "Tender Revisions: Harryette Mullen's *Trimmings* and *S*PeRM**K*T.*" *American Literature* 77.1 (March 2005): 65–92.

Moghadam, Valentine M. *Globalizing Women: Transnational Feminist Networks.* Baltimore and London: Johns Hopkins University Press, 2005.

Mohanram, Radhika. *Black Body: Women, Colonialism, and Space.* Public World Ser. 6. Minneapolis and London: University of Minnesota Press, 1999.

Mohanty, Chandra Talpade. *Feminism Without Borders: Decolonizing Theory, Practicing Solidarity.* Durham and London: Duke University Press, 2003.

Montefiore, Jan. *Feminism and Poetry: Language, Experience, Identity in Women's Writing.* London and New York: Pandora Press, 1987.

Morrison, Toni. *Beloved*. New York: Plume/Penguin Books, 1987.

Mullen, Harryette. *Blues Baby: Early Poems*. Lewisburg: Bucknell University Press, 2002.

———. "'A Collective Force of Burning Ink': Will Alexander's *Asia & Haiti*." *Callaloo* 22.2 (1999): 417–26.

———. "Hauling Up Gold from the Abyss: An Interview with Will Alexander." *Callaloo* 22.2 (1999): 391–408.

———. "Imagining the Unimagined Reader: Writing to the Unborn and Including the Excluded." *boundary 2* 26.1 (Spring 1999): 198–203.

———. "'Incessant Elusives': The Oppositional Poetics of Erica Hunt and Will Alexander." *Holding Their Own: Perspectives on the Multi-Ethnic Literatures of the United States*. Ed. Dorothea Fischer-Hornung and Raphael Hernandez Heike. Tubingen, Germany: Stauffenburg, 2000. 207–16.

———. *Muse & Drudge*. Philadelphia: Singing Horse, 1995.

———. "Optic White: Blackness and the Production of Whiteness." *Diacritics* 24.2–3 (Summer–Fall 1994): 71–89.

———. "Poetry and Identity." *West Coast Line* 30.1 (Spring 1996): 85–89.

———. *Recyclopedia: Trimmings, S*PeRM**K*T, and Muse & Drudge*. St. Paul, MN: Graywolf Press, 2006.

———. "Runaway Tongue: Resistant Orality in *Uncle Tom's Cabin, Our Nig, Incidents in the Life of a Slave Girl*, and *Beloved*." *The Culture of Sentiment: Race, Gender, and Sentimentality in Nineteenth-Century America*. Ed. Shirley Samuels. New York: Oxford University Press, 1992. 244–64.

———. "'A Silence between Us Like a Language': The Untranslatability of Experience in Sandra Cisneros's *Woman Hollering Creek*." *MELUS* 21.2 (Summer 1996): 3–20.

———. *Sleeping with the Dictionary*. Berkeley: University of California Press, 2002.

———. *S*PeRM**K*T*. Philadelphia: Singing Horse Press, 1992.

———. *Tree Tall Woman: Poems*. Galveston, TX: Energy Earth Communications, 1981.

———. *Trimmings*. New York City: Tender Buttons, 1991.

———. "'When he is least himself': Dunbar and Double Consciousness in African American Poetry." *African American Review* 41.2 (Summer 2007): 277–82.

Murphet, Julian. *Literature and Race in Los Angeles*. Cultural Margins ser. Cambridge: Cambridge University Press, 2001.

Murphy, Patrick D. "'The Women Are Speaking': Contemporary Literature as Theoretical Critique." *Ecofeminist Literary Criticism: Theory, Interpretation, Pedagogy*. Ed. Greta Gaard and Patrick D. Murphy. Urbana and Chicago: University of Illinois Press, 1998. 23–48.

Myers, Christopher. "Harryette Mullen, 1999." *Index Magazine* (2001): n. pag. Web. 22 April 2002.

Nielsen, Aldon Lynn. "African-American Prose Poems." *Reading Race: "An Area of Act"*. Ed. Aldon Lynn Nielsen. Urbana and Chicago: University of Illinois Press, 2000. 148–62.

————. *Black Chant: Languages of African-American Postmodernism.* Cambridge: Cambridge University Press, 1997.

————. *Integral Music: Languages of African American Innovation.* Tuscaloosa: University of Alabama Press, 2004.

Oliver, Paul. "Can't Even Write: The Blues and Ethnic Literature." *MELUS* 10.1 (1983): 7–14.

O'Mara, Kathleen K. "Wanda Coleman." *Dictionary of Literary Biography* 130— *American Short Story Writers since World War II.* Ed. Patrick Meanor. Detroit: Gale Research, Inc., 1993. 82–88.

Ostriker, Alicia Suskin. *Stealing the Language: The Emergence of Women's Poetry in America.* Boston: Beacon Press, 1986.

Parrinder, Geoffrey. *African Mythology.* Library of the World's Myths and Legends. London: Hamlyn, 1982.

Pearcy, Kate. "A Poetics of Opposition? Race and the Avant-Garde." *Poetry and the Public Sphere.* Rutgers University conference, 1997. Web. 9 September 2002.

Perelman, Bob. *The Marginalization of Poetry: Language Writing and Literary History.* Princeton, NJ: Princeton University Press, 1996.

Peretti, Burton W. *Jazz in American Culture.* American Ways Ser. Chicago: Ivan R. Dee, 1997.

Perkins, Eugene. "The Black Arts Movement: Its Challenge and Responsibility." *The Black Seventies.* Ed. Floyd Barbour. Boston: Porter Sargent Publisher, 1970. 85–97.

Pinson, Hermine. "An Interview with Lorenzo Thomas." *Callaloo* 22.2 (1999): 287–304.

Pinto, Samantha. "Feminist Subjectivity and the Everyday Blues: The Casual Erotics of Harryette Mullen." *Sound as Sense: Contemporary US Poetry and/in Music.* Ed. Michel Delville and Christine Pagnoulle. Brussels: Peter Lang, 2003. 59–75.

Poetry in Motion. Dir. Ron Mann. Perf. Jayne Cortez et al. Home Vision Entertainment, 1982.

Pollard, Cherise A. "Sexual Subversions, Political Inversions: Women's Poetry and the Politics of the Black Arts Movement." *New Thoughts on the Black Arts Movement.* Ed. Lisa Gail Collins and Margo Natalie Crawford. New Brunswick, NJ: Rutgers University Press, 2006. 173–86.

Porter, Lewis. *John Coltrane: His Life and Music.* Ann Arbor: University of Michigan Press, 1998.

Prettyman, Quandra. "Come Eat at My Table: Lives with Recipes." *Southern Quarterly* 30.2–3 (Winter–Spring 1992): 131–40.

Quinby, Lee. "Ecofeminism and the Politics of Resistance." *Reweaving the World: The Emergence of Ecofeminism.* Ed. Irene Diamond and Gloria Feman Orenstein. San Francisco: Sierra Club Books, 1990. 122–27.

Ramazani, Jahan. *Poetry of Mourning: The Modern Elegy from Hardy to Heaney.* Chicago and London: University of Chicago Press, 1994.

Reagon, Bernice Johnson. *If You Go, Don't Hinder Me: The African American Sacred Song Tradition.* Lincoln and London: University of Nebraska Press, 2001.

Redmond, Eugene B. *Drumvoices: The Mission of Afro-American Poetry.* Garden City, NY: Anchor Books, 1976.

Reich, David. "'As Poets, As Activists': An Interview with Sonia Sanchez." *Conversations with Sonia Sanchez.* Ed. Joyce A. Joyce. Jackson: University Press of Mississippi, 2007. 80–93.

Rexroth, Kenneth. "Jazz Poetry." 1958. *World outside the Window: The Selected Essays of Kenneth Rexroth.* Ed. Bradford Morrow. New York: New Directions Books, 1987. 68–72.

Robbins, Bruce. Introduction. *Intellectuals: Aesthetics, Politics, Academics.* Ed. Bruce Robbins. Minneapolis: University of Minnesota Press, 1990. ix–xxvii.

Roberts, Diane. *The Myth of Aunt Jemima: Representations of Race and Region.* London and New York: Routledge, 1994.

Roberts, Dorothy. *Killing the Black Body: Race, Reproduction, and the Meaning of Liberty.* New York: Pantheon Books, 1997.

Rome, Danielle Alyce. "An Interview with Sonia Sanchez." *Speaking of the Short Story: Interviews with Contemporary Writers.* Ed. Farhat Iftekharuddin, Mary Rohrberger, and Maurice Lee. Jackson: University Press of Mississippi, 1997. 229–36.

Rosemont, Franklin. "Afterword." *Blues and the Poetic Spirit.* By Paul Garon. San Francisco: City Lights Books, 1996. 217–29.

———. "Introduction." *What Is Surrealism?* By André Breton. New York: Pathfinder, 1978. 1–139.

Rosendale, Steven. "Introduction: Extending Ecocriticism." *The Greening of Literary Scholarship: Literature, Theory, and the Environment.* Ed. Steven Rosendale. Iowa City: University of Iowa Press, 2002. xv–xxix.

Ross, Andrew. *No Respect: Intellectuals and Popular Culture.* New York: Routledge, 1989.

Ross, Fran. *Oreo.* 1974. Foreword Harryette Mullen. Boston: Northeastern University Press, 2000.

Salaam, Kalamu ya. "Historical Overviews of the Black Arts Movement." *Modern American Poetry,* 2000. Web. 11 September 2002.

———. "Love and Liberation: Sonia Sanchez's Literary Uses of the Personal." *BMA: The Sonia Sanchez Literary Review* 3.1 (Fall 1997): 57–120.

———. "Sonia Sanchez." *Afro-American Poets Since 1955.* Ed. Trudier Harris and Thadious M. Davis. Detroit: Gale Research, 1985. 295–306.

Sanchez, Sonia. *A Blues Book for Blue Black Magical Women.* Detroit: Broadside Press, 1974.

———. *Crisis and Culture: Two Speeches.* New York: Black Liberation Press, 1983.

———. *Home Coming: Poems.* Detroit: Broadside Press, 1969.

———. *Homegirls & Handgrenades.* New York: Thunder's Mouth Press, 1984.

———. *Ima Talken Bout the Nation of Islam.* Astoria, NY: Truth Del. Corp., 1971.

———. *It's a New Day: Poems for Young Brothas and Sistuhs.* Detroit: Broadside Press, 1971.

———. *I've Been a Woman: New and Selected Poems.* Chicago: Third World Press, 1978.

————. *Liberation Poem.* Illus. Shirley Woodson. Detroit: Broadside Press, 1970.

————. *Like the Singing Coming Off the Drums: Love Poems.* Boston: Beacon Press, 1998.

————. *Love Poems.* New York: Third Press, 1973.

————. *Under a Soprano Sky.* Trenton, NJ: Africa World Press, 1987.

————. *We a BaddDDD People.* Detroit: Broadside Press, 1970.

————. *Wounded in the House of a Friend.* Boston: Beacon Press, 1995.

Sato, Hiroaki. *One Hundred Frogs: From Renga to Haiku to English.* New York and Tokyo: John Weatherhill, Inc., 1983.

Sawaya, Francesca. "Emplotting National History: Regionalism and Pauline Hopkins's *Contending Forces.*" *Breaking Boundaries: New Perspectives on Women's Regional Writing.* Ed. Sherrie A. Inness and Diana Royer. Iowa City: University of Iowa Press, 1997. 72–87.

"Scarify." *Concise Oxford Dictionary.* 10th ed. 1999.

Schenck, Celeste Marguerite. *Mourning and Panegyric: The Poetics of Pastoral Ceremony.* University Park and London: Pennsylvania State University Press, 1988.

Schmid, Julie. "Spreading the Word: A History of the Poetry Slam." *The World in Time and Space: Towards a History of Innovative American Poetry in Our Time.* Ed. Edward Foster and Joseph Donahue. Jersey City, NJ: Talisman House Publishers, Inc., 2002. 636–45.

Selinger, Eric Murphy. "Trash, Art, and Performance Poetry." *Parnassus* 23.1–2 (1998): 356–81.

Shange, Ntozake. *A Daughter's Geography.* New York: St. Martin's Press, 1983.

"Sherley Anne Williams, 54, Novelist, Poet and Professor." *The New York Times* 14 July 1999: A21.

Silliman, Ron. *The New Sentence.* New York: Roof Books, 1987.

Simpson, Megan. *Poetic Epistemologies: Gender and Knowing in Women's Language-Oriented Writing.* Albany: State University of New York Press, 2000.

Smith, Bonnie G. "Introduction." *Global Feminisms Since 1945: Rewriting Histories.* Ed. Bonnie G. Smith. London and New York: Routledge, 2000. 1–10.

Smith, Patricia. *Big Towns, Big Talk.* Cambridge, MA: Zoland Press, 1992.

Smitherman, Geneva. *Talkin and Testifyin: The Language of Black America.* Boston: Houghton Mifflin Company, 1977.

Spady, James G. "Black Jazz Daughter When She Is Singing: The Historical Blues Journey of a Sonia Sanchez." *BMA: The Sonia Sanchez Literary Review* 2.1 (Fall 1996): 1–43.

————. "The Centrality of Black Language in the Discourse Strategies and Poetic Force of Sonia Sanchez and Rap Artists." *BMA: The Sonia Sanchez Literary Review* 6.1 (Fall 2000): 47–72.

————. "Sonia Sanchez: The Consummate Teacher." *BMA: The Sonia Sanchez Literary Review* 3.1 (Fall 1997): 14–23.

Spahr, Juliana. *Everybody's Autonomy: Connective Reading and Collective Identity.* Tuscaloosa: University of Alabama Press, 2001.

Spears Jones, Patricia. *The Weather That Kills*. Minneapolis, MN: Coffee House Press, 1995.

Spretnak, Charlene. "Ecofeminism: Our Roots and Flowering." *Reweaving the World: The Emergence of Ecofeminism*. Ed. Irene Diamond and Gloria Feman Orenstein. San Francisco: Sierra Club Books, 1990. 3–14.

Stein, Gertrude. *Tender Buttons*. New York: Claire Marie, 1914.

Stephens, Jim. *Bright Moments: A Collection of Jazz Poetry*. Madison, WI: Abraxas Press, 1980.

Stone, Carole. "Elegy as Political Expression in Women's Poetry: Akhmatova, Levertov, Forché." *College Literature* 18.1 (February 1991): 84–91.

Sullivan, James D. *On the Walls and in the Streets: American Poetry Broadsides from the 1960s*. Urbana and Chicago: University of Illinois Press, 1997.

Tate, Claudia. "Sherley Anne Williams." *Black Women Writers at Work*. By Claudia Tate. New York: Continuum Publishing Company, 1983. 205–13.

———. "Sonia Sanchez." *Black Women Writers at Work*. By Claudia Tate. New York: Continuum Publishing Company, 1983. 132–48.

Thomas, Gregory V. "The Canonization of Jazz and Afro-American Literature." *Callaloo* 25.1 (Winter 2002): 288–308.

Thomas, Lorenzo. "The Bop Aesthetic and Black Intellectual Tradition." *Library Chronicle of the University of Texas* 24.1–2 (1994): 105–17.

———. "'Communicating by Horns': Jazz and Redemption in the Poetry of the Beats and the Black Arts Movement." *African American Review* 26.2 (1992): 291–98.

———. *Extraordinary Measures: Afrocentric Modernism and Twentieth-Century American Poetry*. Tuscaloosa: University of Alabama Press, 2000.

Thompson, Julius E. *Dudley Randall, Broadside Press, and the Black Arts Movement in Detroit, 1960–1995*. Jefferson, NC, and London: McFarland & Company, Inc., 1999.

Turner, Daniel Cross. "New Fugitives: Contemporary Poets of Countermemory and the Futures of Southern Poetry." *Mississippi Quarterly* 58.1–2 (Winter 2004–Spring 2005): 315–45.

Ulin, David L. "Introduction." *Writing Los Angeles: A Literary Anthology*. Ed. David L. Ulin. New York: Library of America, 2002. xiii–xix.

Van Deburg, William L. *New Day in Babylon: The Black Power Movement and American Culture, 1965–1975*. Chicago: University of Chicago Press, 1992.

Vickery, Ann. *Leaving Lines of Gender: A Feminist Genealogy of Language Writing*. Hanover: Wesleyan University Press, 2000.

Walker, Margaret. *This Is My Century: New and Collected Poems*. Athens: University of Georgia Press, 1989.

Wall, Cheryl A. "Whose Sweet Angel Child? Blues Women, Langston Hughes, and Writing During the Harlem Renaissance." *GRAAT* 14 (1996): 63–72.

Wallace, Michele. *Black Macho and the Myth of the Superwoman*. New York: Dial Press, 1978.

"Wanda Coleman." *Literary Resource Center*. Author Resource Pages, 29 April 2009. Web. 15 July 2009.

Weir, Allison. "Global Feminism and Transformative Identity Politics." *Hypatia* 23.4 (October–December 2008): 110–33.

Werner, Craig. *A Change Is Gonna Come: Music, Race, and the Soul of America.* Rev. and updated ed. Ann Arbor: University of Michigan Press, 2006.

White, E. Frances. *Dark Continent of Our Bodies: Black Feminism and the Politics of Respectability.* Philadelphia: Temple University Press, 2001.

White, Matthew B. "'The Blues Ain't Nothin' But a Woman Want to Be a Man': Male Control in Early Twentieth Century Blues Music." *Canadian Review of American Studies* 24.1 (Winter 1994): 19–40.

Whitehead, Kim. *The Feminist Poetry Movement.* Jackson: University Press of Mississippi, 1996.

Wiegman, Robyn. "Feminism's Broken English." *Just Being Difficult? Academic Writing in the Public Arena.* Ed. Jonathan Culler and Kevin Lamb. Stanford, CA: Stanford University Press, 2003. 75–94.

Williams, David. "The Poetry of Sonia Sanchez." *Black Women Writers (1950–1980): A Critical Evaluation.* Ed. Mari Evans. Garden City, NY: Anchor Press, 1984. 433–50.

Williams, Emily Allen. "Harryette Mullen, 'The Queen of Hip Hyperbole': An Interview." *African American Review* 34.4 (Winter 2000): 701–7.

Williams, Sherley Anne. "The Blues Roots of Contemporary Afro-American Poetry." *Afro-American Literature: The Reconstruction of Instruction.* Ed. Dexter Fisher and Robert B. Stepto. New York: Modern Language Association of America, 1979. 72–87.

———. *Dessa Rose: A Novel.* New York: William Morrow and Company, Inc., 1986.

———. *Give Birth to Brightness: A Thematic Study in Neo-Black Literature.* New York: Dial Press, 1972.

———. "The Lion's History: The Ghetto Writes B[l]ack." *Soundings* 76.2–3 (Summer–Fall 1993): 245–59.

———. "Meditations on History." *Midnight Birds: Stories of Contemporary Black Women Writers.* Ed. Mary Helen Washington. Garden City, NY: Anchor Books, 1980. 195–248.

———. *The Peacock Poems.* Middletown, CT: Wesleyan University Press, 1975.

———. "Remembering Prof. Sterling A. Brown, 1901–1989." *Black American Literature Forum* 23.1 (Spring 1989): 106–8.

———. "Returning to the Blues: Esther Phillips and Contemporary Blues Culture." *Callaloo* 14.4 (Fall 1991): 816–28.

———. "Some Implications of Feminist Theory." *Griot* 6.2 (Summer 1987): 40–45.

———. "Some Implications of Womanist Theory." *Within the Circle: An Anthology of African American Literary Criticism from the Harlem Renaissance to the Present.* Ed. Angelyn Mitchell. Durham, NC: Duke University Press, 1994. 515–21.

———. *Some One Sweet Angel Chile.* New York: W. Morrow, 1982.

————. "Telling the Teller: Memoir and Story." *The Seductions of Biography*. Ed. Mary Rhiel, David Suchoff, William S. McFeely, Anthony K. Appiah, Betty Sasaki, Barbara Johnson, and Marjorie Garber. New York: Routledge, 1996. 179–84.

————. "Tell Martha Not to Moan." *The Massachusetts Review* 9.3 (Summer 1968): 443–58.

————. "Two Words on Music: Black Community." *Black Popular Culture: A Project by Michele Wallace*. Ed. Gina Dent. Dia Center for the Arts Discussions in Contemporary Culture Ser. 8. Seattle: Bay Press, 1992. 164–72.

————. *Working Cotton*. Illus. Carole Byard. New York: Voyager Books, 1997.

Williams, Sherley Anne, and Deborah McDowell. "Conversation." *The Furious Flowering of African-American Poetry*. Ed. Joanne V. Gabbin. Charlottesville: University Press of Virginia, 1999. 194–205.

Wilson, Peter Niklas. *Ornette Coleman: His Life and Music*. Berkeley, CA: Berkeley Hills Books, 1999.

Witt, Doris. *Black Hunger: Food and the Politics of U.S. Identity*. New York and Oxford: Oxford University Press, 1999.

Woodson, Jon. "Jayne Cortez." *Afro-American Poets Since 1955*. Ed. Trudier Harris and Thadious M. Davis. Detroit: Gale Research, 1985. 69–74.

Wyile, Herb, Christian Riegel, Karen Overbye, and Don Perkins. "Introduction: Regionalism Revisited." *A Sense of Place: Re-Evaluating Regionalism in Canadian and American Writing*. Ed. Christian Riegel and Herb Wyile. Alberta, CA: University of Alberta Press, 1997. ix–xiv.

Yasuda, Kenneth. *The Japanese Haiku: Its Essential Nature, History, and Possibilities in English, with Selected Examples*. Rutland, VT, and Tokyo: Charles E. Tuttle Company, 1957.

Young, Kevin, ed. *Giant Steps: The New Generation of African American Writers*. New York: Harper Perennial, 2000.

Young, Kevin, et al. "What's African American about African-American Poetry?" *Fence* 4.1 (Spring–Summer 2001): n. pag. Web. 14 October 2001.

Zafar, Rafia. "Cooking Up a Past: Two Black Culinary Narratives." *GRAAT* 14 (1996): 73–84.

————. "The Proof of the Pudding: Of Haggis, Hasty Pudding, and Transatlantic Influence." *Early American Literature* 31.2 (1996): 133–49.

Zeiger, Melissa F. *Beyond Consolation: Death, Sexuality, and the Changing Shapes of Elegy*. Ithaca, NY, and London: Cornell University Press, 1997.

Zinn, Howard. *A People's History of the United States, 1492–Present*. Rev. ed. New York: Harper Perennial, 1995.

INDEX